HOLE IN THE ROOF

SWAIM-PAUP SPORTS SERIES

Sponsored by James C. '74 & Debra Parchman Swaim
and T. Edgar '74 & Nancy Paup

H O L E
IN THE ROOF

The Dallas Cowboys, Clint Murchison Jr., and the
Stadium That Changed American Sports Forever

Burk Murchison and Michael Granberry

Foreword by Drew Pearson

Texas A&M University Press · College Station

(∞) This paper meets the requirements of
ANSI/NISO Z39.48–1992 (Permanence of Paper).
Binding materials have been chosen for durability.

Manufactured in the United States of America.

Library of Congress Cataloging-in-Publication Data

Names: Murchison, Burk, author. | Granberry, Michael, author. | Pearson,
   Drew, 1951– writer of foreword.
Title: Hole in the roof: the Dallas Cowboys, Clint Murchison Jr., and the
   stadium that changed American sports forever / Burk Murchison and Michael
   Granberry; foreword by Drew Pearson.
Other titles: Swaim-Paup sports series.
Description: First edition. | College Station: Texas A&M University Press,
   [2023] | Series: Swaim-Paup sports series | Includes index.
Identifiers: LCCN 2022021562 (print) | LCCN 2022021561 (ebook) | ISBN
   9781648430961 (cloth) | ISBN 9781648430978 (ebook) | ISBN
   9781648430978 (ebook) | ISBN 9781648430961 (cloth)
Subjects: LCSH: Murchison, Clint, Jr., 1923–1987. | Murchison, Clinton
   Williams, Sr., 1895–1969. | Dallas Cowboys (Football team)—History. |
   Football stadiums—Texas—Arlington—History. | Football
   stadiums—Texas—Arlington—Design and construction. | Football
   stadiums—Texas—Arlington—Finance. | Football team owners—United
   States--Biography. | Arlington (Tex.)—Social life and customs. | BISAC:
   SPORTS & RECREATION / Football | BIOGRAPHY
& AUTOBIOGRAPHY / Sports
Classification: LCC GV956.D3 M87 2023 (ebook) | LCC GV956.D3 (print) | DDC
   796.332/64097642812 23/eng/20220—dc04
LC record available at https://lccn.loc.gov/2022021562

For Elise, for Mother and Dad,
and for babies who grow up to be Cowboys.
—Burk Murchison

In loving memory of my parents,
Mina Gene Wilbourn Granberry and Henry Lee Granberry,
who when I was a third grader in 1960 introduced me
to a new phenomenon: The Dallas Cowboys.
—Michael Granberry

The journey is essential to the dream.
—*St. Francis of Assisi*

Well planned is half built.
—*Leonardo Haber*

CONTENTS

A gallery of photos follows page 85

FOREWORD

When I signed with the Dallas Cowboys as an undrafted free agent in 1973, the team was already cruising to immortality. In 1966, the Cowboys ignited a streak of twenty consecutive winning seasons that lingered until 1985. I was privileged to be a part of "America's Team" during that incredible run, which no other team has equaled.

When I retired after the 1983 season, Clint Murchison Jr. had owned the Cowboys throughout my playing days. And I played all of my home games with the Cowboys in the stadium he created—Texas Stadium.

Burk Murchison, his son, and coauthor Michael Granberry have assembled a fascinating history of the life and times of Clint Jr. and his Xanadu of a stadium where, I'm proud to say, many of my accomplishments took place.

It does not surprise me that all five of the Cowboys' championships occurred when the Cowboys called Texas Stadium their home. It provided a rock 'n' roll atmosphere for a wide receiver catching passes from my friend and fellow Hall of Famer Roger Staubach. With Roger as my quarterback for seven wondrous seasons, I became First Team All-Pro in 1974, 1976, and 1977. I am honored to have joined Roger in the Cowboys' Ring of Honor, which was founded at Texas Stadium.

Murchison and Granberry have done a great job in feeding us the flashbacks of the most memorable moments in Cowboys history. And though it happened on the road, I was thrilled to read their account of the "Hail Mary" game, when, in the final seconds, I caught the pass from Roger that allowed us to beat the Minnesota Vikings on December 28, 1975. That come-from-behind victory allowed the Wild Card Cowboys to play in the Super Bowl weeks later.

In commending this awesome book, I wish to echo the words I said in my Hall of Fame induction speech, when I paid tribute to "the late great Clint Murchison, the original owner of the Dallas Cowboys. Thank you for your ownership and drive to set the blueprint of what the Dallas Cowboys still are today."

Why stop there? I now wish to use other words from my Hall of Fame speech to describe *Hole in the Roof*, this history of my forever team, the Dallas Cowboys, that all of us have been waiting so patiently to read:

"The wait is over!"

And I, for one, am happy that it is. Enjoy.

—Drew Pearson

ACKNOWLEDGMENTS

We began this project a long time ago—2011, to be specific. And in those eleven years, we have interviewed more than 100 people and pored through not hundreds but thousands of documents as ancient as the early 1960s, when the Dallas Cowboys began playing in the Cotton Bowl. Sadly, some of the people we interviewed are no longer with us, but we wish to thank them—as well as dozens of sources who are, happily, still with us—for their matchless contributions to *Hole in the Roof*.

And, of course, our journey would not be complete were it not for our friends at Texas A&M University Press who were from the start enthusiastic about *Hole in the Roof* and did an extraordinary job in helping us land the plane. In that regard, we wish to thank editor-in-chief Thom Lemmons, managing editor Katie Duelm, and the marketing team of Christine Brown and Kyle Littlefield. We also wish to thank Christine Decker and her Pennsylvania team, who did such a great job with editing. We extend a special thank-you to our ace indexer, Joanne Sprott, who took on the task when the deadline wasn't far away.

We wish to thank author and literary agent James Donovan for his help, as well as Jonathan Thorn, the official archivist of the Dallas Cowboys.

And there are so many more—Former Cowboys executive Joe Bailey; Mitch Lewis, whose father enriched the Cowboys for years with his marketing genius; Kevin Kendro and the Irving Archives and Museum; and the family members of so many men with connections to the story: Robert Power; Ed Smith; Charles Pistor; Melvin Shuler; Steve "Cottontail" Schneider; and Texas Stadium architect Warren Morey.

Tearfully, we also wish to thank the late great Alan Peppard, a good friend to both Burk Murchison and Michael Granberry, who introduced Michael to Burk and recommended that the two collaborate on *Hole in the Roof*. Alan, we miss you.

And lest we forget, we owe a big thank-you to Vinny Minchillo, who said the book was destined to have only one title: *Hole in the Roof*. Thank you, Vinny!

Promotion is, of course, a huge part of any book's success. In that regard, we wish to thank our friends in the East Texas hamlets of Athens and Winnsboro, plus the two-man team of *Intentional Grounding* at The Ticket in Dallas, David Moore and Robert Wilonsky, who had us on the air when we were, so to speak, still in the pre-season. In that regard, we also wish to thank Brandon Murray with the Dallas Public Library, which put together a Zoom panel that included not only us but also Cowboy greats Cliff Harris and Charlie Waters, in honor of the 50th anniversary of Texas Stadium.

Last but not least, we must thank our families, who were so patient and helpful, in particular our wives, Elise Murchison and Nancy Churnin, whose advice as a bestselling children's book author has been invaluable in helping us pinpoint and grow our audience.

In full gratitude, we are happy to have *you* as part of that audience, to whom we say: We hope you enjoy *Hole in the Roof* as much as we did in pushing it across the goal line.

HOLE IN THE ROOF

Prologue

I N THE SPRING of 2000, a 31-year-old Egyptian national showed up at a federal office in Florida seeking a $650,000 loan from the Department of Agriculture. He said he hoped to buy a twin-engine, six-passenger crop duster on which he could add a large fuel tank. His name was Mohamed Atta. His loan was denied. He reacted to his rejection by threatening to slit the throat of loan manager Johnell Bryant, who told him she was skilled in the martial arts, which scared him away. Before that moment, however, Bryant said he asked specifically about two iconic buildings: the World Trade Center in New York and Texas Stadium in Irving, Texas. He was curious about the latter's hole in the roof, which Dallas Cowboys linebacker D. D. Lewis once famously said existed "so that God can watch his favorite team."

On September 11, 2001, barely a year after asking about the hole in the roof, Atta spearheaded a terrorist attack that flew hijacked airliners into the Twin Towers of the World Trade Center, killing 2,749 people in the Towers and on the ground nearby.

Spared the wrath of terrorists, Texas Stadium enjoyed a happier fate.

The stadium with the hole in its roof served as the home of "America's Team" from 1971 until the end of the 2008 football season, after which its primary tenant moved to what became AT&T Stadium in Arlington, Texas, where taxpayers funded $325 million of the overall daunting tab of $1.2 billion. It represented a new vanguard in American stadia, just as its predecessor had when it opened for football on a sunlit afternoon on October 24, 1971, with halfback Duane Thomas notching its first score on a 56-yard touchdown run that served as a lyrical foreshadowing of what would happen months later: the Cowboys captured their first championship, beating the Miami Dolphins in Super Bowl VI in New Orleans by the lopsided score of 24–3.

The hole in the roof appeared for years as one of the opening shots in the hit CBS television show *Dallas*, which gave to the world the iconic villain J. R. Ewing, a Texas oilman. The character, made famous, or infamous, by actor Larry Hagman (whose mother, Mary Martin, played the title role in the original Broadway production of *Peter Pan*), hot-wired a ratings bonanza that introduced the world to the hole in the roof.

J. R. crumpled to the floor with a gunshot wound in the cliffhanger episode that aired on March 21, 1980. Viewers the world over had to wait until November 21, 1980, to learn the answer to the question that sparked international curiosity: Who Shot J. R.? The answer to the mystery revealed itself in what was then the highest-rated episode in television history, titled "Who Done It?," luring an estimated 83 million viewers—more than the number of voters in that year's presidential election.

Despite Texas Stadium being demolished by the city of Irving in 2010, the hole in the roof lives on. It is now a signature element in the design of AT&T Stadium, whose own version of the hole in the roof appeared in the opening moments of the TNT remake of *Dallas*. The new stadium has yet to lay claim to a Super Bowl-winning Cowboys team. The team last won it all in Super Bowl XXX in Tempe, Arizona, on January 28, 1996, when the Cowboys beat the Pittsburgh Steelers to capture their fifth Lombardi Trophy. All five of the Cowboys' Super Bowl trophies were acquired when the team made its home in Texas Stadium, spanning the seasons from 1971 to 1995.

Texas Stadium and its hole in the roof would not have existed had it not been for the Cowboys' founder, Clint Murchison Jr. His father, Clint Murchison Sr., was one of the most iconic names in the history of Texas oil, the world that gave rise to J. R. Ewing.

We could not tell the story of Clint Jr. without sharing our view that all good stories fall into three categories: history, comedy, or tragedy. But the most compelling contain elements of all three. And so it is with the story that our book, *Hole in the Roof*, will expose between its front and back covers.

As with all great stories, ours has a beginning, a middle, and an end. And just as the beginning of the Cowboys' epic saga must start with Clint Jr., so his story begins with his dad, Clint Sr.

We, the authors, are Burk Murchison (one of Clint Jr.'s four children) and Michael Granberry, who grew up in Dallas and who, like his coauthor, began following the Cowboys from the moment they were founded in 1960. One of Michael's most esteemed colleagues in a newspaper career spanning more than 50 years was the late Bryan Woolley, whose thousands of bylines include a moving profile of Clint Jr.

In that article, which unfolded with the eloquence and elegance of a talented writer, Woolley described Clint Sr. as having a "nose for oil." If true, Clint Sr.'s nose became nothing less than a beacon for wealth, teleporting him from backwater West Texas boom towns into the horror of the Great Depression, from which he emerged a multimillionaire.

In 1953, *Fortune* magazine published a two-part profile of Clint Sr., who then controlled 103 companies, ranging, in Woolley's words, "from such traditional Texas interests as oil, gas, cattle and banks to a fishing tackle company, tourist courts, a silverware factory, Martha Washington Candy and *Field and Stream* magazine,"[1] which flourished in the golden age of magazines.

"Even those who know a little," *Fortune* wrote, "don't pretend to understand how Clint got mixed up in so much outlandish stuff, or how he keeps track of it all without going batty or broke." His wealth in 1953 was estimated at $300 million—and growing. In 2022, such a sum would exceed $8.364 billion. And yet, his wealth continued to grow. Exponentially.

The elder Murchison died in 1969, almost a decade into Clint Jr.'s Cowboys experiment, which his father only reluctantly supported, despite the fact that, by the time Clint Sr. died, the Cowboys were a sports-world juggernaut. They were arguably professional football's most popular team, despite falling short of a championship—until they won Super Bowl VI on January 16, 1972.

After its patriarch passed away, the family empire prevailed under a partnership called Murchison Brothers. It represented an alliance of the founder's sons, older brother John and younger brother Clint. Despite sporting radically different personalities, the two agreed to co-own the Cowboys via their partnership, with each owning half of the 90 percent of total ownership. In later years, the joke became, "They talk about Clint being low-profile, but he was a carnival-barker show daddy compared to John, who most Cowboys fans didn't know existed." In later years, however, John played an excruciatingly important role in the history of the Cowboys—albeit in death, which triggered the fall of Clint Murchison Jr.

John was two years older than Clint Jr. and was, by all accounts, the careful, judicious partner. John was more conservative than daring, more measured than maniacal. He also happened to be far more socially adept, comfortable in high society in ways his brother never was nor hoped to be. John collected art as an investment. He sat on the board of the Dallas Museum of Fine Arts, which lingered in Fair Park, in the shadow of the Cotton Bowl, until 1984, when it moved to downtown Dallas as the newly christened Dallas Museum of Art.

And in that respect alone, irony abounds, one of many we share in *Hole in the Roof*. New York–born J. Erik Jonsson, a chap of Swedish descent who served as mayor of Dallas from 1964 to 1971, and Fair Park guardian Robert B. Cullum, who owned a supermarket chain that took as its namesake fairy tale hero Tom Thumb, thwarted at every turn Clint Jr.'s quixotic crusade to construct a stadium in downtown Dallas, which he hoped to buttress with a lavish new performing arts center and art museum. The Jonsson-Cullum forces adamantly and repeatedly said no, ridiculing the notion as civic silliness.

Clint Jr. saw a downtown stadium as a far better home for his rapidly improving team than what he called the "fully depreciated" Cotton Bowl in Fair Park.

He also longed for a symbol of redemption—a state-of-the-art stadium that could go a long way toward restoring a depressed downtown in the wake of President John F. Kennedy's assassination on Elm Street in Dallas in 1963. It would, he believed, give the Cowboys and their fervent fan base a spiffy new home that would pay an added dividend: it would serve as a catalyst in rebuilding a damaged Dallas and healing a wounded populace who bristled at the nickname "city of hate."

But when it came to the Dallas elite, Clint Jr.'s ideas were met by scoffs, not support.

Broke and dying, Clint Jr. sold the Cowboys in 1984, the same year the art museum abandoned Fair Park, only to resurface downtown as the anchor of the Dallas Arts District. Its seventy acres now eat up multiple blocks, housing museums and a school for the performing arts, in addition to the Dallas Symphony Orchestra, the Dallas Opera, and the Tony Award-winning Dallas Theater Center.

This was, for the most part, exactly what Clint Jr. had envisioned. While the arts would eventually move downtown, the Cowboys never did. As we show you later, the city of Dallas twice rejected America's Team, failing to cut a deal that forced the twenty-first-century Cowboys to look elsewhere for a new home, which turned out to be Arlington.

We document that story as well, showing you how, in the end, it comes back around to Clint.

Hole in the Roof takes you on a deep dive into the personality and passions of Clint Jr., while extending a more than passing hello to everyone else who was part of his world. And what a world it was.

Its cast of supporting actors included silent brother John. John excelled, in Woolley's words, in "such three-piece-suit enterprises as banking and insurance. John was nothing like his father, whereas Clint was everything like his dad—a gambler, a risk-taker extraordinaire."[2] In that respect, Clint Sr. and Jr. resembled a more modern billionaire: current Cowboys owner Jerral Wayne "Jerry" Jones. Jerry is a fellow risk-taker who made his money by becoming what feels to us like an oxymoron—an *Arkansas* oilman. Even so, the Arkansas oilman deserves 100 percent of the business chops he gets. He paid a record $140 million for the Cowboys in 1989 and made the team the most valuable sports franchise in the world. *Forbes* magazine assessed its value in 2021 at $5.7 billion—the sixth consecutive year the Cowboys were ranked as the world's most valuable sports company.

Jones saw what Clint Jr. envisioned with the creation of Texas Stadium. From the beginning, Clint saw it as far more than a place to play games. Rather than being a city-owned rental facility, à la the Cotton Bowl and dozens like it across America, where the only real perk was a hot dog and a Coke (or in Texas, a Dr Pepper), Clint cast the stadium in an adventurous new light, and Jones *got it*. Clint was the first American sports owner to see the stadium as the primary source of revenue, even more so than television. Jones may not have been aware of it when he bought the Cowboys, but to his credit, he was a quick study. And now it's no secret that AT&T Stadium remains the underpinning of the Cowboys' financial empire, the pandemic notwithstanding. During the outrageously troubled 2020 season, thirteen NFL (National Football League) teams—*thirteen*!—had exactly zero attendance, including the new $5 billion SoFi Stadium, which houses the Los Angeles Rams and Los Angeles Chargers, who until the 2021 kickoff had played before zero—that's right, *zero*—fans in the stands in Inglewood, California, where the capacity is 70,000. Carving out their own reality, the 2020 Cowboys continued their reign of having the League's highest attendance, with Jones luring 197,313 fans to Arlington. By the end of June 2021, Texas had seen almost three million cases of COVID-19 and more than 52,000 deaths—putting it third in the nation, trailing only California and New York in deaths and only California in cases.

Jones even managed to land the January 1, 2021, Rose Bowl game, which, because of the pandemic, could not be played in its traditional home in Pasadena, California.

In terms of what stadiums could mean to the foundation of a franchise, Jones took what Clint envisioned—and put it on steroids.

In biblical terms, the story of the Cowboys' financial empire is one of Clint begat Jerry. And in the Murchison empire, Clint Sr. begat Clint Jr.

"He's as remarkably like his father as he was remarkably unlike his brother," radio icon Gordon McLendon once said of his friend Clint Jr. "His father—we all referred to Clint Sr. as 'The Boss'—loved to go into businesses of every description. Clint Jr. did too. His father loved to stay borrowed up to the hilt. Clint Jr. did, too. They depended on inflation to take care of things. They believed the people who borrowed money and invested it in land and other things that appreciate with inflation would win. And those who saved their cash were going to be the losers."[3]

The Boss, Clinton Williams Murchison Sr., was fond of saying he liked to do business through a formula expressed through the homespun homily "financin' by finaglin'." Clint Sr. soon thrust himself into a pantheon of Texas wheeler-dealers that enumerated such fellow giants as Sid Richardson, H. L. Hunt, and Hugh Roy Cullen, American folk heroes in the making. (Perhaps it's no coincidence that H. L. Hunt's son, Lamar, also founded a professional team, the Dallas Texans, who began playing in the Cotton Bowl in 1960, at the same time the Cowboys did, but who, after winning the American Football League Championship in 1962, became the Kansas City Chiefs a year later, only months before the Kennedy assassination in November 1963.)

Richardson, Hunt, Murchison, and Cullen accomplished their meteoric rise through an alchemy of luck and risk, whose payoff was best captured in the lyrics of the 1960s television comedy *The Beverly Hillbillies*, about a poor mountaineer who was "shootin' at some food," when "up through the ground come a bubblin' crude. Oil that is, black gold, Texas tea."

Clint Sr. was born in 1895 in Athens, a small hamlet in East Texas. His grandfather founded the First National Bank in Athens. His father was its president. After high school, he enrolled at Trinity University, then in Waxahachie, where he was expelled three weeks later for shooting craps. The university offered to reinstate him if he would rat out his fellow gamblers—he refused. He returned to Athens and worked in the bank until the outbreak of World War I, when he joined the army. In 1919, he made his way to Fort Worth, with nary a penny in his pocket. There he teamed up with boyhood friend Richardson, who was nibbling at the edges of a scary new enterprise—oil leases.

Because the risk-taking pair won far more than they lost, they stayed afloat. And prospered. Boy, did they prosper. Just one story in the folklore is how one night, Clint Sr. drove to Wichita Falls, near the Oklahoma border, fueled by a rumor he'd heard about a wildcat well ready to start pumping black gold. When he got to Wichita Falls, he yanked his buddy out of a poker game. He and Richardson drove to the site, and sure enough, smelled the black gold bubblin' up. They slapped down $50,000 on the spot to buy the leases. (In today's dollars, that's more than $750,000.) By noon the next day, they'd returned to Wichita Falls, having tripled their profit in 24 hours by flipping the leases for $200,000 (more than $3 million in today's dollars). All in a day's work.

Clint Sr. became an obsessive wildcatter, riding a stunning string of luck that by 1927, when he was 32, had netted him $6 million, a fortune he'd made entirely through oil. In today's dollars, that's north of $87 million. And yet, it was money that Clint Sr. and his wife would not be able to share. She died in 1926, leaving him to raise three small sons—John, Clint Jr., and Burk, who died from pneumonia when he was 11. Coauthor Burk Murchison is named for the uncle who died.

As Robert Murchison, Clint Jr.'s youngest of four children, notes, "Their brother Burk, Dad's best friend, died when John was 13 and Dad, 12." Clint Jr. and John, Robert adds, "could not have been more different. As a child, Dad was small and sickly and shy to a fault. He was socially aloof to the point many considered downright rude. He only had a few childhood friends. He rarely exchanged pleasantries and ignored people he knew when he would see them on the street or in the elevator. Yet, he was the rainmaker of his generation."[4]

The death of his mother and closest brother took its toll on Clint Jr. in other ways. Robert Murchison notes that "Pop was out of town much of their childhood looking after his business interests, thus John and Dad were raised by a loving aunt, grandmother and wonderful servants."[5]

And then, more change.

Looking for a new chapter after the death of his wife and son, Clint Sr. moved to Dallas, where he rapidly expanded his burgeoning portfolio. "At that time, he was well on his way to success and wealth in gas and oil,"

Fortune wrote, "and if he had been alone in the world he might never have wandered. But since he had two sons in their teens, whose business talents were unpredictable, it seemed unwise to keep all their legacy in one immensely risky petroleum basket."[6]

Clint Sr. shipped John and Clint off to prep school. John later went to Yale but quit to join the Army Air Corps when World War II broke out. Clint Jr. became enamored of education and its extracurricular dividend—football, which gave him his own identity beyond his dad. Despite being a scrawny 5 foot 6, 120 pounds, he played halfback on an intramural team at Lawrenceville, his New Jersey prep school. He made Phi Beta Kappa in electrical engineering at Duke University in Durham, North Carolina, and earned a master's degree in mathematics at the Massachusetts Institute of Technology (MIT), which was at the time the country's toughest school for science and engineering. It was, however, a natural fit for Clint Jr., who for the first and only time in his life was surrounded by people whose intelligence mirrored his.

In *The Murchisons: The Rise and Fall of a Texas Dynasty*, author Jane Wolfe writes how Clint Jr. thrived in "a milieu of intellectuals from Harvard, MIT, and Wellesley. Even in this environment, Clint Jr. was viewed as a scientific genius and an eccentric. He loved to spend an evening at the home of a professor, or a fellow graduate student, where the conversation about mathematical or scientific theory lasted well into the morning hours."[7]

Clint Jr. had begun as an undergraduate at MIT but was soon derailed by World War II, which led to his induction in the Marine Corps, via the US Navy's V-12 program. Through the accelerated officers' training program, he was sent to Duke, where he obtained his bachelor's degree in electrical engineering. After leaving the Marine Corps, he married and returned to Boston, this time to pursue a graduate degree in math at MIT.

Soon after Clint Jr. left MIT to return to Dallas to stake his place in the family business, Clint Sr. received a letter from the MIT professor with whom Clint Jr. lived as an undergraduate. As Wolfe notes in her book, "The professor told Murchison that it was a great loss to science that his son Clint had gone into business."[8]

Clint Sr. appreciated the kindness, but in his mind, academia was no place for a Murchison. "At their father's knee," Woolley wrote, Clint Jr. and John "learned how to wheel and deal."[9] Soon, Clint Sr. was sharing *his* idea of an education, designed to ensure enduring wealth and chisel the Murchison name into the granite of high society.

"Money is like manure," Clint Sr. once famously told his boys, echoing a line written by Thornton Wilder in his 1954 play, *The Matchmaker*, but adding his own special spin: "If you spread it around, it does a lot of good. But if you pile it up in one place, it stinks like hell."

According to *Fortune*, Clint Sr. "declares one of his best assets is a full knowledge of the use of credit. His borrowing, which has been an immensely profitable business practice, has become an addiction."[10]

He liked to use what bankers called "leverage"—use a small amount of capital and a large loan to gain control of a company with large assets. The assets of the company being acquired are then used as collateral for the loan.

As Woolley wrote, "The Boss and his sons got into the construction business, for instance, with only $20,000 of their money and an $80,000 promissory note. The company they acquired was Tecon, which over the years would remove the overhanging shale that threatened to close the Panama Canal and would build the tunnel under Havana Harbor, the St. Lawrence Seaway and other multibillion-dollar projects around the world."[11]

This next part is important, because it underscores the model Clint Jr. followed with the Cowboys: Once Clint Sr. established or acquired a company, he left its operations to others, in the same way that Clint Jr. appointed Tex Schramm to be his president and general manager and Tom Landry his head coach. The two men sustained their roles for almost three decades—until Jones bought the team. In other words, as Cowboys fixtures, they lasted even longer than Clint.

"His executives had the authority to make important decisions without consulting him, and he never coached from the corner or second-guessed them,"[12] Woolley wrote. Dare we say it, but that was precisely the model that became the antithesis of how Jones runs the Cowboys. As Jones said on the night in 1989 that he proclaimed himself the Cowboys' new impresario, he would be involved in *everything*—"down to the jocks and socks." The Murchison way was the polar opposite.

Clint Jr.'s risk-taking would lead him to the world of professional football and allow his team to succeed. During their first five seasons, the Cowboys lost $3 million and failed to win more than five games a season.

When it all came to an end in 1984—the tragic part of the story—Clint Jr. had lost everything, and risk-taking was largely to blame. His failure is just one of the ways *Hole in the Roof* embraces a double meaning.

Even so, Clint Jr. created a football team that compiled a record twenty consecutive winning seasons, from 1966 through 1985; appeared in five Super Bowls, winning two; and came to be known as *America's Team*.

Clint Jr.'s success can be attributed largely to Schramm, a marketing genius; Landry, one of the game's great coaches; and Gil Brandt, who, as director of scouting, revolutionized the way players are recruited by using newfangled technology—computers—long before computers were commonplace. Schramm, Landry, and Brandt all have bronze busts in the Pro Football Hall of Fame.

What about Clint? What most of America doesn't know is that he, too, was revolutionary. He changed where and how games are played, not only in professional football but also in baseball, basketball, and colleges and high schools. To wit: In 2017, Katy, Texas, unveiled a $72 million high school facility, which carries luxury boxes for corporate sponsors. In case you're wondering, Katy taxpayers paid for most of it.

Texas Stadium became the prototype of the twenty-first-century stadium, whether it hosts high school games in Katy, Texas, or serves as the $5 billion launchpad that opened in 2020 as the shared home of the Rams and Chargers. Clint taught the sports world how stadiums could be so much more than where games are played.

This is the journey we share—how Clint Murchison Jr. created the prototype, giving the Cowboys and the rest of professional sports the blueprint of a new model. We may also surprise you by showing you the ways in which the sports world has taken Clint's model and corrupted it in ways that he more than anyone would loathe.

In telling you the story, we will show you how it serves as history, comedy, and tragedy, but most of all, as a rollicking read, every bit as fascinating as a Texas character named Clint Murchison Jr., the creator of *your* Dallas Cowboys, who fostered their own rare world beneath the hole in the roof that seized the attention of terrorists and sports fans alike.

CHAPTER ONE

Lone Star Chutzpah

Texas. It *had* to be Texas.

When Clint Murchison Jr. was building his dream stadium—the stadium that changed stadiums forever—he knew it could have only one name.

Texas Stadium.

When Clint hired the president and general manager who would oversee the Dallas Cowboys from 1960 to 1989, he picked the man with the unmistakable first name: Texas, as in Texas E. Schramm.

But that's the least of it when it comes to Texas and the role it played in the lifeblood of the Murchison family.

Clint Jr. graduated Phi Beta Kappa from Duke University with a degree in electrical engineering, while serving in the Marine Corps as part of the elite officers training program. After World War II, he entered MIT in Boston to pursue a master's degree in mathematics. There, he was in the early days of marriage to his Texas sweetheart, Jane Coleman, who soon became pregnant with the couple's first child.

Predictably, if the child turned out to be a boy, he was going to be named Clint Murchison III. It was his destiny. But within the larger scope of the expanded Murchison family, what to name the boy was the least of it.

It was *where* the child would be born that was causing concern, even panic.

Clint Murchison Sr., whose oil empire was passed to his sons, Clint and John, was growing more and more concerned about *where* his first grandchild would enter the world. It could not be—*would* not be—in Massachusetts. That was Yankee land. And no child of the Murchison family was going to be born in Yankee land.

So, the patriarch of the Murchison family did what any giant of an oil-rich family would do: he arranged for Clint and his wife to board his private DC-3—dubbed "the Flying Ginny," which Clint Sr. had named for his second wife, Virginia Murchison—and fly to an air force base in San Antonio, where Jane's mother lived, so that Clint III would be born in Texas.

It was not going to happen any other way. Because Clint Sr. decreed that it wouldn't happen any other way.

Clint Jr. was the son of one of the Big Four of Texas oil. They were, in addition to Clint Sr., Sid Richardson, H. L. Hunt, and Hugh Roy Cullen. Sons of two of the four ended up as owners in the NFL.

Clint's older brother, John, was born in 1921. Clint followed in 1923. Their youngest brother, Burk, was born in 1925 but died a decade later from pneumonia at age 11. Anne Murchison, the mother of the three boys, died when Clint Jr. was 2 years old.

In 1928, the widowed Clint Sr. moved his boys to Dallas, where it didn't take long for Clint Jr. to develop a fascination with football, one of the few things that could—and did—separate Clint Jr. from the shadow of Clint Sr.

His was a famous, powerful father, but football offered Clint Jr. a stake in his own identity, his own passion.

He was scrawny at 5 foot 6, 120 pounds, and yet he proved he could hold his own as a halfback in intramural football at the Lawrenceville School, a New Jersey boarding academy. Through his days at Duke, the Marine Corps, and MIT, his interest in football never waned. Instead, it grew exponentially stronger. It was *his* thing, not his father's.

He returned to Dallas in the late 1940s, when he and brother John began the process of building their own identities, their own empire.

Granted, most of their wealth was inherited. Interests passed on from Clint Sr. included the Daisy Manufacturing Company (Daisy made BB guns), *Field & Stream* magazine, Henry Holt and Company (later known as Holt, Rinehart and Winston), and Delhi Gas Pipeline. Companies that Clint Sr. founded also included Southern Union Gas, Florida Gas, and Trans-Canada PipeLines.

As Robert Murchison, Clint Jr.'s youngest child, says of "Pop," his grandfather, "He was fearless and operated beyond the familiar economic beacons without concern for financial resources."

"Hunt not for gain but sport" was the motto carved into the wainscot across from the fireplace in his living room. He was a true sportsman, says Robert Murchison, adding, "When asked how he judged a man's character, he answered, 'By the way they hunt, fish, and play poker.'"

His sons tried their best to emulate his example. Clint Jr. and brother John did manage to launch their own successful companies, including numerous real estate projects, as well as Centex Corporation—destined to become the largest home builder in the United States—and the Tecon Construction Company, which flourished for years.

But the one thing Clint Jr. longed to own more than anything else was a pro football team.

So, in 1952, the year General Dwight D. Eisenhower was elected president for the first of two terms, Clint Jr. laid his eyes on the business he most hoped to enter—professional football.

That same year, Giles Miller and his brother Connell, who were sons of the founder of Texas Textile Mills, had bought a franchise in the NFL with the help of a cluster of Texas oilmen. They paid $300,000 for the New York Yanks, including the assumption of a lease at Yankee Stadium that cost $200,000. And they moved the hapless franchise all the way to Fair Park, where it took on a new name, the Texas Rangers. But by September 1952, when the woebegone team played its first game in the Cotton Bowl, it did so as the Dallas Texans.

Its debut unfolded on September 28, 1952, when the 17,499 fans present included an aspirational Clint Murchison Jr., who had purchased twenty season tickets in advance.

Texas governor Allan Shivers proclaimed it "a new era in sports in Texas." It would take years, however, before Shivers's prophesy would make sense.

From the moment the season began, the Texans were swimming in red ink. Owner Giles Miller sent co-owner Harold Byrd to lobby the all-powerful Dallas Citizens Council for a loan of $250,000, simply to allow the Texans enough capital to finish the season.

In what became a foreshadowing of what Clint Jr. would endure, the answer was an unqualified no. Their support, they informed Byrd, was earmarked for the Dallas Symphony Orchestra and Fair Park—for fine art, not football.

Byrd responded by saying that it was time to "call in the dogs, piss on the fire and go home."[1]

Which was exactly what Clint Jr. hoped to hear. It was like hearing the young woman you've had a crush on for years tell you, sadly, that she and her boyfriend were splitting up. So, what did Clint do? He pounced.

For the first time, but by no means the last, he approached NFL commissioner Bert Bell and offered to buy the Dallas Texans. Bell said no, informing Murchison that the Texans were already committed to new owner Carroll Rosenbloom, who planned to move them from Dallas to Baltimore, where they would become the Colts.

All he ever wanted, Clint said, was "the fun of being able to see professional football in my hometown."

Deterred but hardly defeated, he inquired about another erstwhile team, the San Francisco 49ers. No, Bell said, the team we want you to buy, the one you *should* buy, is the listless Chicago Cardinals. Murchison shifted gears again, inquiring about the Washington Redskins and managing to get owner George Preston Marshall to agree to a sale, with a hulking caveat. Marshall would turn over ownership of the Redskins to Murchison for $600,000, with the condition that he continue to manage the club for another five years. Reluctantly, Clint said yes.

But at the eleventh hour, Marshall moved the goalposts again, saying he would have to manage the team for at least a decade, forcing an angry Clint to back out. Marshall's reneging on the deal lit the fuse to a feud that lingered for decades, involving live chickens, bad songs, and CIA-like spy missions. The nastiness of the Murchison–Marshall feud remains at the heart of professional football's fiercest rivalry.

Soon after Clint told Marshall to go to hell, a strange coincidence emerged: Marshall had an equally bitter falling-out with Barnee Breeskin, the Redskins band director who had written the music to the Redskins' fight song, a song Marshall loved as much as life itself. Breeskin had been associated with the Redskins since the team moved to Washington from Boston in 1937. He was the leader of the Redskin Wigwam Band, which played in a teepee high above Griffith Stadium.

Breeskin's collaborator on "Hail to the Redskins" was Corinne Mae Griffith, an American film actress, producer, author, and the one-time wife of George Preston Marshall. She was popular, she was beautiful, and she had been nominated for an Academy Award for Best Actress for her performance in the silent film classic *The Divine Lady*.

Married four times, she was Marshall's wife from 1936 to 1958. When their relationship reached its nadir, she took to calling him the "Marshall without a plan."

As former Cowboys player Pat Toomay wrote years later in a lively essay for ESPN: "Breeskin, smelling an opportunity for revenge in the strained negotiations, approached Murchison lawyer Tom Webb and asked if he'd like to buy the rights to 'Hail to the Redskins.' Webb agreed, paying $2,500. He figured this would at least be good for an occasional joke on Marshall."[2] And boy, was he right.

Around that time, Murchison developed a new strategy. He approached George Halas, the powerful owner and coach of the Chicago Bears, who headed the NFL expansion committee. He asked Halas to help him acquire his own team, an expansion franchise that would carry his imprimatur from the start.

And, you guessed it, the main opposition to Dallas having a team came from Washington Redskins owner George Preston Marshall, who deemed Dallas part of his vast Southern territory. Yes, it sounds ridiculous, but he was serious. Marshall felt threatened at Murchison's would-be intrusion because of radio. As improbable as it seems, he actually believed that his Redskins radio network was a mighty force, with tentacles that reached as far south and west as North Texas, which, of course, Clint Jr. regarded as balderdash.

Marshall told the other owners no, he would *never* vote for a Dallas expansion franchise, and besides, he said, Murchison was "obnoxious."

Then, much to his astonishment, Marshall found out that Murchison had acquired the rights to his beloved "Hail to the Redskins." Breeskin had written the music, but Marshall's wife had written the lyrics, so Marshall had made the song the centerpiece of his elaborate pregame and halftime shows.

Michael Meredith, the son of "Dandy" Don Meredith, the first player signed by the Dallas Cowboys—Don was literally *the* first Cowboy—remembers his dad telling him the story about the Redskins' song and how it played a gargantuan role in the birth of the 'Boys.

Corinne, an East Texas girl from Texarkana, had a fond memory of Dandy Don playing at nearby Mount Vernon High School and got the idea of helping Dandy's new team, albeit with her own dark motive mixed in. She arranged a meeting with Dandy Don at Dallas's tony Adolphus Hotel, a gathering fueled partly by attraction but mostly by wanting to get back at her estranged husband. Moments after his college football eligibility ended on the afternoon of November 28, 1959, with a forgettable 19–0 loss to Texas Christian University in Fort Worth, Meredith signed a "personal services contract" with Clint, who so wanted the charismatic All-American from Southern Methodist University (SMU) to be his first player. Clint agreed to pay Meredith an astonishing $30,000 a year, which much later remained one of the biggest salaries in the pre–Big Television era of the NFL. (Duane Thomas, the Cowboys' No. 1 draft choice a decade later in 1970, was, for instance, paid $20,000 a year.)

"Corinne was married to George Marshall," Michael Meredith said. "She had divorced him, but she had co-written the Redskins' fight song and owned the rights. She sold them for nothing, just to get back at George. Clint went to the owners' meeting in Miami in January of 1960. George Marshall had pioneered the NFL halftime show, invented it. It meant a huge amount to him.

"Clint said, 'You'll never play that song again. And there's now a restraining order. Halftime shows are over. You're done, unless . . . you want to rethink the Cowboy vote.' And Marshall buckled. He got his song back for free, but the Cowboys got a franchise."[3]

As Toomay writes: "Back then, the Redskins band was a small army in buckskins and headdresses, snappy and well-drilled, featuring a chorus line of prancing Indian princesses. Many fans thought the band, the princesses and Marshall's halftime pageants were more entertaining than the team itself."

When word of Murchison's "dirty trick" leaked out, Toomay said that one Washington columnist wrote that taking "Hail to the Redskins" away from Marshall would be like "denying 'Dixie' to the South, 'Anchors Aweigh' to the Navy, or 'Blue Suede Shoes' to Elvis."[4]

Angrily, Marshall agreed to a deal: vote for the Dallas franchise and you get back the rights to the song. Clint paid the entry fee of $50,000, and on January 28, 1960, the NFL gave birth to its newest team—in Dallas.

The money didn't stop there, of course. The Murchison brothers paid an additional $550,000 to acquire players from other teams in a hastily arranged, ill-conceived expansion draft. Fate would soon play yet another role in the Cowboys' strange evolution. NFL commissioner Bert Bell had blocked Clint at every turn, but in 1959, while watching a game between the Philadelphia Eagles and Pittsburgh Steelers—teams he had once served as coach—Bell died of a heart attack. His replacement, Pete Rozelle, who became commissioner in January 1960, proved to be not only easier to deal with but also a staunch Murchison ally in the years to come. During his days with the Los Angeles Rams, Rozelle reported to a general manager named Tex Schramm, the newly named president and general manager of the Cowboys.

Even with hurdles imposed by Bell and Marshall now removed, Clint faced a new set of problems. He had competition from another favored son of Texas' oil elite. Lamar Hunt, the son of H. L. Hunt, had also approached Bell about owning a franchise. He, too, wanted a team in the NFL, and he, too, had his arm twisted about buying the Chicago Cardinals, who no one seemed to want. He continued to beg Bell, not for an existing team, but rather for an expansion team, and Bell always said no.

Told that expansion was "off the table," Hunt got fed up. So, he gathered together like-minded men to form a rival league—the newly created American Football League, whose inaugural franchises were the New York Titans, the Boston Patriots, the Buffalo Bills, the Denver Broncos, the Oakland Raiders, the Los Angeles Chargers, the Houston Oilers, and the Dallas Texans, who, along with Murchison's Cowboys, would share the 75,504-seat Cotton Bowl.

Murchison responded by lobbying the League to let him field a team in the Cotton Bowl in 1960, rather than in 1961—thus putting him on equal footing with Hunt's Texans. To wait any longer, decreed Halas, would give Hunt and the Texans an unfair advantage. So, overnight, Dallas went from having no professional teams to having two.

Hastily, Clint Jr. named his team the Dallas Rangers. But even that turned out to be a foul ball. He soon realized that Dallas's minor-league baseball team was called the Rangers, so he turned to Tex Schramm, who recommended the name Cowboys. It stuck. The truth is, Schramm had strongly objected to the name Rangers and persuaded Clint to change it.

Michael Meredith notes, however, that Clint really liked the name Rangers, because his own grandfather had served in the Texas Rangers law enforcement agency. Schramm talked him out of it.

As any 2021 branding expert would attest, thank your lucky Lone Stars that Cowboys stuck. In another stroke of genius, Schramm also decided on the single blue star as the team's signature element. But as Michael Meredith points out, Tom Landry's wife, Alicia, had a lot to do with the team adopting a lone star as its logo. Alicia Landry had inspired the use of the star by telling Cowboys management, repeatedly, that husband "Tommy" was her "star." So, no one can discount the role played by two women, Alicia Landry and Corinne Mae Griffith.

It also helped that Schramm was a shrewd master of branding. His consultants included Jack Landry (yes, that really was his last name), who had made the Marlboro Man an icon of national advertising, back when cigarettes could still be promoted on billboards and television screens.

"Everything Tex did was focused on making the team unique and different," says Joseph A. Bailey III, who went to work for the Cowboys on a full-time basis in 1970, but who became part of the team when he was only 13, helping the trainer and equipment manager during training camp. Bailey's father was a cardiologist, who treated Clint Sr. and Clint Jr. and other family members. One of the elder Bailey's closest friends was Thomas Webb Jr., a former FBI agent, who later spent 30 years as a lobbyist for the Murchison family.

Schramm, Bailey says, learned a lot from his days in Los Angeles. He had gone from being the general manager of the Rams, where he hired future NFL commissioner Pete Rozelle to be the team's PR guy, and where, Bailey says, "he learned the importance of the star system." Soon, Schramm moved to CBS, where he revolutionized coverage of the 1960 Winter Olympics in Squaw Valley, California, by appointing network news superstar Walter Cronkite as anchor of the telecast. That alone helped revolutionize television coverage of the Olympics. Murchison understood Schramm's brilliance at branding, but Murchison had his own ideas.

Aside from being the millionaire offspring of Texas oil giants, Murchison and Lamar Hunt had another thing in common: they could see that professional football was a game rapidly on the rise, poised to seize the attention of postwar America. And why? Its 100-by-50-yard grid and its speed were a perfect match for television, far more than its geographically expansive and plodding competitor, baseball.

As proof, they offered as evidence the 1958 NFL Championship Game, which some call the "greatest game ever played." Played in Yankee Stadium, the Baltimore Colts—yes, the former Dallas Texans—came from behind to tie the New York Giants, sending the game into sudden death overtime. Running back Alan Ameche scored the winning touchdown, giving the Colts a championship and launching professional football as a sport suited perfectly to America's new technological phenomenon, television. Even if it was, at the time, black and white television.

CHAPTER TWO

The First Cowboy

Clint knew he needed a popular first player, so even before hiring his head coach, Murchison inked Don Meredith to his famously worded "personal services contract," a term the pale-eyed quarterback used often, with a telling wink.

The team had a name, a president, a general manager, and its "first Cowboy," a winsome kid from the Piney Woods of East Texas named Dandy Don.

Now he needed a coach. And soon he had one of those, a World War II bomber copilot whose planes dropped bombs on Nazi-held territory. He was Tom Landry, a native Texan and former Longhorn who served as defensive coordinator for the badass New York Giants.

The Cowboys were admitted to the League too late to participate in the 1960 college draft, prompting Murchison to sign one other player, New Mexico running back Don Perkins, to a second "personal services" contract. The NFL honored the contracts, albeit with the arranged protocol of the Colts drafting Perkins in the ninth round and the Bears picking Meredith in the third. Bears owner George Halas made the pick to help ensure that the expansion Cowboys had their potential franchise quarterback. They were, after that, utterly devoid of any advantages, something Halas and the other owners must have been aware of. They weren't stupid. The draft in those days was held much earlier than it is now, which made it impossible for the Cowboys to take part.

In exchange for keeping Meredith and Perkins, the Cowboys gave the Bears their third-round choice in the 1962 NFL draft and sent their ninth-round choice to the Colts.

Omitted from the 1960 draft, the Cowboys entered the League with a crushing disadvantage. They were at least permitted the strange option of being able to grab players via the expansion draft, through which they picked thirty-six players—hence the additional $550,000 they were forced to pony up to the twelve other owners. The other teams were allowed to protect twenty-five players from a thirty-six-man roster, giving Dallas 24 hours to pick three players from a pool of unprotected players, who were, at best, woefully mediocre. In other words, Dallas got to pick from the eleven worst players on each team, many of whom were older veterans at the end of their careers.

In an effort to shore up their glaringly deficient roster, the Cowboys signed veteran quarterback (and Meredith mentor) Eddie LeBaron from the Washington Redskins and wide receiver Billy Howton from the Cleveland Browns. LeBaron, who was 5 foot 7, only an inch taller than Clint Jr., was nicknamed "the little general."

The Cowboys opened the season in the Cotton Bowl, drawing a surprising 30,000 fans (leaving, however, 45,504 empty seats). The next week, they lost to the Philadelphia Eagles before an announced Cotton Bowl crowd of 18,500. Poor attendance and mediocrity defined the Cowboys' debut season, with estimated crowd size sinking to a dismal 10,000 during a rainy November game against the San Francisco 49ers.

Cotton Bowl officials didn't bother to install turnstiles until several years later, so 10,000 may have been a generous estimate.

At one point, peering down from the press box, unable to spot even a single fan—the crowd, as it were, had nestled under the overhang to avoid the downpour—Clint made a vow to himself to never again sit in the press box. Instead, he would confine himself to the lower deck, giving him the privilege of feeling the heat from at least a few warm bodies—fellow spectators. Even then, the lack of humanity was jolting. During the waterlogged game against the Niners, the crowd looked more like a khaki-clad army than seasoned football enthusiasts. Easily explained, as Clint ruefully admitted—it was, after all, "Boy Scouts-are-let-in-free day."

The dreariness continued unabated until December 1960, in the next to last game of the season, when the Cowboys fashioned a thin ray of promise:

A 31–31 tie in Yankee Stadium against the New York Giants. The team finished 0–11–1.

The Dallas Texans had a better go of it in 1960, having started on equal footing with all the other teams in the AFL. They drew an estimated 42,000 to the Cotton Bowl for their first home game against the Los Angeles Chargers.

But from that early season peak, the crowds diminished—to 37,500; 21,000; 21,000; 20,000; 12,000; and 18,000.

Looking back from an altitude of 2021—when Jerry Jones charges almost $400 apiece for the cheapest reserved seats at Jerry World—the Cowboys charged $4.60 for a reserved seat from 1960 through 1962. Even on the 50-yard line, to see such players as Jim Brown and Y. A. Tittle. General admission (read it: end zone) was $2.75. From 1963 to 1965, the price of a reserved seat escalated to $5.50, with general admission costing $3.50. From 1966 to 1968—when, finally, the Cowboys recorded three consecutive winning seasons—reserved seats jumped to $6 apiece, with end-zone seats costing $4. A personal story: as a teenager, coauthor Granberry used his paper-route money to buy three season tickets for himself, his dad, and his brother.

Despite such incredibly low prices, Cowboys' attendance fared no better in 1961 than it had in 1960. Gazing back at the team's down-then-up narrative, it's not hard to find the beginning of the turning point. It came in 1961, when, finally, the Cowboys landed the first pick in the first round of the NFL draft—and didn't miss. Indeed, they couldn't have gotten it any better. They picked a future Hall of Famer in defensive tackle Bob Lilly. (In 2020, in celebration of the League's centennial, Lilly was named one of the hundred best players in NFL history.)

They traded for future superstar linebacker Chuck Howley and signed running back Amos Marsh as a free agent. Even so, frustration continued, especially in the rivalry with the AFL. Dallas drafted talented linebacker E. J. Holub, who signed with Dallas—but with the Texans, not the Cowboys.

Schramm made a genius move, however, by lobbying NFL owners to allow the team to enter its second season as members of the Eastern Conference. Geographically, it made no sense, but with Dallas in the same conference as New York, Philadelphia, and Washington—the epicenter of print-dominated news in 1960s America—Schramm knew that playing in the Eastern Conference would grease the wheels for a marketing bonanza. It's among the reasons that, in 2021, the most valuable sports franchise in the world for multiple years in a row was not a team from New York or London. It was the

Cowboys, with a daunting value of $5.7 billion. Would that have happened had they been in the Western Conference? We think not.

During their first year, the Cowboys played every team in the East and West at least once, rounding out a twelve-game season. One of the reasons the Cowboys got their wish of playing in the Eastern Conference had a lot to do with *shared* ticket sales, a socialistic concept that arguably made the NFL a sports-world juggernaut. The NFL in this respect has long been different from Major League Baseball, which takes a Darwinian approach. Revenue sharing allows such franchises as the Green Bay Packers in tiny Green Bay, Wisconsin—whose population is barely more than 100,000 even today—to not only exist but also flourish. (Dallas suburb Plano is almost three times bigger than Green Bay.) In baseball, teams in San Diego and Tampa, Florida, simply don't play on a level playing field with the New York Yankees or Los Angeles Dodgers. Nor will they unless the paradigm is changed. Or the owners of those teams choose to spend their own millions, as the Padres' owner is now doing to compete with the Dodgers.

Because NFL owners shared ticket revenue, then as now, the owners of the Eastern Conference laid down a welcome mat for the Cowboys, who played in the 75,504-seat Cotton Bowl—which was at the time one of the League's biggest stadiums. So, credit the Cotton Bowl with playing a huge role in the Cowboys' success. Its size allowed an entrée into the Eastern Conference, which in turn dramatically heightened the Cowboys' profile and potential for marketing. In other words, it was one more example of "follow the money." Even to this day, the Cowboys share the NFC East with Philadelphia, Washington, and New York. Which, again, makes no sense.

Not that it helped on the field, at least not in the early days. The Cowboys finished 1961 with a 4–9–1 record, which was, of course, far better than their winless inaugural campaign. Attendance continued to be a problem, with an October game against the New York Giants drawing an estimated 41,500. But then a November game against the Washington Redskins drew only 17,500, and again, that was an estimate, maybe even a benevolent estimate.

Clint had figured out by this time that, regardless of crowd size, the Cotton Bowl left much to be desired from the fan's experience. It was either too hot or too cold, exposing the Cowboys' clientele to searing heat, blinding rain, and cold that, during late-season games, often resembled an arctic blast. It wasn't Green Bay, but it was hardly San Diego.

Fans in the Cotton Bowl sat on splintery wooden benches, and those under the "overhang"—seats below the upper deck—often craned their necks, having to peer around obstructed views. It could be so much better, Clint determined, and in the future, it would have to be.

After winning four of their first seven games, the Cowboys plummeted in the season's second half. They failed to win any of their final seven, managing only a 28–28 tie in the Cotton Bowl against Washington.

But something was beginning to happen, quietly, amid the shadows that often engulfed the Cotton Bowl in late afternoon. The Cowboys were building a killer defense, which did not escape the attention of Tex Maule, the ace football writer for *Sports Illustrated*. The future looked bright, though it would take a while—as in years.

Tom Landry had earned a reputation as a defensive genius with the New York Giants, where a fellow assistant was an offensive guru named Vince Lombardi. Landry had, however, excelled as a halfback with the Texas Longhorns and would soon flex his muscles as an offensive coach. (As history later showed, the soon-to-be-defined destinies of Landry and Lombardi were fully intertwined.)

As Landry evolved, so did the Cowboys, with the 1962 season serving up the chance to acquire even more building blocks. They included defensive lineman George Andrie and defensive backs Mike Gaechter and Cornell Green. The selections of Gaechter and Green offered a blueprint that became a Cowboys trademark—pick a good athlete, even if he'd played other sports or hadn't played football. Green was a college basketball player, while Gaechter excelled in track.

The bad news about the 1962 season? Attendance fell dramatically, maybe because the Cotton Bowl had installed a turnstile system, or maybe because fans were already tired of a team enduring its third straight losing season.

The Cowboys opened the 1962 season at home against Washington, drawing only 15,730. A Dallas high school game that year between Bryan Adams and Samuell drew a bigger crowd.

Attendance rose for the second game of the 1962 season, but as much as any in Cowboys' history, it underscored the frustration that bedeviled Clint's team.

The matchup against the Pittsburgh Steelers drew 19,478, and the Cowboys would have won the game had it not been for a holding penalty in the end zone.

Eddie LeBaron threw what appeared to be a 99-yard touchdown pass to Frank Clarke, another rising star, but a holding penalty in the end zone, called against offensive lineman Andy Cverko, wiped out a 6-point touchdown and added 2 points to the Steelers' tally. A player charged with holding in his own team's end zone automatically results in a two-point safety, which proved to be the margin of victory with the Steelers winning 30–28.

In many ways, the Cverko holding penalty, which nullified what would have been to this day the longest touchdown pass in Cowboys history, symbolized the team's earliest frustrations. And it opened the door to the ribald humor favored by Clint Murchison Jr. and his best bud, Steve "Cottontail" Schneider.

It was, of course, an earlier era, one in which letter-writing thrived, and the funnier the better. So, Schneider could not pass up the chance to send *Dallas Times Herald* sports columnist Dan Jenkins his own take on the busted play, dated September 25, 1962:

> I am a geologist, so I know a lot about pro-football rules and officiating. Therefore, I feel that I am obligated to explain the controversial call in the Cowboy-Steeler game on Sunday.
>
> Actually, the call was right and should stand but not for the reasons stated by the officials, who were too embarrassed to tell the true story. Here is what really occurred.
>
> The play itself was as clean as a whistle—except possibly for Bobby Layne's yelling, "Look out for the water bucket," as Frank Clarke came by the Steeler bench at full speed looking back over his shoulder for LeBaron's pass. The comedy of errors really is attributable to "Old 36," the head linesman. You see, "Old 36" used to be a tournament golf referee before his eyesight got so poor he couldn't see golf balls anymore, and not wanting to stop his officiating career, he looked around for a sport that used a larger ball.
>
> Now "Old 36" still has retained some of the practices of his golf days, one of which is spotting the location of the ball on the field with a coin. He was using shiny new dimes Sunday, and these caught the eye of both Big Daddy Lipscomb of the Steelers and Andy Cverko of the Cowboys. Unknown to the spectators, much of the vicious line play was really a result of Lipscomb and Cverko going for the dime when the ball was snapped.
>
> At the time of the critical play, "Old 36" had lost about $1.80 in dimes and was rightfully getting sore. To add to his misery, his hay fever was acting up requiring that he blow his nose continuously. "Old 36," determined to get his dime back for a change, dove into the pack of players before the play was even over, and in the three-way scrap that ensued with Lipscomb and Cverko over the dime, his soggy handkerchief slipped from his pocket. This is where the trouble began. Before the handkerchief could be recovered by "Old 36," it had been spotted by the referee, Emil Heintz, who raced forward gleefully blowing his whistle to stop the play. And then, as if pre-arranged, at just the precise moment, a flock of pigeons flew low over the group of dumbfounded players and officials on the field. Referee Heintz caught a glimpse out of the corner of his

eye of the oncoming bird formation and quite naturally threw his hands above his head in a protective manner. Before he realized that he had inadvertently given the signal for a safety, two points were on the scoreboard for the Steelers, to everyone's surprise including Heintz. Unfortunately, once a decision is made, it cannot be changed.

To cover up, "Old 36" charged Cverko with holding, bitter because Andy had come up with the dime. Coach Landry was mad, the Cowboy fans were mad, but Frank Clarke was the maddest of them all as he walked back down the field with the football under his arm and the Steeler water bucket on his foot.

My cousin, Cottontail, says the Cowboys need a good dropkicker. But I say this year they would be better off to trade their top draft choice for a couple of good referees.

If that wasn't enough to gin up Clint's wickedly devilish sense of humor as a way of coping, his rivalry with George Preston Marshall (GPM) was.

On November 4, 1962, Clint exacted his revenge.

But one first must go back to November 19, 1961, when Clint and his buddies cooked up their initial attack on GPM.

The Cowboys were playing the Redskins in their gleaming new home, one they shared with baseball's Washington Senators—who, ironically, in 1972, became the Texas Rangers, playing just a few miles from the Cowboys' new home, Texas Stadium. That, too, fueled the DC–Dallas sports rivalry, since North Texas stole the capital city's Major League Baseball team, with Washington not getting a replacement until 2005, when the Montreal Expos became the Washington Nationals.

Back to Clint's military-style attack on November 19, 1961, and the question: Was it inspired by stadium envy? Perhaps, but it *was* funny and lastingly memorable. And if anyone deserved it, GPM did. He was, for one, a notorious racist (more about that in a moment).

In his essay for ESPN, former Cowboy Pat Toomay wrote about it as well as anyone ever has:[1]

> Three Murchison cronies who lived in Washington, plus Bob Thompson, a Texan who was also well-known in the capital, decided to have a little fun with Marshall for being such a jerk when Clint was trying to buy his team.
>
> So, the night before the game, operatives snuck into D. C. Stadium and spread chicken feed all over the field. The next day, when a team of Alaskan sled dogs would pull Santa Claus onto the field at halftime, a bunch of hungry chickens would be released to gobble the feed. CBS would be televising the festivities live. The thought of those chickens wandering around as the dogs showed up made Murchison's buddies howl.

The day of the game, two crates of chickens were smuggled into the stadium, stashed in a dugout and covered with a tarp. All told, there were seventy-six chickens, seventy-five white, one black. At the time Marshall was the only NFL owner who hadn't signed an African American player.

Before we resume Toomay's account, we need to dwell on this particular point a bit longer. Marshall was so entrenched in keeping the NFL an all-white league, long after Jackie Robinson had broken baseball's color line in 1947, that he once explained his antipathy with signing Black players by making this outlandish statement: "We'll start signing Negroes when the Harlem Globetrotters start signing whites."[2]

GPM didn't budge until 1962, when he allowed—albeit reluctantly and defiantly—a trade for Bobby Mitchell, an African American, who went on to become one of the greatest players in the history of the game. Mitchell, who caused plenty of problems for the Cowboys on the playing field, was inducted into the Pro Football Hall of Fame in 1983.

As Thomas G. Smith reveals in his book, *Showdown: JFK and the Integration of the Washington Redskins*,[3] Marshall was *forced* to change. In 1961, the Redskins were preparing to become primary occupants of the gleaming new DC Stadium (renamed RFK Stadium after the assassination in 1968 of Democratic presidential candidate Robert F. Kennedy).

The stadium sat on federal land, so in effect, President John F. Kennedy's interior secretary, Stewart Udall, served in 1961 as the de facto landlord of DC Stadium. Udall gave Marshall the first of two ultimatums, according to *Showdown*: "If you do not hire a Black player, you will not be able to use this new stadium." Marshall refused. As Smith writes, "Udall backed off, and the Redskins did play in their new stadium for the 1961 season." But Udall persisted, slapping GPM with a second threat, saying that, "if you don't integrate in 1962, you will not be able to use the stadium." Smith writes: "He told Marshall to sign or trade for a Black player, turning the 1962 draft into a showdown. Marshall refused to draft an African American, so he sent coach Bill McPeak to do it for him." As fate would have it, the Redskins benefited enormously from what happened in the '62 draft.

Washington selected Syracuse running back Ernie Davis—who was also African American—as the first pick in the '62 draft, taking the player widely regarded as the best in the draft and potentially one of the best ever. In other words, a steal. Surprisingly, they then traded Davis—who, unbeknownst to the Redskins and everyone else in the NFL, was dying of leukemia and would never play a down of professional football—and in return scored big.

In the trade, the Cleveland Browns were thrilled to get Davis, whom they believed would be a bridge to the next generation by following in the footsteps of the great Jim Brown, arguably the best running back in NFL history. In return, the Redskins got Bobby Mitchell *and* first-round draft pick Leroy Jackson—for a player who would soon be dead. Mitchell ended up a Hall of Famer and remained with the Redskins for years, ascending to the job of assistant general manager. He said in later years that he never felt any direct racism from Marshall but in the early years got plenty from Redskins fans.

Now, back to Toomay's account of Murchison's mischief against GPM, during the '61 season finale:

> All went well until just before halftime when a Redskins official wandered by and heard the chickens. He queried the guard, who tried to buy his silence with a [$100 bill]. The official called the police. Both the guard and the chickens were arrested.
>
> Predictably, Marshall was furious when he heard about the prank. He filed a complaint with commissioner Pete Rozelle. He named Thompson as a conspirator. He made ominous threats. But Marshall's pique only heightened the pranksters' resolve. The following year, as the Cowboy game drew near, one member of the group vowed, "There will be chickens in D. C. Stadium."

Chapter Two of the Chicken Attack did indeed occur less than a year later, on November 4, 1962, within weeks of the peaceful resolution of the Cuban Missile Crisis. That perilous moment placed the United States and the Soviet Union on the threshold of nuclear war, when the United States discovered that the Soviet Union had installed, in Fidel Castro's Communist Cuba, a fleet of nuclear warheads. They were 90 miles from Miami, locked and loaded and aimed at the United States.

Ending it without a catastrophe was arguably President John F. Kennedy's finest hour, serving as a prelude to this: what an irony his final day as the American president would play in the Cowboys' own history a year later.

But in the post-missile crisis days of 1962, everyone needed a laugh. And Clint and his buddies were more than happy to give them one.

The stage was set. Cowboys versus Redskins in DC Stadium on November 4, 1962. As Toomay wrote:

> I wish I'd been there. As Dallas columnist Sam Blair reported: "A few minutes before kickoff it happened. The Indian princesses pranced onto the field, followed by the Redskin band playing 'Hail to the Redskins.' As they reached midfield, four banners were unfurled from the upper deck of the stadium. The

banners said: CHICKENS. One was at each 50-yard line and in the center of each end zone."

The banners were the cue for the acrobats, reported Blair. "Dressed in chicken costumes, they rushed down through the stands, tumbled over the rail and dashed onto the field. Each man carried a bag, from which he tossed colored eggs as he ran. One guy was grabbed by stadium guards and gave up easily but the other was dedicated to his task."

By now the band was playing the National Anthem so no one could stop the man in the chicken suit as he zigzagged through the formation. According to Blair's account, "He pulled one real chicken out of his bag and released it. Then he wriggled away from some stadium guards, jigged up and down, shook his feathers. The real chicken was captured and carried out, but the man was elusive. As stadium guards pursued, he ran out to the middle of the field, turned a cartwheel, fell and sprawled on the 30-yard line. Then, as the teams began to run on the field, the man leaped up, climbed into the stands, and dashed up the steps. The Cowboy Chicken Club had succeeded!"

In the game itself, the 'Skins, 4–2–2 coming in, disintegrated before a standing-room-only crowd, as [Redskins quarterback Norm] Snead completed only 11 of 27 passes in a 38–10 Cowboys' rout. The next morning, the game story in the *Dallas Morning News* detailed the Redskins' demise. The scoring summary, in agate type, was the usual breakdown of stats. Only the last line was different:

Attendance—49,888 (and one chicken)."

Them were the days.

But, hey, that wasn't all. The night before the successful (human) chicken attack in 1962, pranksters had given GPM a sneak preview by sneaking into his plush hotel suite and inserting a large, live turkey in the bathroom. *Gobble, gobble.*

What ensued was apparently not a pleasant experience.

"Chickens are nice," Marshall said, "but a man shouldn't fool with a mad turkey."

Oddly, the story line involving Marshall added yet another chapter in 2020. Shortly after the killing of a Black man named George Floyd by Minneapolis police, demonstrations erupted across the country. The Redskins responded by removing a memorial to Marshall that had stood outside RFK Stadium for years. In addition, they expurgated the Marshall name from all official team material, including their Ring of Fame, history wall, and website.

Curiously, Jordan Wright, Marshall's granddaughter, told the *Washington Post* that she did not object to the statue being removed.

"No, not at all—not one damn bit," she said. "I was glad to see it come down. It's past time to see it go."

And in the summer of 2020, pressured heavily by corporate sponsors, the Washington franchise decided after 87 years that it was also time to ditch the name *Redskins*. The main objection came from FedEx, which told Redskins owner Daniel Snyder—who had stated adamantly in the past that he would *never* drop the Redskins name—that it would sever its contract with the franchise, resulting in $45 million of lost income for Snyder. FedEx was not alone. Fox Business reported in July 2020 that "a group of 87 investment firms and shareholders demanded that PepsiCo, Nike and FedEx cut ties with the team unless officials agree to change the name."

So, finally it happened. *Redskins* was out and *Washington Football Team* was in. Until, of course, they could figure out a less offensive moniker than *Redskins*, a name that made the notorious George Preston Marshall feel all mushy inside. In 2022, the team finally rebranded itself as the Commanders, prompting DC sports wit Tony Kornheiser to say that headline writers would undoubtedly shorten the name to "Commies," for a team whose home market holds the seat of American democracy.

And therein lies a compelling tie-in with *Hole in the Roof*: Until Texas Stadium spearheaded the change, individual franchises did not carry their own corporate sponsorships. Those existed only under the banner of the NFL, which then shared the revenue equally with all its teams. FedEx is one of many examples of the latter generation. For FedEx to even be able to give directly to an individual team and not the league as a whole was brought about indirectly by Clint and Texas Stadium but put into overdrive by Jerry Jones. As for Snyder finally, reluctantly giving in to the name change, we offer the three little words stated by Watergate source Deep Throat in the book and movie *All the President's Men*: "Follow the money." Or, as network executive Don Ohlmeyer, the first hired producer of *Monday Night Football*, once famously said to broadcaster Tony Kornheiser: "The answer to all your questions is money."

The George Preston Marshall story line accentuated the fact that, in his prime, Clint Jr. was a truly funny man. There are so many examples, so many grin-worthy stories to be told, we can't share them all. But we have to share this one.

Only a week after the human-chicken prank in Washington, the Cowboys were scheduled to return home for a game in the Cotton Bowl.

And what do you know, Clint's team surprised everybody by drawing 45,668 to a game against the New York Giants. For 1962, it was a damn good crowd. But Clint himself may have had something to do with the jacked-up attendance.

New York restaurateur Toots Shor counted among his closest friends Supreme Court chief justice Earl Warren *and* Clint Murchison Jr. So, he told the Cowboys owner weeks in advance that he really, really wanted to fly to Dallas to see the game. So, Clint complied. One morning in New York, a massive truck pulled up in front of Shor's legendary Manhattan restaurant. Delivery personnel brought in box after bulging box. A puzzled Shor opened the card that came with the last of this massive shipment and found his answer: Clint had delivered to Shor 10,000 tickets to the Giants–Cowboys game in the Cotton Bowl and added a note of wry explanation:

"In case you want to bring any of your friends with you, I am also sending you Sections 1, 2, 3, and 4."

CHAPTER THREE

Bizarre beyond Belief

T HE 1963 SEASON was easily one of the strangest in Cowboys history. The team opened with four straight losses, but amid the failure, slivers of hope began to surface. For one, the Cowboys no longer shared Dallas or the Cotton Bowl with the red-shirted Texans. After winning the AFL championship in 1962, beating the Houston Oilers in overtime, Lamar Hunt stunned Dallas and the Cowboys by announcing he was moving the team to Kansas City to become the Chiefs. Reluctantly, even glumly, Texans fans were forced to ponder the unthinkable:

They would have to become Cowboys fans.

Whether that made a difference, the Cowboys enjoyed an immediate bump at the gate. They drew 36,432 to the Cotton Bowl for their first game against the St. Louis Cardinals and 28,710 to their second, against mighty Jim Brown and the Cleveland Browns.

On October 13, 1963, they won their first game of the season, beating the Detroit Lions 17–14 before a Cotton Bowl crowd of 27,264. It proved to be a noteworthy game and weekend for several reasons.

For one, you could easily make the case that the "fully depreciated" Cotton Bowl (Clint's name for it) was in its glory on that Friday, Saturday, and Sunday. The day before the Cowboys' first win of the season, No. 2 Texas beat No. 1 Oklahoma 28–7 in what amounted to a makeshift national championship during their annual State Fair of Texas blood match.

But the night before *that*, in a game that launched a colossal gridiron weekend, Southern Methodist University pulled a stunner by upsetting Navy and its future Heisman Trophy–winning quarterback, Roger Staubach, 32–28.

Navy lost only two games that season, finishing as the No. 2 team in the country behind national champion Texas, which defeated Staubach and Navy in a return trip to the Cotton Bowl on January 1, 1964.

Talk about memorable moments. The triple-header served as one of the sweetest page-turners in Cotton Bowl history, but something even more noteworthy went down during the Navy–SMU game. Dallas fans were unknowingly introduced to their future through the neon persona of Captain America, Roger Staubach, who would leave the academy at the end of the season and spend five years in the US Navy, including service in Vietnam, before returning as a Cowboys rookie in 1969.

Three weeks after Staubach and Navy lost to SMU under the fair's "Friday Night Lights," as Staubach dubbed it years later, the Cowboys crushed Washington in the Cotton Bowl, drawing a listless 18,838.

Two weeks later, they beat the Philadelphia Eagles and drew 23,694, which hardly mattered—America was one way before the game and one way after. The Eagles–Cowboys game took place on November 17, 1963, only five days before Dallas history, American history, and Cowboys history endured a permanent change.

Firing from a sixth-floor window, a sniper named Lee Harvey Oswald assassinated President John F. Kennedy on Elm Street in Dallas, placing the Cowboys in the crosshairs of Assassination Aftermath.

What happened to the team that day and two days later, when they flew to Cleveland for an ill-advised trip, charted their future for decades. As America's Team, they helped heal a wounded Dallas more than any other single force. They were the catharsis, Dallas's Angels of Redemption, whether they wanted to be or not. They were the unlikely counterbalance to the "city of hate," the label inflicted on Dallas in post-assassination America.

But the impact of the city's darkest moment reached even deeper, extending its tentacles to the stadium debate that would engulf Clint Murchison Jr., the Cowboys, and Dallas itself in the years, even decades, to come.

Looking back at the assassination on its fiftieth anniversary in 2013, it was easy to see the damage it had done to downtown, which became a ghost town in the aftermath of Kennedy's death. A state-of-the-art stadium in downtown Dallas, housing the blue-starred Cowboys, would have gone a long way toward repairing the city's image, not to mention the steroid-like effect it might have had on downtown real estate.

The Texans' departure and the cloud of gloom hovering over Dallas made Clint want to leave the bedraggled Cotton Bowl even more. He was tired of its extreme weather, its obstructed views, its cramped, splintery seating, its smelly restrooms, its carny-like concession stands, and the increasingly grisly crime invading its surrounding neighborhoods. The team's fans and the city of Dallas deserved better, he thought. Clint had an idea, but as T. S. Eliot once wrote: "Between the idea and the reality falls the shadow."[1] Clint would soon be wallowing in a giant shadow cast by the Dallas establishment.

One must first understand the impact of the assassination on Clint's team, which in 1963 was enduring its fourth consecutive losing season, with little to show for it. What the team endured on one of the strangest weekends in American history gave the Cowboys little hope for expecting that anything might be different in the future. And yet, in so many ways, it proved to be a turning point.

On Saturday, November 23, 1963, hours after President Kennedy was assassinated in Dealey Plaza, the Cowboys reported to Love Field for a trip to Cleveland.

The players were shocked at having to go. During the flight, they stared out the window at the whirring propellers of their Douglas DC-7, courting a sense of dread over what might await them on the shores of Lake Erie.

It was bothersome to many that Don Meredith, the team's happy-go-lucky quarterback, was sitting stoically, staring out the window. Meredith's world had gone into upheaval the day before, when, right after lunch, Friday's pregame practice was interrupted by a trainer gone bonkers.

"He came running up, yelling, 'Kennedy's been shot! Kennedy's been shot!' And everything just kind of went crazy from there," Meredith said in a 1982 interview with coauthor Michael Granberry. "And," he said, "it stayed crazy."

Meredith was 25, enduring the ups and downs of his own difficult life, which included a 1963 divorce from his college sweetheart, with whom he shared a daughter. The Cowboys were nothing to brag about, trapped in the midst of a 4–10 season.

Since being founded in 1960, Dallas's expansion franchise had put the *m* in mediocrity.

And now a new problem: they were from Dallas, which, minutes after Kennedy's death, had wormed its way into infamy.

Commissioner Pete Rozelle, citing JFK's "avid love of sport," ignored the pleas of his fellow National Football League executives, including Clint, to cancel the weekend's games.

Pierre Salinger, JFK's press secretary and Rozelle's college classmate, had told him the president would have wanted the games to be played, which Rozelle said later—regrettably—drove his decision. "It has been traditional in sports for athletes to perform in times of great personal tragedy. Football was Mr. Kennedy's game. He thrived on competition," Rozelle said in a statement, sending the Cowboys to Cleveland.

Defensive tackle Bob Lilly grew up as a West Texas kid loving football, but this was one game he didn't want to play. Lilly soon discovered that the people of Cleveland didn't want to see him either.

As the Cowboys' bus pulled up in front of the aging Cleveland Hotel, Lilly and his teammates were stunned to see that bellhops, normally in a frenzy to help football players, were turning a cold shoulder, wanting no part of the team from Dallas.

The Cowboys unloaded their own bags and took them to their rooms. The icy reception prompted Don Perkins, the team's star running back and an African American who had felt discrimination more than once in the years preceding the 1964 Civil Rights Act, to say he felt "tainted."

"I just wanted to go hide somewhere," Perkins said.[2]

The reception in Cleveland made the players especially nervous about eating out as a group, which they did before every road game. Lilly and roommate George Andrie found a diner near the hotel and retreated to a corner where no one could see them. "I didn't blame people for being mad at us," Lilly told the *Dallas Morning News* in 2003. "I think I probably would've felt the same way."

Rodger Jones, an editorial writer now retired from the *News*, was a boy living in Cleveland on the Sunday of the ill-fated game. Jones's father was the baseball writer for the *Plain Dealer*. His family never missed a Browns home game. But they wouldn't be going to this one, he told his son. The elder Jones felt it was inappropriate to go to a game that day, especially to see a team from Dallas.

Browns owner Art Modell picked up on the hostile vibe and began a series of preemptive measures. As soon as he heard Friday's news, he placed a frantic call to Rozelle, begging him to cancel the seven games scheduled that weekend.

"Trust me," Modell told the commissioner. "Don't play those damn games."[3]

Rozelle refused to budge, even arguing the point that playing the games was a good thing. It made no sense to Modell, who reminded him that network television would carry Kennedy news 24/7 and preempt every game, which is precisely what happened.

Rozelle's intransigence prompted Modell to go into "battlefield" mode, stationing police sharpshooters throughout the 83,000-seat Cleveland Municipal Stadium. As players took the field, men toting weapons stood guard on the roof of the aging building.

"I felt like George Patton," Modell told the *News* in 2003. "It looked like an armed camp when I got through with it."[4] Psychologically, Modell took yet another precaution: he ordered the public-address announcer to refer to the visiting team only as "Cowboys," never "Dallas."

Tight end Lee Folkins, one of Meredith's favorite targets, loved the pregame ritual of being a visiting player, hearing the "buzz" that came from the hometown crowd when the white-shirted Cowboys walked on the visitors' field for the first time.

"But when we ran out, it was so quiet, you could hear a pin drop," Folkins said. "It really struck me how quiet it was. One person yelled out, 'Dallas, go home.' But that was it. The rest of the time, it was scary quiet."

With pregame preparations over, the Cowboys huddled in the small, cold locker room and waited. They sat quietly, nervously, staring at the floor.

Shortly before kickoff, reports began to circulate that Jack Ruby, a Dallas nightclub owner, had fatally shot Lee Harvey Oswald, the suspected presidential assassin, in the basement of the Dallas police station.

Months earlier, during the Cowboys' final days of preseason training in Dallas, Folkins and Meredith were cooling off from a hot August workout by swimming in the pool of the team hotel on North Central Expressway. There, they met two women who told them they worked as strippers at the Carousel Club. They invited Meredith and Folkins to join them later that night, which they did.

They stayed only a few minutes, Folkins said. They were so turned off by the "obnoxious" owner of the club, Ruby, that they got up and left. Folkins was stunned to hear that the same odd man who owned the Carousel was the guy who'd turned yet another page in the assassination narrative.

He concedes, a half century later, that it's one of the bizarre footnotes of that era in Dallas history that the great Don Meredith would have been sitting, if only for a few minutes, at the same table as Ruby.

Meredith, Folkins, and the other Cowboys trundled up the steps of the baseball dugout and onto the soggy turf of Municipal Stadium to brace for kickoff. What no one told them was that, at that moment, a tribute to the slain president was occurring on the field. Four uniformed officers, marching in regimented formation, carried the flag at half-staff. The only sound one heard was the officer's feet—until the Cowboys interrupted.

Suddenly, the crowd of more than 55,000 turned surly, emitting what sounded like the growl of a massive, menacing bear. "There we were," Meredith said, "with the little stars on our helmets." The team responded with what the quarterback called a truly "awful effort. It was a listless game, pathetic, the eeriest I've ever been involved in."[5]

The Cowboys lost, 27–17. Meredith completed thirteen of thirty passes for 93 yards. Jim Brown, the great Cleveland running back, rushed for 51 yards. The flight home was quiet, the propellers of the DC-7 humming outside. At one point, Folkins said, the pilot came over the PA system to tell them a bit more about Ruby killing Oswald, which only added to the sense of numbness.

None of them knew it at the time, but for the Cowboys and Dallas, the Kennedy assassination had opened the door to a strange new world.

"The assassination," Meredith said in 1982, sipping coffee and smoking cigarettes at his home in Beverly Hills. "I was going through some fairly severe growing pains. So was the city, so was the nation. Everybody was really, really frustrated. A terrific amount of anxiety was everywhere, just ripping it all apart. Dallas began to change almost overnight. Attitudinal changes. It seemed like the cork finally blew, and all the craziness came gushing out."[6]

Unbeknownst to Meredith, "the craziness," as it were, would soon drop its own weird footnote in the life story of a 21-year-old from Cincinnati, Ohio, destined to become Dandy Don's successor as the next iconic Cowboys quarterback.

As the winner of the 1963 Heisman Trophy—college football's highest individual honor—Staubach was due to appear on the cover of the November 29, 1963, edition of *Life*, America's signature magazine. Preliminary issues were already printed. As he noted years later in an interview with the *Washington Post*, Budd Thalman, the sports information director at the

Naval Academy, asked the man from *Life*: "Is there anything that could keep Staubach off the cover?"

"Only a catastrophe," said the man from *Life*.

Then, of course, the catastrophe happened. The image of Roger Staubach on the cover of *Life* had to be replaced, overnight, by shocking images of what Meredith called "the craziness" gushing out of Dallas.

CHAPTER FOUR

Dare to Be Different

THE 1964 SEASON began with the Cowboys losing four of their first six games. One game ended in a tie, adding up to yet another mediocre record of 5–8–1. In the same way the assassination had served as a pivotal moment the year before, 1964 delivered its own weird karma.

For one, Clint stunned the Dallas sports media by telling them they were right, by God! He *did* need to do something about Tom Landry.

What the sports media had in mind, of course, was Landry's immediate termination. So, Clint responded the way only Clint would, awarding Landry *a 10-year contract*, despite four consecutive losing seasons.

The '64 season would, of course, be the fifth.

In addition to Clint's decision to prolong by a decade the Landry era, whose upside was so difficult to see, the season was noteworthy for another reason. The Cowboys had begun to pride themselves on signing players who had not played football in college. They included ace defensive back Cornell Green, who joined the Cowboys in 1962 after not playing football at Utah State University. He was selected in the 1962 National Basketball Association draft but not the NFL draft. But as a Cowboys player, Green was damn good, becoming a five-time Pro Bowl selection and four-time first-team All-Pro cornerback. And, in 1972, he got a Super Bowl ring.

The Greening of the Cowboys secondary was, in many ways, an extension of the team's obsession with doing things differently. Clint had a degree from MIT, and in hiring scouting director Gil Brandt, who relied almost exclusively on computer technology—an alien concept to the NFL and even the country in 1964—he charted a course that would separate the Cowboys from the rest of the League.

It's important to note that Clint would soon do the same with stadiums, creating a model and launching a trend that, as we've said, continues to define the NFL more than half a century later.

In 1970, Clint wrote a piece for the *Dallas Cowboys Insiders Newsletter* in which he cited 1964 as a turning point in his feelings about the Cotton Bowl.

"By 1964," he wrote, "it had become obvious that the Cotton Bowl, a grand lady in her day, suffered from terminal illness. That year I had to resort to mild trickery to have the restrooms whitewashed; later a high school band member was to suffer heatstroke before water fountains were installed; and on, and on and on. The question arose as to whether the Cotton Bowl should be repaired, or a new stadium built; and if the latter, where."[1]

It would take several more years for the stadium debate to position itself front and center. In the meantime, the Cowboys were more preoccupied with how to win games. And part of that formula involved doing things differently, as it would in the not-too-distant future with *where* the games were played.

In the aftermath of the Kennedy assassination, America was changing, its black-and-white world giving way to a new kind of color. A band from England called the Beatles seized the world's attention, popping up on the *Ed Sullivan Show* in early 1964 (less than 3 months after Kennedy's death) and changing pop culture forever. Their hair was long. Girls screamed when they sang. They dared to be different.

And so did the Cowboys, in more ways than one.

In 1964, the Cowboys signed Pete Gent, who'd excelled on the Michigan State University basketball team from 1962 to 1964 but who, like Green, had not played a down of college football. The lanky Gent signed as a wide receiver and had a knack for making seemingly impossible catches. And yet, he would come to be known for a radically different reason.

Gent's tenure as a Cowboy, marked by a slew of injuries that lingered for five seasons, gave him the chance to make lemonade out of lemons. His Cowboys tenure became grist for a literary mill, resulting in a favorably reviewed novel called *North Dallas Forty*. Gent the novelist exposed the underbelly of professional football and offered a less-than-flattering portrait of a coach modeled on—who else?—Landry. But those elements—signing basketball players and having your team profiled in a novel that would soon become a Hollywood movie—only served to amplify the Cowboys' increasingly high profile.

Clint knew he would never have the mojo he needed to ask for a new stadium with the Cowboys never once managing a winning season. But in 1965, they came tantalizingly close, finishing for the first time with something other than a losing record. The final tally was 7–7, which was, at least, progress.

In keeping with its philosophy of signing good athletes, regardless of football acumen, the Cowboys stunned the NFL in 1965 by admitting onto their roster track superstar Bob Hayes, billed as the "world's fastest human." Hayes won two gold medals at the 1964 Tokyo Olympics and in 1972 became the only person to win an Olympic gold medal *and* a Super Bowl ring. In Tokyo, he tied the world record in the 100-meter dash with a winning time of 10.06 seconds, despite borrowing a teammate's left shoe at the last minute.

Later that day, he ran in the 4×100-meter relay final. One of the French runners taunted American Paul Drayton, saying, "You can't win. All you have is Bob Hayes." Hayes ran an incredible anchor leg in that relay, delivering yet another gold medal in a world-record 39.06 seconds, prompting Drayton to respond, "That's all we need, pal."[2]

Hayes alone forever changed how defense is played in the NFL, catching twelve touchdown passes in 1965, mostly by outrunning, by quite a margin, the helpless defensive backs who tried in vain to cover him. In other words, you can prove irrefutably that Bob Hayes alone gave rise to a new invention: The "zone" defense, which every pro team still uses.

In 1965, hope was beginning to fill the Cotton Bowl, however slowly it happened to brew. The Cowboys won the season opener at home, beating the New York Giants, 31–2. But the most hopeful sign was the crowd—59,366. Attendance at the second game was even better. The Cowboys beat the Washington Redskins 27–7, drawing 61,577. They were inching, however incrementally, toward a sellout—their first.

It would finally happen on November 21, 1965, when the Cowboys played host to Jim Brown and the Cleveland Browns, whom the Cowboys had never beaten. Dallas came into the game with a 4–5 record, losing five straight games, starting with the third game against the St. Louis Cardinals.

Don Meredith was beginning to be booed—unmercifully—with not one but two outstanding rookie quarterbacks, Craig Morton and Jerry Rhome, waiting on the bench, squirming to take his job. It only got worse in the game against Cleveland.

A truly Meredith moment allowed sportswriter Gary Cartwright, the Cowboys' beat writer for the *Dallas Morning News* through much of the 1960s, to record a seminal moment in his own career.

Cartwright came up with a lead for his Browns–Cowboys game story that, to this day, remains a staple of sports-writing folklore.

Meredith had marched the Cowboys to the Browns' 1-yard line, with 4 minutes, 34 seconds remaining and the Browns ahead, 24–17. What may have mattered most to Clint, however, was the staggering statistic recorded that day in the Cotton Bowl. For the first time ever, the Cowboys had sold out the aging stadium, luring to Fair Park a cacophonous standing-room-only crowd of 76,251. It signified not only the largest Cowboys' crowd but also the largest crowd in the history of the storied Cotton Bowl (up to that point).

And then came "the moment."

Rather than have the Cowboys run the ball, Meredith hurled a wobbly first-down pass, which caromed into the arms of a Cleveland defender.

Hunched in the press box on deadline, Cartwright crafted a lead that serves as a lasting parody of turn-of-the-twentieth-century sports-writing icon Grantland Rice:

"Outlined against a gray November sky, the Four Horsemen rode again. You know them: Pestilence, Death, Famine and Meredith."[3]

That, legendary sportswriter Dan Jenkins would say later, "was one of the greatest leads ever."[4]

Indeed, it was, but the growing antipathy with Meredith carried a dark side, one his son, Michael Meredith, revealed in a 2017 interview with the *Dallas Morning News.*

The elder Meredith suffered devastating injuries, both physical and emotional, that belied the moniker "Dandy."

He was, at times, booed mercilessly. Once at a four-way stop sign, the driver to his left urged Meredith to go ahead. But as he entered the intersection, he saw the other driver lurch toward him, Michael says, hitting the quarterback on the driver's side of the car, at full impact, then racing away in what could have resulted in a fatal hit-and-run.

Somehow, Michael says, the team kept the incident out of the newspapers (which the Cowboys had the power to do in those days).

Despite the fans turning on Meredith, and in utterly creepy ways, Clint felt the team was close. Where they played, however, was another matter.

By the end of 1965, Clint was sick, with an illness we'll call "Houston Envy."

CHAPTER FIVE

Houston Envy

S IGMUND FREUD, THE father of psychoanalysis, coined the term *penis envy*. In the history of Texas Stadium, the term would have to be: *Houston Envy*.

In 1965, Clint Murchison's Cowboys were 5 years old and languishing in their usual mediocrity. Tepid seasons of five victories, eight losses, and one tie in 1962 and 1964 were the best they could muster. Dallas's fickle fans wondered openly if maybe the wrong team had left town, since the Texans had captured the AFL Championship in '62 before fleeing to Kansas City to reemerge as Lamar Hunt's Chiefs.

That left the Cowboys still ensconced in the "fully depreciated" Cotton Bowl, which made the hubris of Houston even harder to stomach.

The Bayou City had long courted a feeling of inferiority about its smaller neighbor to the north, but no more. Houston was never more bullish than in the spring of '65, when it seized the imagination of the nation 4 years before men would walk on the moon by opening the $45 million Harris County Domed Stadium, soon to be christened the Astrodome.

No one had ever heard of such a thing, and yet, it was another big event in the technological renaissance of the 1960s.

By unveiling the so-called eighth wonder of the world, which Houstonians not even half-jokingly likened to the Hanging Gardens of Babylon and the Colossus of Rhodes, Texas' largest city didn't just apply heat to its rivalry with Dallas—it poured gasoline all over the fire of their long-contentious relationship. No other city in the world could claim a stadium big enough for baseball and football, with a roof and an air-conditioning system that kept the temperature hovering at 72 degrees, 24 hours a day.

"Texas was generally agog, and Dallas was feverish with civic envy," Pulitzer Prize–winning author Larry McMurtry wrote in his 1968 book of essays, *In a Narrow Grave*. "The letters columns of the *Dallas Morning News* were soon clogged with plaintive little epistles telling the editors how much better life would be if only Dallas had a dome. For a time, there was even a move afoot to dome the Cotton Bowl."[1]

Murchison marveled at the chutzpah and political cunning of Judge Roy Mark Hofheinz, who brought Major League Baseball to Houston and sold the Bayou City on the notion of building a domed stadium.

Hofheinz had been a state representative from 1934 to 1936, the county judge of Harris County from 1936 to 1944, and the "boy mayor" of Houston from 1953 to 1955. He had served as campaign manager for Lyndon B. Johnson during LBJ's ascendancy to both the House of Representatives and the Senate. When the Astrodome opened, LBJ was in the White House and was, of course, the judge's No. 1 guest on opening night. (Former president LBJ reappeared six years later at the opening of Texas Stadium.)

Like Murchison, Hofheinz dreamed big dreams, the difference being he usually needed someone else's money to make them happen. He did, however, deserve an enormous amount of credit for changing the course of Houston sports history. He landed the city a baseball expansion franchise in 1960, mainly by selling the skeptical owners of the National League on his grandiose vision for the world's first indoor stadium. It would mean having to play outdoors, however, from 1962 through 1964, as the Colt .45s, in heat and humidity that only mosquitoes as big as catchers' mitts seemed to enjoy.

Portly, with slicked-back hair and thick horn-rimmed glasses, Hofheinz may have looked like an unlikely champion, but he alone did much to make Houston the capital of sports envy.

The Astrodome sported a 642-foot-wide dome—the largest ever built. It was five times the diameter of Rome's Pantheon and could fit under its roof an eighteen-story hotel with room left over for New York City's Madison Square Garden.

Murchison was enormously intrigued with Houston's achievement and the political will summoned by Hofheinz to get it built. One element in particular captivated his curiosity more than any other. He had seen "skyboxes" or so-called luxury suites at Aztec Stadium in Mexico City, where the wealthy would drive up to the door of the suite and park. Once inside, they would sip champagne and nibble on caviar while peering at the sunken playing field far below.

As cool as that was, the Astrodome piqued his interest even further. On opening night, Houston's new creation drew back the curtain on fifty-four skyboxes, one of which was Hofheinz's private apartment. The other fifty-three were leased to wealthy businesses and individuals in Houston. The leases ran for 5 years, with the cost based, according to the book *The Houston Astrodome* by Craig A. Doherty and Katherine M. Doherty, "on how many seats they had for viewing the events." In 1965, writes the authors, "the smaller boxes had 24 seats and cost $15,000 a year, while the 30-seat boxes cost $18,000 a year."[2]

Murchison reveled in the concept, believing there would be a market among affluent fans for buying such boxes, which would prove to be, in the increasingly expensive world of professional football, a source of *unshared* revenue too enticing to pass up. The Cowboys' owner also loved the fact that the Astrodome skyboxes "were," as the Doherty couple noted in their book, "decorated in a variety of styles and themes, and each box had a name that fit its décor, such as Las Vegas, New England, Old South, and Egyptian Autumn. All the rooms had closed-circuit TVs for viewing the events, and many of the boxes had stock prices displayed constantly so that those attending the events could keep up with their investments. The boxes also had many other luxury features: private elevators and special food-and-beverage services were all part of the lease price."[3]

Even a Hofheinz mistake ended up whetting the Murchison appetite. When the Astrodome opened, outfielders found it difficult and almost impossible to catch routine fly balls: the glare spreading through the stadium skylights flat out blinded them. Feverishly, workers painted over the skylights, saturating them with 700 gallons of white acrylic paint. That *did* stop the glare, but it also killed the natural grass growing on the playing field, making it bare and yellow. Almost overnight, Hofheinz huddled with the Monsanto company to create a new product: AstroTurf. Murchison soon realized that any new stadium of his would also need artificial turf as the best way of coping with Texas' volatile weather.

The opening of the Astrodome signified a turning point, not only for the future of stadiums but also for Houston as a major American city. In 1961, the National Aeronautics and Space Administration (NASA) opened the

Manned Spacecraft Center in Houston, leading to one of the famous lines in movie history, when Tom Hanks in *Apollo 13* says, "Houston, we have a problem."

On that night in 1965, a year of turbulence that saw riots explode in the LA neighborhood of Watts and the number of Americans fighting in South Vietnam almost double, Houston provided a refuge of hope and change. Hofheinz welcomed to the Astrodome on its opening weekend more than 200,000 baseball fans. They got to see Dallas resident Mickey Mantle single and slug a home run before the New York Yankees succumbed to the Astros in an exhibition game. Texas governor John Connally threw out the first pitch, while LBJ watched from Hofheinz's private box.

Hofheinz's box *was* incredible, sprawling 17,000 square feet over four levels. It soon became the place to be for the nation's glitterati.

Houston was no longer a backwater; Hofheinz and the dome were the reason why.

But Texas' best writer saw it as opening the door to something else. He had no idea how prophetic he would become.

"In Texas," McMurtry wrote—although he could have said, *in America*, having no idea how far-flung the stadium boom would be by the early twenty-first century—"there is always room for something bigger. Soon some enterprising native will think of something new and even more extraordinary . . . Perhaps it will be a glassed-in aerial roadway from River Oaks to the Petroleum Club, or a mink Beatle wig to put over the Dome on cold days. Whatever it is will be bigger, better, sexier, more violent, and, above all, *costlier*, than anything we've had before."

CHAPTER SIX

Finally, a Turning Point

Make no mistake, there were things Clint liked, even loved, about the Cotton Bowl. He loved the sight lines, the fact that its wooden stands all but hugged the field. Twelve out of fifteen teams in the NFL in 1966 played some or all of their home games in dual-purpose stadiums, most of which were ancient.

In the Western Conference in 1966, the Green Bay Packers played four home games at Lambeau Field, a football-only venue in tiny Green Bay, Wisconsin, that opened in 1957, and three at Milwaukee County Stadium, known mostly as a baseball venue since opening in 1953.

The Baltimore Colts shared Memorial Stadium, which opened in 1950, with its primary tenant, baseball's Orioles.

The San Francisco 49ers played in Kezar Stadium, a football-only basin bowl whose roots went back to 1925. And that wasn't even the oldest stadium.

The Rams played in the Roman-like Los Angeles Coliseum, which opened in 1923, when Warren G. Harding was president. The Coliseum was used primarily for football, with the NFL forced to share it with the USC (University of Southern California) Trojans. Its past also included offering temporary housing to baseball's Dodgers, after they moved to LA from Brooklyn, New York, in 1958, and before they built the legendary Dodger Stadium in Chavez Ravine.

The Coliseum's most famous role was hosting the 1932 Olympics, which created an aesthetic misery. Because of the need to accommodate track and field, its seats were waaaaay, waaaaay back from the field. This would later become a widespread disadvantage, with the 1980s trend being new stadiums that were forced to accommodate both baseball and football. For Clint, the frustrated architect, it was an element he despised.

The Chicago Bears played in ivy-ancient Wrigley Field, which opened in 1914, the first year of World War I, and the Detroit Lions played in Tiger Stadium, which had opened in 1912, the same year as the sinking of the *Titanic*. It, too, was built for baseball.

In the Eastern Conference, it was even more lopsided. The Cowboys and the Philadelphia Eagles, who played in Franklin Field, which had opened in 1895, were the only teams out of the eight in the conference that staged their home games in a football-only facility. The Cleveland Browns, St. Louis Cardinals, Washington Redskins, Pittsburgh Steelers, Atlanta Falcons, and New York Giants all played in doddering urban baseball parks.

In fact, all eight stadiums in the conference were old, including the Cotton Bowl, which broke ground at the height of the Great Depression, in 1930, the same year a pair of Texas kids named Bonnie Parker and Clyde Barrow became serial bank robbers. As incredible as it sounds, the Cotton Bowl in 1966 was actually one of the League's *newer* stadiums.

You could almost hear Clint screaming at his fellow owners, "When are you going to change!" Clint was also deeply influenced by what was happening in his own city. World-renowned architect Frank Lloyd Wright had designed the Kalita Humphreys Theater, a jewel of an arts venue that opened in Dallas in 1959. The Kalita compelled Clint to wonder: Why couldn't stadiums duplicate the same sleek architecture and the same feeling of warmth, elegance, and comfort? Seven years after Wright's futuristic Kalita opened its doors, the NFL was playing almost all its games in city-owned rental facilities, made for baseball, not football, and where the only amenity fans could expect was a boiled hot dog and a warm Coke. Or, okay, a Dr Pepper.

Clint was arguably the first NFL owner who recognized that the League needed new stadiums—and fast—and preferably football-only venues built for twentieth-century football fans.

"Clint was a true visionary," said Gary Cartwright. "He understood from the beginning that the league had already outgrown its stadiums, even the ones that were fairly new—and especially the Cotton Bowl, which basically dated back to the [1930s]. Clint was promoting luxury boxes, retractable roofs and other modern amenities before almost anyone in sports, and when he had a vision he acted on it."

Of course, it would take a good long while before Clint could bring to fruition the visions that danced in his head. A few years before his death, legendary sports columnist Blackie Sherrod told Michael Granberry about a Clintian moment he found impossible to forget.

This was the early 1960s.

"He always told me, 'Fifteen to 20 years from now, you won't have any use for a 90,000-seat stadium, because your TV screen will be as big as your wall and built into it like wallpaper.'"[1]

The first time Clint told him that, Sherrod said, he walked to his car and muttered under his breath, "Damn, this guy is *nuts*."

In its own way, even the Cotton Bowl inspired Clint, whetting his architectural appetite for what was good and gutting what wasn't. He wanted to keep what made the Cotton Bowl cool and toss in the trash bin of stadium history what made it a tired relic destined for obsolescence.

He loved its sight lines and its closeness to the field, and he longed to export to any new home the kick-ass way it helped to enable a raucous, sold-out, *football* crowd.

Such crowds became commonplace during the Cowboys' breakout season of 1966.

Four years later, James Taylor would write a song called "Fire and Rain," which contained the lines, "I've seen sunny days I thought would never end."

That kind of joy oozed like melted butter in the Cotton Bowl in 1966, when two words captured the essence of the Cowboys' early season: *Meredith* and *Hayes*. The two were killing NFL defenses. The Cowboys' season opened in the Cotton Bowl, where 60,010 watched Meredith and Hayes annihilate the New York Giants, 52–7. Hayes caught touchdown passes from Meredith of 74 and 39 yards. He finished with six catches for 195 yards. Meredith threw for 358 yards. The Giants' defense had no clue how to cover Hayes, especially on a "man-to-man" basis.

The Cowboys won the next week, beating Minnesota 28–17 and drawing 64,116 to the Cotton Bowl. On October 9, 1966, they drew 69,372 to the Cotton Bowl and beat Philadelphia, 56–7, with Meredith and Hayes once again crushing the defense.

Three weeks later, they beat the Pittsburgh Steelers 52–21 and played three consecutive road games before returning to the Cotton Bowl for a seminal moment.

On November 24, 1966, Tex Schramm and the Cowboys launched an ongoing trend by becoming the first team to host an afternoon game on Thanksgiving Day, a turkey day ritual that continues more than half a century later.

Clint lobbied heavily for the Thanksgiving showcase to become the first professional football game broadcast in color on national television. Which it was, but not before a flurry of game-week modifications. Technical experts hired by CBS in the weeks leading up to the game concluded that the lights in the Cotton Bowl—mounted on toothbrush-like vertical stands that are still in place—were inferior for the high-tech standards of color TV. Even though the game was scheduled to start in the late afternoon, an overcast sky or rain or second-half darkness could reveal how woefully inferior such lighting was. The toothbrush stands could and should remain in place, everyone agreed, but there had to be *more* lighting. So, in concert with CBS and the NFL, the Cowboys persuaded city officials to let them install additional lighting. Almost overnight, the ancient vertical stands shared the enhanced lighting belt with horizontal banks of far brighter illumination—both of which remain to this day. Murchison marveled at how much brighter the stadium became and how terrific the playing field looked on Thanksgiving Day. It also gave him ideas for how to light up any future stadium.

Problem was, they had welcomed to Dallas on Thanksgiving Day the Cleveland Browns, a team they had never beaten. The game drew 80,259, which at that point was the largest crowd in Cotton Bowl history. And Dallas *won*. Even today, players who played in the game call it *the* turning point in Cowboys history, because at that point, they knew they'd arrived.

The 1966 Thanksgiving Day game proved scrapbook-worthy for yet another milestone. It marked the introduction of Tommy Loy, a terrific solo trumpeter hired by Clint to play the national anthem before every home game, a streak that took him from beyond the grass of the Cotton Bowl to the artificial turf at Texas Stadium. Loy played "The Star-Spangled Banner" on Thanksgiving Day 1966 and continued playing it at every home game through December 18, 1988—the last game played under the Cowboys' *second* owner, H.R. "Bum" Bright. (Much more about him later.)

"He was my dad, but I had no idea how good he was, what an influence he was on other musicians and how well known he was," his daughter, Lindi Loy, told coauthor Michael Granberry. "His name Loy was even the answer to a *New York Times* crossword puzzle. The clue was: 'Cowboy trumpeter.' And the answer, of course, was Loy."[2]

Coauthor Burk Murchison says his dad got the idea to have a solo trumpeter play the anthem based on having seen Montgomery Clift play a trumpeter in one of his favorite movies, *From Here to Eternity*.

Lindi Loy says her father got a call in November of 1966 from a man who said, "You're the best trumpet player in Dallas."

The unidentified man told him to be at the Cotton Bowl at 10:00 a.m. the next day—Thanksgiving Day—hours before the Cowboys would take the field in what turned out to be that pivotal victory over the Browns before the largest crowd ever assembled at the Cotton Bowl.

Loy auditioned first, followed by a high school band. The man in charge said, "Mr. Murchison will let you know."

"Dad thought, 'Well, obviously, they're not going to pick me, but at least I get to stay for the game!' Five minutes before kickoff, the man said, 'Mr. Murchison has decided to go with the trumpet solo,'" Lindi recalls.

And, of course, he went with Tommy Loy for not just that game but for the duration of his ownership of the Cowboys.

And there was more.

His highest-profile moment happened to Loy at the end of 1970 season, when the Cowboys made their first Super Bowl appearance, in Super Bowl V, against the Baltimore Colts.

And that experience is now embedded in family folklore. Singer Anita Bryant was supposed to perform the national anthem but called in sick, leaving the NFL with almost no time to find a replacement. Tex Schramm spoke up and said, "I have a guy who can play the anthem for you."

Loy got the call the night before the game. He and his wife hopped a flight from Love Field to Miami the next morning, in time for him to blow his horn before an international television audience while decked out in a white blazer and black bow tie.

"It was really meaningful to him. My dad was a patriot," Lindi says. "It was an honor, a privilege. He took it very seriously. And, of course, he loved the attention, because he was a natural performer."

Loy stopped performing at Cowboys home games before the start of the 1989 season, when Jerry Jones took over. Upset over the firing of legendary coach Tom Landry, he resigned, his daughter says.

Loy was honored, Lindi said, to perform a trumpet solo of the national anthem at Landry's memorial service at the Meyerson Symphony Center in 2000, his last official act as a Cowboys soloist.

But as Lindi noted, three years ago, the Cowboys did a very cool thing by bringing back the tradition of the trumpet-solo anthem. The new trumpeter is jazz musician Freddie Jones. During the 2013 season, the Cowboys invited Lindi and her sisters to a game and sat them on a platform near Jones as he played the anthem.

Each sister was given a Cowboys jersey emblazoned with the No. 22, "representing," Lindi says, "the 22 years Dad played the anthem." One sister held the Cowboys blazer her dad used to wear; another held his trumpet.

With the singular power of Tommy Loy added to the mix, what could go wrong? The Cowboys finished the 1966 season with three more victories, drawing another overflow crowd of 76,965 to the Cotton Bowl on December 4, when they beat St. Louis, 31–17. That gave them a 10–3–1 record for the season and the Eastern Conference championship.

And it put them in the playoffs for the first time ever against the Green Bay Packers on, no less, January 1, 1967.

Suddenly, Dallas, Texas, was a bona fide major league sports *city*, with a football team that looked almost unbeatable. But it only got better from there. The cool thing was, should they beat the Packers, the season would keep going. They would play the Kansas City Chiefs—yes, the old Dallas Texans—in the NFL–AFL Championship Game, now known, of course, as the Super Bowl.

That's right, the Cowboys and Texans had a chance of squaring off in Super Bowl I. Clint could hardly wait.

Before we tell you about the 1966 NFL Championship Game, played in the Cotton Bowl on January 1, 1967, we feel compelled to share the behind-the-scenes drama going on in the months and even years leading up to that austere New Year's Day.

That was an incredible game. It solidified the Cowboys as high-profile players on the national stage. And from an athletic standpoint, it substantiated their owner's case for finding the team a new home.

Clint was famous for being a master at delegating authority. Tex Schramm ran the front office. Gil Brandt ran the scouting operation. And Tom Landry coached the team. But Clint alone masterminded the push for a new stadium, and to a large extent, he did so with stealth precision.

In the beginning, he was hopeful, giddily so. And why wouldn't he be? The entire nation could see what an incredible sports team he had placed on the field, one whose brand lingers well into the twenty-first century. He may have assumed, shortsightedly, that the powers that be in Dallas would see it the same way he did, that the Cowboys ought to be in a lavish new stadium in downtown Dallas. What a great thing that would be for a city deeply wounded by the 1963 assassination of President Kennedy.

But those guys didn't see it Clint's way at all.

The Astrodome opened in 1965, and while many perceive that Clint and the Cowboys did not begin plotting their exit from the Cotton Bowl until 1966 and 1967—when the team finished each season by playing the Green Bay Packers in the NFL Championship Game—that is simply not the case. Clint's antipathy with Fair Park and the fully depreciated Cotton Bowl began long before.

In their excellent book *The Dallas Cowboys and the NFL*, authors Donald Chipman, Randolph Campbell and Robert Calvert,[3] all professors of history at North Texas State University when the book was released in 1970, posit a different timeline:

> [Clint] became seriously concerned with the need for improved stadium facilities [as early as 1963]. He recognized the inadequacies of the Cotton Bowl, and he knew that other major sports cities had begun to improve their sports facilities only after years of planning and organization for the effort. Television, especially with the widening use of color equipment, provided ever-tougher competition for the fan's interest.
>
> Murchison believed the Cowboys had to have a stadium attractive enough to encourage people to leave their television sets and go out to a game. "The amount of discomfort," he still maintains, "that people will put up with is decreasing as the quality of television is increasing." The Cowboy owner began to think in terms of a new football stadium that would avoid the problems of the Cotton Bowl and at the same time be attractive in itself.

Murchison believed from the beginning, the authors contend, "that the best solution for the City of Dallas was a new downtown stadium and adjoining center for the performing arts," and the city's visual art museum. In that respect, Clint was way ahead of his time. While Dallas has blown it twice in terms of providing the nation's most popular football team a new home within the city limits, the arts community began to follow his lead—but not until 1984.

That year, the Dallas Museum of Fine Arts abandoned Fair Park and moved downtown, renaming itself the Dallas Museum of Art. A few blocks down Flora Street, the $360 million AT&T Performing Arts Center opened in 2009, financed in a no-new-taxes environment with only $18 million in public money and solidifying the area that came to be known as the Dallas Arts District. An area once home to used car outlets now includes the Meyerson Symphony Center (opened in 1989), the Crow Museum of Asian Art (opened in 1998), and the Nasher Sculpture Center (opened in 2003).

Enriching the once-desolate area even further is 5.2-acre Klyde Warren Park, a lovely green space atop the Woodall Rodgers Freeway that opened in 2012, connecting Dallas's uptown with its downtown. That same year, the Perot Museum of Nature and Science relocated its primary campus downtown, where by 2015 it had welcomed more than one million visitors.

The last holdout, Broadway Dallas—formerly known as Dallas Summer Musicals—still resides in the Music Hall at Fair Park, which opened in 1925, just 5 years before the opening of the Cotton Bowl.

The only thing missing on the downtown landscape are homes for the Cowboys and Texas Rangers, who entertained notions of moving to downtown Dallas before settling for a retro-design baseball stadium in suburban Arlington in 1994. The Rangers' new $1.2 billion stadium, equipped with air-conditioning and a retractable roof, opened in Arlington in 2020—albeit without a single fan in the stands because of the ongoing spread of COVID-19.

Clint could see the need for becoming downtown centric when others in Dallas could not. By 2015, cities across the country—Seattle, San Francisco, San Diego, Denver, Phoenix, Pittsburgh, Cleveland, Minneapolis, Indianapolis, Atlanta, and others—had opened either football or baseball stadiums as a way of enhancing their downtown core. Minneapolis offers the best example of what Clint had envisioned: its downtown area includes a new arena for hockey and basketball, a new outdoor Major League Baseball stadium, and one of the sexiest new indoor stadiums in the National Football League. In addition to all *that*, downtown Minneapolis also includes the world-renowned Guthrie Theater and multiple museums. Downtown Dallas in 2021 is home to the Dallas Mavericks of the National Basketball Association and the Dallas Stars of the National Hockey League, and that's it—no other sports.

What we're telling you is, Dallas's failure as a downtown-centric sports city can be traced directly to Clint Murchison Jr. and the city's hostile rejection of him and his football team, the Dallas Cowboys—yes, *the Dallas Cowboys!*—in the 1960s. One could also argue that were it not for the efforts of Mayor Ron Kirk, who spearheaded the effort to have the $420 million American Airlines Center opened in downtown Dallas in 2001, *all four* of Dallas's major-league sports franchises would now make their home in suburban Arlington. For those who say cities have no business financing sports venues—and in so many ways, they have a compelling argument—it should be noted the city of Dallas paid off its taxpayer debt for American Airlines Center in 2011, with interest, years ahead of schedule.

Clint's demands for a downtown venue became far more public during the halcyon seasons of 1966 and 1967, but the truth is, he may have wanted to leave the Cotton Bowl soon after the Cowboys began playing there in 1960, two months before John F. Kennedy defeated Richard Nixon for the presidency.

He had no other option for a stadium in 1960, and nearly a decade later, he learned the hard way how entrenched the city was about Fair Park and the Cotton Bowl.

As a graduate of MIT, with an advanced degree in math, Clint saw the world in purely analytical terms. But when it came to Fair Park and the Cotton Bowl, and its seasonal rite, the State Fair of Texas, Dallas was all emotion.

As Clint noted in his book *Clint's Corner*, "The Fair was originally proposed in 1886 by the downtown merchants of this City." In 1936, the year of the Texas Centennial and one many view as a turning point in the history of Dallas, "the Fair received great impetus when Dallas was selected as the site for the Texas Centennial Exposition."[4]

And from this, he wrote, "a new concept evolved; the Fair became, not just a 16-day-a-year event, but the location for a year-round sports, entertainment, cultural and amusement complex. Those charged with promoting the Fair began to promote this multi-faceted notion. Eventually, the site of a rural fair became the location for our museums, performing arts theaters, sports palaces, and you name it. It grew like Topsy, without plan."

When it came to Fair Park and the Cotton Bowl, Dallas's feelings were like those of Tevye in *Fiddler on the Roof*, whose signature song—"Tradition"— had been sung so many times at the Music Hall.

Who was Clint, many wanted to know, to be challenging tradition?

It was William Shakespeare, who in *Julius Caesar* wrote: "Timing is everything. There is a tide in the affairs of men which when taken at the flood leads on to fortune."

In Clint's case, the timing could not have been worse. And when it came to a new home in downtown Dallas, there was certainly no fortune.

To realize his dream of building a new home for the Cowboys, in the downtown core of the city he loved, he would have to win over, as it were, the city's mayor, J. Erik Jonsson, whose own sons admitted he cared nothing about sports, and Robert B. Cullum, board president of the State Fair of Texas, whose love of Fair Park bordered on obsession. No one was more emotional about Fair Park than Cullum, who was also one of the city's most powerful men.

Nor was Clint the best salesman in the world. Noted Dallas journalist Lee Cullum, Bob Cullum's niece, said Clint lacked the social skills of his fifty-fifty partner, brother John Murchison, who, unlike Clint, was active on the board of the Dallas art museum and far more engaged with civic and philanthropic endeavors.

But when it came to the Cowboys, John was clearly a silent partner. Clint commandeered the task of finding the Cowboys a new home as a solo endeavor.

"John had a lovely way about him," says Lee Cullum. "Everybody loved John. Clint was very introverted. Not a people person, whereas Uncle Bob was the quintessential people person. Erik Jonsson was very much admired, and I always found him to be warm and wonderful."

So, to a large extent, Clint didn't fit in. The combination of his personality, which many regarded as eccentric, to put it mildly, coupled with Dallas's political climate at the time, made landing a downtown stadium a truly quixotic task. Not that Clint was immune to quixotic missions. Some would say the idea of founding a professional team in Dallas in 1960 was a quixotic quest. And, well, look how that turned out.

Lee Cullum is especially insightful in explaining the situation that Quixote Clint found himself in. The Dallas Citizens Council, and by extension the Citizens Charter Association, controlled city politics, creating a situation more like the Kremlin than *Mr. Smith Goes to Washington*. At the time, the Dallas City Council did not include single-member districts. The council consisted of at-large candidates who were appointed to run and win any election. Yes, it was an oligarchy, and despite his wealth, Clint was as far removed from the inner circle as Jimmy Stewart would have been at Lenin's Tomb.

There were other complications, which, to use a football analogy, left Clint about three touchdowns behind before the game even started. While it's true that Erik Jonsson cared nothing about sports, he cared deeply about the future of the Cotton Bowl. So why was that? It had all the components of a political land mine.

"Mayor Jonsson needed to get along with South Dallas," Lee Cullum says.

And the reason is fascinating. The bellwethers of Jonsson's post–Kennedy assassination makeover of Dallas were his beloved city hall, designed by I. M. Pei; the cornerstone of his 1967 Goals for Dallas endeavor; and—here comes his legacy—Dallas/Fort Worth International Airport.

Incredibly, the bond referendum for the airport failed by 2,260 votes when first presented to the voters on June 6, 1967, leaving the normally placid Jonsson shocked and enraged. There was no way he could weather the risk of offending *any* potential voters, which talk of a downtown stadium would have done. Unfortunately, for Clint, the airport bond referendum failed at the precise moment he was gearing up for *his* push.

As funny as he was, Clint's humor may not have been his best weapon in winning an argument with the mayor. Keep in mind, the D/FW Airport referendum had failed on June 6, which, by all accounts, had rendered the mayor apoplectic.

The day after the airport vote failed, in June of '67, Jonsson went to a breakfast meeting with the Oak Cliff Chamber of Commerce and all but exploded.

"He lectured them on the essential need for the airport and said they didn't do their job to get out the vote," recalled former city manager George Schrader. "I never saw him lecture anybody like he did there. He was always a velvet-gloved guy. But he took them off that day."

So, less than a month later, he was in no mood for Clint's one-of-a-kind humor, but that's what he got, applying another coat of ice to an already frozen lake.

Not that Clint belittled the mayor's accomplishments. Quite the contrary. He greatly admired Jonsson for his intellect and his achievements. Way back in 1930, Jonsson signed on with Geophysical Service Inc., which became Texas Instruments. Under Jonsson's firm hand, the company's research and development wing could later take credit for its landmark invention of silicon transistors. That was *huge* and precisely the kind of achievement that the MIT-educated Clint would have marveled at.

But when he mentioned it in one of his letters—which he did on July 3, 1967—well, let's just say it didn't win brownie points with the mayor. The letter reads as follows:

> Dear Erik: I noted in the morning paper your comment that until the Astrodome was built, everyone thought the Cotton Bowl was pretty good. Of course, until the transistor was developed, people thought the vacuum tube was pretty good. Sincerely, Clint.

Ouch. Again, Clint's timing was not the best.

Developer Vincent Carrozza, whose knowledge of Dallas history is second to no one's, is one of those who understood what Clint was up against.

Carrozza's own association with the Murchison family goes back to 1958, when he was hired by W. W. Overton, president of the Texas Bank and Trust Company and an associate of Clint Murchison Sr., to assist in buying 10 acres of prime real estate in downtown Dallas. Overton had grown concerned that Dallas was losing the strength of its inner core, as the city began to migrate farther east.

"The politics of the time," Carrozza said, "did not favor federal dollars for revitalization." That was due largely to one man, US Representative Bruce Alger, a Republican in the Democratic-controlled House of Representatives, and the right-wing darling of North Dallas.

"Alger was so popular," Carrozza said, "that bankers were fearful of opposing him publicly. Other cities were moving forward with revitalization"—financed with federal dollars—"but because of Alger, Dallas was not."

So, it required what's known in the football world as an end around. Overton Sr. went to Murchison Sr. and asked for help (read, *cash*) in buying 10 acres of real estate, bounded by Dallas's three principal streets, Elm, Main, and Commerce, and extending from Akard Street to Lamar Street. "And create there," Carrozza said, "a kind of Dallas Rockefeller Center," which, in the original concept, called for three skyscrapers.

Clint Sr., Carrozza said, agreed to put up the money, which would be used to acquire, as secretly as possible, no fewer than 250 properties.

The resulting development came to be known as One Main Place, which, despite failing to meet its original goals, became a hallmark of downtown redevelopment, giving Carrozza even more credibility.

Around that time, Carrozza paid a visit to the offices of Joe Dealey, then the publisher of the *Dallas Morning News*. Peering out the window to the east, Dealey expressed concern about a hamburger stand going in nearby.

"What do you think about me buying that block?" he asked Carrozza.

Carrozza knew the area, where WFAA-TV, then owned by the *Dallas Morning News*, had recently purchased 6 acres. Owner of the remaining 40 acres was the Cotton Belt railroad company. At Dealey's behest, Carrozza developed a master plan for the area, including the 6 acres bought by WFAA and the land owned by the railroad company, which added up to almost 50 acres.

Fast-forward to 2011, where the twenty-three-story Omni Dallas Hotel now stands as the entry point to the Kay Bailey Hutchison Convention Center, underscoring Carrozza's point that this was one valuable property whose full potential was nowhere near being realized in the 1960s.

Clint was one of those who knew exactly how valuable the land could be. And he was surprised at how affordable it actually was. He wanted it—*longed* for it—to be the new home of the Dallas Cowboys. Think about it: the Cowboys' home stadium could have been sitting on the same piece of land as the Omni Dallas Hotel, with the city skyline shimmering in the background.

Excitedly, he told Carrozza that he wanted the land for the Cowboys' new home *and* an adjoining development that would include new homes for Dallas arts institutions.

Clint most coveted the 40-acre parcel owned by Cotton Belt, which sat near the site of what later became the Convention Center and the Omni. Carrozza says that, even after the city of Dallas expressed no interest in helping Murchison acquire, much less pay for the property, he continued to want it—badly.

"So, Clint started making comments that appear in the press about some property in that area," Carrozza says. "Vague comments but comments that caused me great alarm. I saw this and said, 'Oh, my God.'"[5]

Despite Carrozza having been a Murchison ally, this is where the two parted ways, which helped doom the dream of a downtown stadium.

"I, Vince Carrozza, didn't want a stadium there," says the developer, who complained to Overton, who arranged a meeting.

"We went to Clint and we said, 'Clint, this is not good. We may lose all these other downtown properties with all this stuff you're saying in the paper.' He said, 'Well, sorry, Vince, but I want to build a stadium there, and I want the city to do it.' I said, 'Clint, that is never going to happen. You will never get the city to approve your building a stadium there.' I knew it, because I knew Erik Jonsson."[6]

Born in 1901, J. Erik Jonsson was the only child of Swedish immigrants, who had settled in Brooklyn, New York, in the late nineteenth century. They were poor. Jonsson's father had wanted his son to forgo college so he could take over the family cigar store. Jonsson spurned his father's advice to earn a degree in mechanical engineering at Rensselaer Polytechnic Institute. He paid his own way through with what Jonsson biographer Darwin Payne calls "an astonishing series of part-time jobs."

Jonsson became machine shop supervisor and later office manager of an oil exploration company, which he managed to transform into Texas Instruments, the wildly successful electronics firm. Through that endeavor, he became a civic stalwart in his adopted city of Dallas.

Through heartbreak comes opportunity, a truism that defined Jonsson as much as anyone. On November 22, 1963, President Kennedy was scheduled to speak at the Dallas Trade Mart soon after his motorcade parade through the city's downtown streets. Jonsson had been appointed to emcee the event, but instead, he became the bearer of the worst possible news: the president of the United States had been fatally wounded on Elm Street.

In the aftermath, Jonsson soon emerged as the city's mayor, replacing Earle Cabell, a Democrat whom city officials championed as the replacement for Alger, whose right-wing politics were no longer welcome in a Dallas struggling to overcome its national blemish as the "city of hate," the place where a president had been murdered at the end of an otherwise blissful parade, and where the lead suspect was gunned down in the basement of the Dallas police station two days later.

In short, Jonsson had become politically indestructible. "Erik Jonsson rehabilitated the city in the post-JFK assassination era," says Darwin Payne, who later became Jonsson's biographer. "The city had suffered a trauma of the worst sort. Its reputation was at the bottom of the heap nationally and internationally. He brought hope, and he brought real concrete achievements to the city that continue to impact our lives and also our reputation."[7]

He was, Payne says, "very much a dominant individual — he got his way on things," with the stadium being Exhibit A. "He was a man of vision, but when it involved large sums of money or time or effort, he generally took charge of it. I don't want to make him sound too hardheaded, but he was very strong-willed. He was also at the peak of his popularity and power."[8]

None of which was good news for Clint.

Backed by the Citizens Charter Association, and with his power intensified in the wake of the assassination, Jonsson had a say in every decision. If he didn't want it, it wouldn't happen. That soon became abundantly clear to Clint.

And, to put it bluntly, Carrozza says, Jonsson didn't like Clint. "Erik was furious with Clint because of something that had happened earlier. Once, he had gone to Clint, asking for money for a project that meant a lot to Erik. Clint said no. That didn't sit well with Erik, who for one wasn't used to hearing the word 'no.' So he says to me, 'You know, Vince, I wasn't born with a silver spoon in my mouth like Clint was. He wants a downtown stadium? Sorry, it ain't gonna happen. Not on my watch.'"[9]

And again, the mayor was especially sensitive to the needs of South Dallas, far more than Clint may have realized.

Longtime South Dallas resident Don Bryant says the south end zone of the Cotton Bowl became a microcosm of the Cowboys' South Dallas fan base.

Until the Cowboys and Dallas Texans began play in the Cotton Bowl in 1960, integrated football was almost nonexistent. Not counting occasional appearances by Black players in the lineup of the visiting team in the annual New Year's game in the Cotton Bowl—Jim Brown and Ernie Davis of Syracuse University were the main examples—all the players were white.

Until 1966, when SMU signed Jerry LeVias, no Black player had been awarded a scholarship in any football program in the Southwest Conference. Before LeVias, Baylor University had allowed onto its roster a single Black player, but he was a walk-on, meaning he didn't have a scholarship.

The big SWC schools—Texas, Arkansas, Texas Tech, and Texas A&M—failed to sign any Black players until the late 1960s, shortly before a landmark desegregation ruling by a federal judge in 1970.

So, in terms of integration, the Cowboys and Texans brought much-needed change to the Cotton Bowl, which did not go unnoticed by the Black community. But Lee Cullum is right: Mayor Jonsson would have taken an enormous political risk, vis-à-v is his narrow majority for a game-changing airport, by alienating Black voters, which he might have done by backing the Cowboys' exit from the Cotton Bowl.

For Bryant and others in South Dallas, the issue of the Cowboys leaving the Cotton Bowl touches off an emotional land mine more than half a century after their departure. "The Black churches of South Dallas changed their ministry solely because of the Cowboys,"[10] Bryant says. "The pastors changed the starting time of the service, for no other reason than to accommodate Cowboy home games in the Cotton Bowl. In the old days, the service would start at 11 and go to 1 or 1:30. The pastors were willing to sacrifice, willing to make the change, for only one reason: To remain in control of their membership."

Bryant waxes nostalgic about "thousands of Black fans walking from their homes to the Cotton Bowl to see the games. Everybody knew their seats, and you didn't take nobody else's seats. No sir. We filled that south end with thousands of people, all Black. In South Dallas, everything stopped from 11:30 until after the Cowboy game was over."

Bryant relished what the Cowboys' Cotton Bowl days did for South Dallas, but so did people throughout the city. They may not have known it at the time, but they became the living embodiment of a golden era in sport, when there were no luxury suites, when the millionaire from North Dallas sat next to the shoeshine man and paid the same price.

Bryant didn't want it to end. And it's probably a safe bet that Robert Cullum, Jonsson's ally and in the end Clint's adversary, felt the same way.

As his niece, Lee Cullum, will tell you, Bob Cullum came from a long line of grocers, who as she says "*loved* the State Fair. He loved everything about it."[11] As Lee points out, Bob Cullum served for years as chairman of the board of the State Fair of Texas. And today, the main drag in front of the entrance to the fairgrounds is named Robert B. Cullum Boulevard.

A native of Dallas born in 1912, Bob Cullum was a graduate of SMU. Along with his brother Charles, they assumed the reins of the family business. They eventually took over Toro Food Stores, a failing chain they renamed after a children's fairy tale hero, Tom Thumb.

Today, Tom Thumb is part of Albertsons, which in 2015 acquired Tom Thumb from Safeway, which at one time was the second-largest supermarket chain in North America, with more than 2,200 stores and more than 250,000 employees.

Civically, Cullum served on the board of the State Fair of Texas and became its president from 1967 to 1969, the very years in which Clint lobbied hard to leave the Cotton Bowl. He served as president of the Dallas Chamber of Commerce from 1964 to 1965 and served on the board of directors of Dallas Power and Light, the Dr Pepper Company, and, of course, Republic National Bank.

"Bob Cullum was at the time an extremely powerful person," Carrozza says, and for Clint, the problem was doubly severe—he was Jonsson's No. 1 ally.

Even before the stadium issue came to a head, Clint was having as much luck getting his way with these two as Lyndon Johnson was in ending the Vietnam War. Sadly, for Clint, Cullum's dislike for Clint may have been exceeded only by Jonsson's.

No one was more aware of this than Carrozza, one of the most well-connected power brokers in Dallas.

"Bob once said to me, 'Vince, the trouble with Clint is, he wants to row the boat all the time. He won't let anybody else row the boat.'"[12]

Such an accusation is almost laughable when one considers that Clint hired three men to run the Cowboys—Schramm, Landry, and Brandt—and left them alone. Few others in the history of professional sports have been as hands-off as he was. Even so, Clint could be stubborn and obstinate about things he really cared about.

Let's concede, for one, that the stadium issue was different. Although Schramm exercised almost total control over the business side of the Cowboys, Clint reserved stadium issues for himself.

It had to have been dispiriting to learn that even his friend Carrozza was not on his side when it came to a downtown stadium.

"I went to yet another meeting and said, 'Clint, I don't want the stadium there. That property has far more value for the city being developed with housing and office buildings.'"[13]

At one point, Carrozza said he told Clint, "It's not the right thing to do, and I'm upset about it. He said, 'Fine, Vince, you go your way and I'll go mine.'"

Carrozza says the collective disposition of the men involved was such that political compromise simply wasn't possible. Cullum would not admit it, of course, but his row-the-boat analogy applied equally to him and the mayor.

Had the parties involved been even remotely willing to compromise, it might have resulted in a new stadium, albeit at Fair Park. Carrozza contends that Murchison *might* have gone for that.

But it's apparent, looking at his own writings, in the pages of *Clint's Corner*, that he believed Fair Park was hopelessly doomed.

"By 1964, it had become obvious that the Cotton Bowl, a grand lady in her day, suffered from terminal illness," Murchison wrote.[14]

That same year, the State Fair commissioned a study, allowing a California research firm to find that "it would cost more to renovate satisfactorily the old stadium than to build a new one."

The fair accepted the findings, Murchison wrote, "and it was Bob Cullum's decision to build a new stadium." Murchison then commissioned his own study, which concluded that by a 4-to-1 margin, Dallasites preferred a location "other than the Fairgrounds."

Further research enabled Murchison to discover that a downtown Dallas location "would provide parking for 8,000 cars. Within five blocks [the distance from the present Cotton Bowl to the gates of the Fairgrounds] there were already available 14,000 additional parking spaces. The project could be financed without cost to taxpayers [through parking revenue, and without requiring season ticket holders to purchase option bonds]. Finally, as an added dividend, the city would obtain 10 acres of land adjacent to the stadium as a location for an art museum and a music hall."[15]

The reaction?

"I exposed the plan to civic leaders," Murchison wrote. "Great, they said. Merchants liked it; hotel operators liked it; restaurateurs liked it; convention promoters liked it; the president of the Dallas Citizens Council liked it so much he even proposed expanding the concept; both newspapers loved it."

But when it came to the most powerful person he had to convince, "Erik Jonsson hated it," Murchison wrote. "He never told me why; in fact, he didn't tell me anything for over a year."

Once Jonsson made up his mind, Clint wrote, "he, like Caesar, did not deviate."

Clint said he met with Jonsson and Cullum one last time to "commit the Cowboys to play at the fairground location if a new stadium were built there, provided the taxpayers were informed as to the extravagance of the alternative. [For reasons too involved to set forth here, the stadium proposed by the State Fair would have cost the taxpayers at least $15 million more than one downtown.] Finally, the verdict came, as sure and swift as a Turk's scimitar," Murchison wrote.

"There is no stadium in my plans in the foreseeable future," intoned the mayor, "because of other more pressing requirements."

And, in Clint's words, "thus was born Texas Stadium."[16]

But, of course, it wasn't born yet. During the Cowboys' fantastically memorable 1966 season, when they emerged as having the makings of a potential dynasty, it became painfully clear to Clint that, despite the team's luster, the powers that be were disinclined to reward them with a palatial new home, no matter how cool it might have been for Dallas as a whole.

As Clint once told Blackie Sherrod, "In one sense, it won't be an Astrodome. In another sense, it will be better. We can play everything in it but baseball. That was the point in wanting a downtown Dallas stadium. It would have been even more dramatic. Even in Irving, it still will be a dramatic thing for Dallas."[17]

As it was, the pre-Irving ingredients just didn't add up. You had an all-powerful mayor who didn't like sports and who didn't like Clint, and the mayor was adored. No one in post-assassination Dallas dared challenge J. Erik Jonsson, who simply never understood the role a winning team could play in healing a damaged city. In Dallas circles, he was known as "King Erik," proving that more than anyone the mayor symbolized Dallas's system of government as a purebred autocracy. Without its blessings, you were nowhere. And in the king's corner was Bob Cullum, whose passion for the Cotton Bowl and Fair Park knew no bounds. And, of course, neither guy liked Clint, who, for many people, *could* be difficult to like.

Lee Cullum is right—maybe he should have involved brother John as a full-time lobbyist. He might have carried more weight with Jonsson and Cullum, who were part of his world, not Clint's. Jonsson grew up poor. Clint hadn't.

But as 1960s Cowboys beat writer Gary Cartwright once said in an interview, the divisions ran even deeper. "Clint and Erik did not travel in the same social circles or subscribe to the same politics," Cartwright told co-author Granberry in a 2004 interview. "I imagine that Erik thought that Clint was a socialist snob, and I'm fairly sure that Clint thought that Erik was a reactionary clod."[18]

So, on a bitterly cold day in December 1966—days before the Cowboys would play the Packers in the NFL Championship Game—Clint quietly agreed to a meeting with an eager band of suitors from the city of Irving.

Dallas is not exactly a haven for ice storms, but when they happen, they happen with a vengeance.

Clint and twenty members of city government in Irving, Texas, carefully maneuvered their cars up the icy, winding road that led to the Dallas Gun Club.

Clint had arranged the meeting with the help of his friend, Max Thomas, a gun club member who knew the officials in Irving. The purpose of the meeting? To begin to explore suburban Irving as a possible alternative home for the Cowboys. No matter how eccentric he might have appeared to some, Clint had his own valuable business and social network, which included Max Thomas. Without his friendship with Thomas, chances are Clint never would have pursued Irving as an option. Thomas later became highly instrumental in steering Clint to the property that became the eventual home of Texas Stadium.

"Clint told me that he still wanted to build the stadium in downtown Dallas," said Dan Matkin, then the mayor pro tem of Irving. "But he had been rebuffed time and again by the Dallas leadership."[19]

Clint had also been stymied in trying to meet with Irving's mayor Lynn Brown, who expressed no interest whatsoever in having the Cowboys move to Irving—and never did.

Matkin admits that, up until the time Clint Murchison Jr. entered their lives, running Irving, Texas, was not exactly big-time stuff. It involved, to a large extent, buying fire trucks, building parks, and trying to complete a new water tank across from the hospital.

Irving businessman Melvin Shuler asked Matkin to meet with Clint, who already had in his office, during the Cowboys' first winning season, a model for how he wanted a new stadium to look.

Losing patience with Dallas leadership, Clint "was allegedly looking at sites in Irving, Richardson and even Austin," Matkin says. "I have no idea whether that was correct. But he certainly did talk to us."[20]

Robert H. Power, then an Irving councilman, got a call from Max Thomas, on a night just before the initial Gun Club confab. Thomas asked why Mayor Brown had refused to talk to Clint.

"I said, 'Hell, I don't know anything about it,'" Power said.[21]

Before the Gun Club session, Power agreed to meet with Clint, "whose thoughts and ideas sounded far-fetched at the time but quite interesting to contemplate."[22]

Once they ascended the icy hill, brewed coffee, and settled themselves in the Gun Club, Power and his colleagues grew increasingly more intrigued.

This could be a turning point for Irving, they reasoned. Dallas may be making a mistake, from which they could benefit—enormously.

"The *biggest* mistake that Dallas made," Power says, "is that Erik Jonsson referred to Clint Murchison Jr. as 'Sonny boy.' Clint was not a person that you called Sonny. He was the highest-ranking member of his class at MIT. He had projects going on throughout the world. His Tecon Corp. was one of the major construction companies in the world. He was a most interesting and I think brilliant person. I don't know that I've ever met with a mind and a humor such as Clint had."[23]

Lee Cullum is right. When it came to Dallas, Clint had "no cards to play." Jonsson's condescension fueled Clint's desire to find a new hand to play somewhere else. Power and Matkin realized immediately that they could provide an alternative that would benefit Clint *and* the Cowboys and Irving.

Of course, it's hard to keep a secret when twenty-something people meet over coffee on a chilly morning and discuss something as exciting as the Dallas Cowboys fleeing Dallas for lil' ol' Irving, Texas.

Among those at the meeting was Bill Stevens, then the head of Irving's Chamber of Commerce and a man described by Power as "a devoted supporter of the city of Irving."[24]

Stevens would play an enormous role in letting the stadium cat out of the bag, as it were, but first there was the matter of the Cowboys and Packers deciding who would represent the NFL in Super Bowl I, against the former Dallas Texans. And Clint *had* to pay attention to that. After all, the entire nation was.

The NFL Championship Game played in the Cotton Bowl on January 1, 1967, was a crazy, emotional thrill ride. For an aspirational Clint, it showed the world how incredibly good his team had become and why they deserved a better home.

Little did he know, but the 1966 season would become the first of twenty consecutive winning seasons for the Cowboys, a feat no other team had matched before, and no other team has managed to equal in the more than half a century since the Cowboys and Packers met to decide the NFL champ of 1966.

It was one of the first NFL title games broadcast in color, and in retrospect, it's crazy to realize that the game was blacked out in Dallas, even though the Cotton Bowl had sold out days in advance. It would be the early 1970s before the NFL would amend its ridiculous blackout rule by at least permitting the home team to televise the game if it sold out 72 hours in advance. It actually took a threat by President Richard Nixon in 1973 to force the NFL to permit at least partial airing of NFL games to the home-team audience.

Clint ended up using the game as lobbying material for edging the Cowboys from the confines of Fair Park, but make no mistake, the game played on January 1, 1967, was easily one of the best football games ever played in the aging stadium. Looking back at the game through the lens of history, it boggles the mind to think that a game of such quality, now deemed so important in the annals of the NFL, would have cost only $10 a ticket. Regular-season games during 1966 went for $6 apiece in the Cotton Bowl, and end-zone seats were even cheaper.

The Cowboys ended six years of futility by finding their mojo in 1966, with Don Meredith throwing bombs to Bob Hayes. The team's margin of victory during the season was overwhelmingly a by-product of Meredith–Hayes dominance—52–7, 47–14, 56–7, and 52–21 were four final scores during a 10–3–1 season that landed the Cowboys in their first championship game, against the defending champs, the Green Bay Packers, coached by Vince Lombardi, whose name now appears on the annual Super Bowl trophy.

In those days, the winner of the Western Conference (Green Bay) played the winner of the Eastern Conference (Dallas) in the League's solitary playoff game. But 1966 was different, because for the first time ever, the winner of that game got to go to a grudge-match championship between the winner of the National Football League and the upstart American Football League. Years later, that inaugural event would come to be known as Super Bowl I. The AFL designee turned out to be the Kansas City Chiefs, who from 1960 to 1962, when they captured their first AFL championship, were the Dallas Texans, who shared their home field, the Cotton Bowl, with the Cowboys. For kids growing up in Dallas in the 1960s, it was pure heaven to have not one but *two* professional teams in the Cotton Bowl.

And the ultimate reward came on January 1, 1967, when the weather was football-perfect, with the temperature at kickoff hovering in the mid-50s.

Parking in surrounding neighborhoods, fans walked excitedly to the gates of the emerald-field Cotton Bowl. The walk itself signified the beginning of the end of an era. Rich walked with poor, Black with white, and we were one. Luxury suites did not exist. The guy from Highland Park sat next to a guy from Pleasant Grove who sat next to a guy from South Dallas. No one wore a team jersey. And no one cheering for the other team dared show up or make a sound. Thousands of men wore coats and ties, punctuated by a fedora or Stetson. Thousands of women wore dresses, the same worn to church earlier that day.

But the best thing about it all was the shared humanity, the egalitarian bliss that Cowboys games at Fair Park had become. On January 1, 1967, we were three years removed from the Kennedy assassination. We needed the healing balm the Cowboys could offer. The Cowboys belonged to Dallas and to all of us who lived there. We reveled in their joys and suffered in their losses—together. If it rained, we all got wet.

As good as the team was in 1966, the so-called experts said Dallas could never beat the Packers, who exuded a confidence and experience that felt more like hubris. But we, the Cotton Bowl crowd, were determined to take them on.

Moments after the game began, the clunky, primitive Cotton Bowl score-board informed us that the Cowboys were losing already, 14–0. Fathers began to console their sons, saying, "Hey, let's wait until *we* get the ball. Heck, we haven't even gotten the ball yet."

Green Bay scored on its opening drive, with Elijah Pitts snaring a 17-yard pass from quarterback Bart Starr. The normally sure-handed Mel Renfro fumbled the ensuing kickoff, and Jim Grabowski returned it 18 yards to give Green Bay a two-touchdown lead before Dallas's first play from scrimmage. Grim.

Dallas responded quickly.

Don Meredith soon had the Cowboys clawing back. He led them on a 13-play drive, with Dan Reeves slicing through the Packers for a 3-yard touchdown. The Packers punted on the next drive, and Dallas drove 59 yards to tie the game at 14 on a 23-yard touchdown run by Don Perkins. At that point, you could feel the electricity begin to mount. It was palpable, fueled by the loudest crowd in Cotton Bowl history.

Early in the second quarter, Starr threw a 51-yard touchdown pass to Carroll Dale. But Dallas came back again, driving 68 yards to the Packers' 4-yard line. Green Bay held, with Dallas settling for an 11-yard field goal by Danny Villanueva.

With Green Bay leading 21–17, the Packers tried a 30-yard field goal, which the Cowboys blocked, in what became a foreshadowing of second-half dramatics.

Trailing 21–17 early in the third, Cowboys defensive back Warren Livingston recovered a fumble on the Cowboys' 21-yard line, preventing an even bigger Packers lead. Dandy juiced it up again, taking the Cowboys on a 13-play drive. Dallas settled for another field goal, cutting the Packers' lead to 21–20.

Starr, truly a Cowboys' antagonist in those days, responded with a 16-yard touchdown pass to Boyd Dowler, giving Green Bay a 28–20 lead heading into the final quarter.

In the fourth, Bob Hayes fielded a punt on his own 1-yard line and was swarmed over inside the 5. Dallas punted, enabling Green Bay to take over on the Cowboys' 48. With third down, 19 to go, Cowboy killer Starr threw a 28-yard touchdown pass to Max McGee.

At that point, Dallas found itself all the way back where it started, facing a 14-point deficit with Green Bay leading 34–20. But then came a turning-point play, the kind that defines great moments in great games. Hall of Fame defensive tackle Bob Lilly, sent in by Coach Landry for special-teams duty, blocked the extra point attempt, keeping the score at 34–20.

And why was that significant? NFL rules did not yet offer the two-point conversion, so Lilly's block was huge. It kept the game within the two-touch-down mark of 14 points, as opposed to a seemingly fatal 15 points.

The Cowboys amped it up on the next drive, underscoring our long-held belief that, as great as he was, Bob Hayes often fell woefully short in big games. Needing a deep threat more than he ever had, Meredith turned instead to underrated wide-out Frank Clarke, who came up huge. Meredith hurled a 68-yard touchdown pass to Clarke, cutting Green Bay's lead to 34–27. Clarke was just getting started.

The Cotton Bowl crowd was never louder than when Clarke caught that pass. We had hope, with 2 minutes, 12 seconds left.

On the Packers' next drive, linebacker Dave Edwards sacked Starr for an 8-yard loss.

On fourth down, Dallas applied heavy pressure to the Green Bay punter. He squeezed out an effort of a measly 17 yards, giving Dallas the ball on Green Bay's 47 with 2:12 remaining. This was big-time stuff, in Fair Park, no less, where CBS was broadcasting the game nationwide (except in Dallas!).

Meredith threw 21 yards to Clarke. Don Perkins ran for 4 more. Dallas had the ball on Green Bay's 22. The next play illustrated why Lombardi's Packers were true greatness. Meredith tried gallantly to hit Clarke for what would have been the tying touchdown, in the corner of the south end zone. But Packers defensive back Tom Brown, knowing he was beaten, interfered with Clarke before he could catch what appeared to be a perfect pass. It saved a touchdown, but the interference penalty gave the Cowboys a first down on the Packers' 2-yard line.

And that's the point—Brown *saved a touchdown.*

At that moment, the crowd had gone completely bonkers. Dan Reeves gained a yard on first down. On second down, Dallas was a yard away from tying the game and sending it into what was then known as *sudden death.* Overtime rules would not be adopted until 2012. The League allowed ties back then, except, of course, in playoff games. And there was no question that, at that point, Dallas had all the momentum. Lombardi's Packers teetered on the edge of sudden death, and we, the 74,152, were eagerly willing to inflict it on them.

Then came what ABC's *Wide World of Sports* referred to darkly in those days as "the agony of defeat." Left tackle Jim Boeke jumped offsides, sending the Cowboys in reverse, back to the 6. Reeves dropped the second-down pass, making it a far more difficult third and goal from the 6. Reeves had been scratched in the eye on the previous play, giving him double vision. Chalk that up to mistake No. 2.

Mistake No. 3 was this: Bob Hayes, whose crushing impairments as a blocker kept him on the bench in goal-line situations, was inexplicably in the huddle, waiting for the play to be called.

Meredith connected with Pettis Norman on a 4-yard pass, returning the ball to the 2. But then it was fourth down. And even then, his pass to Norman was woefully low, so much so that Norman had to fall to the ground to catch it. If Meredith's pass had hit Norman in the chest, chances were he would have scored.

Few in the crowd knew it, but Norman had scored in a much more important way weeks earlier. He had gone to Coach Landry to ask why the Cowboys were segregated on road trips. If you value the importance of team, why are Black players separated from white players on the road? Landry agreed. Almost immediately, he made roommate assignments alphabetical, meaning that Pettis Norman would room with center Dave Manders, who was white and who soon became one of his best friends. Norman's success at changing things was just the beginning. He became one of Dallas's most passionate athlete-activists, who came to be friends with Dr. Martin Luther King Jr. Norman wasn't alone. Teammate Mel Renfro became an outspoken fair-housing advocate in Dallas, a city the Cowboys and Texans had already changed by insisting on the abolition of Jim Crow laws in local hotels, so that prior to the Civil Rights Act of 1964, the home and visiting teams could stay without racial barriers.

But on that day in the Cotton Bowl, Norman, Renfro, and, yes, Bob Hayes were focused on overcoming the Green Bay Packers, who would soon produce plenty of second-guesses.

With Hayes and not Frank Clarke assigned to block Green Bay's All-Pro linebacker Dave Robinson, he brushed Hayes aside and entangled Dandy Don in his massive arms. The Cowboys' quarterback could manage only a desperation heave, which Green Bay intercepted in the end zone.

Dallas got its chance at revenge almost exactly 1 year later, in what came to be known as the Ice Bowl, played on December 31, 1967. With the mercury plunging to 15 below zero, the Packers won *again*, in an even bigger heartbreaker, with Starr scoring in the final seconds on a quarterback sneak, giving Green Bay and Lombardi their place in immortality—albeit by a fraction—2 years in a row.

Thus, the Cowboys suffered two of the most wrenching losses in NFL history on the first and last day of 1967. Despite the losses, the Cowboys provided a welcome respite from an otherwise grim year, during which the number of US troops in South Vietnam rose to almost half a million. We had the Cowboys, and we had the Beatles, who in '67 released a cool little album called *Sgt. Pepper's Lonely Hearts Club Band.*

The Packers had reduced the fans of the Cotton Bowl Cowboys to being our own Lonely Hearts Club Band. Even so, we will never forget the game that occurred more than 50 years ago in Fair Park. Win or lose, it remains—and always will—one of the greatest ever played. And it set the stage more than any other for the ambitions of the Cowboys owner.

CHAPTER SEVEN

Irving or Bust

A FEW WEEKS later, in early 1967, the head of the Irving Chamber of Commerce was invited to speak at a Lions Club meeting in the Dallas suburb of Farmers Branch. His name was Bill Stevens, who would soon prove terrible at keeping a secret.

"Bill got carried away in extolling the virtues of the city of Irving," Power says, "and he said, 'We're even going to have the Dallas Cowboys!'"[1]

Unbeknownst to Stevens, a reporter for the *Dallas Times Herald* was attending the meeting and immediately returned to his office to write the scoop about the Cowboys' possible relocation to Irving.

"All hell broke loose," says Power, who soon received a call from Clint, who was in New York. "And he said, 'I want you to hold a press conference.'"[2]

So, they held a press conference in the offices of the Irving Chamber of Commerce. Those hosting the presser supplied Clint's model for the new stadium and said, yes, "there were discussions" about the Cowboys possibly moving to Irving.

The legendary Blackie Sherrod, then a *Times Herald* sports columnist, showed up at the press conference. He got Clint on the phone and asked what he thought about the announcement being made prematurely, and in Power's words, "Clint responded by saying, 'All momentous occasions are announced through the Farmers Branch Lions Club.'"[3]

Fast-forward to the spring of 1967, when Irving was having its mayoral election. Bob Power ran against two other candidates, one being incumbent Lynn Brown, who had been steadfast in opposing a Cowboys' stadium in Irving.

Not that Irving politics have ever been a great source of intrigue, but this election radiated intrigue, and years later, disagreement about what really went on. Power contends that he had decided to run for mayor, no matter what. But in his document buried in the city archives, Melvin Shuler disputes that.

Leading up to the 1967 election, Clint was so frustrated over Dallas's rejection and Mayor Brown's refusal to even meet with him, that he said to Power and Shuler (according to Shuler's manifesto): "I want to move my franchise to Oklahoma City, because Irving and Dallas do not want me."[4] Not that he really wanted to do that, but the remark underscores his deepening frustration.

That led, according to Shuler, to Clint agreeing to option the acreage near highways 183, 114, and Loop 12 that Shuler and Max Thomas wanted to develop. "Alright, by gosh, I'll block it up," Shuler quotes Clint as saying.[5] But that prompted the Cowboys' owner to impose a condition.

"OK, I'll do it," he said. "But in the meantime, y'all get you a new mayor."[6] Clint also had another concern: if the stadium fell through, he fretted over being stuck with having to pay for all that land with up to $150,000 from his own pocket to cover the option on land valued at $3.2 million. In response, the Irving delegation said he could develop it as a regional mall, which satisfied him to the extent that he was willing to secure the land.

Shuler writes that he told Power that he, Shuler, could not run, because of his pending divorce and fears that he wouldn't be elected anyway. But Power could be, he thought.

"But I don't have the money," Shuler quotes Power as saying.[7]

That problem was quickly solved, Shuler writes, when "Clint immediately sent me two checks for a campaign fund for Bob."[8]

That was by no means the end of Clint's financial commitment to Irving. Dallas's power elite had Clint by the balls, which is why he turned to Irving in the first place. He was desperate. But Irving officials—who have long cast themselves as white knights in the Clint story—were as skilled at ball-clanging deal-making as their neighbors in Dallas. They knew they had Clint in a corner. And why did they have him in the corner? Because they knew he would never allow his team to play in the Cotton Bowl on a long-term basis. For Clint, that would truly be defeat.

So, Clint ended up buying the so-called teardrop—the 85-plus acres bordered by highways 183, 114, and Loop 12 that would become the future home of the Dallas Cowboys.

The 85 acres were made up of eighteen separately owned parcels. To consolidate the acreage, Clint summoned ace real estate broker Gene Cronin, who accomplished the mission *and* created enormous, anticipated value for the benefit of his client and friend.

Clint paid for the acreage with his own money, but in the home stretch of negotiations, Irving officials twisted the screws, thereby proving that, just like his adversaries in Dallas, they too knew how to play hardball. In the end, they got their way, stipulating in the agreement that *they*, not Clint, would own the land *and* the Dallas Cowboys stadium that served as its centerpiece. In other words, neither he nor his heirs would be able to develop the land at the end of the Cowboys' use of the stadium. We should note also that while Clint paid $3.2 million to make it happen, he was later reimbursed, albeit without a penny of interest. So, all he got back was his cost. Even though, by consolidating the property, he had greatly enhanced its value.

Finances were one thing, politics another.

Clint also realized that, with the incumbent Brown remaining in power as mayor, Irving would cease to be an option as a new home for the Cowboys. And that was yet another corner Clint was forced into—it was power on with Power, at his own expense.

During the campaign, Power chose to soft-pedal the stadium issue. Even so, he promised voters that it would never involve city money—that is, taxpayer money. And it *never* did.

During Power's rise to power as mayor of Irving, Clint's campaign boasts turned out to be anything but exaggeration. Once the stadium was built, he said, the name "Irving" would be mentioned so many times on national television that, under normal circumstances, it would cost the city "$500 million a year to buy that kind of advertising."

As Shuler writes, "This was mid-'60s TV rates. It's even truer today."[9] By 1980, when the prime-time soap opera *Dallas* entered its third season on CBS, vaulting to the top of the Nielsen ratings, Texas Stadium's hallmark hole in the roof appeared weekly on national television.

Despite all that, despite even the windfall of Clint financing the Power campaign, he barely won the election. Scratch that. He actually came in second, but because there was a third candidate, a runoff ensued. He won the runoff—barely—raising the question, what would have happened to the Cowboys had Power not been victorious? Might they have moved to Oklahoma City? If football is a game of inches, it may also be said that the Cowboys remaining in North Texas proved to be a victory eked out by political inches.

Once Power was in, negotiations heated up. The city brass made a deal with the Irving newspaper, lest its staff leak any more premature stadium stories. A reporter was allowed to sit in on all meetings but had to hold off on writing anything until city staff gave him the green light. So much for journalistic integrity.

In the meantime, the Cowboys remained in the Cotton Bowl, with a team fully expected to challenge the mighty Packers yet again.

But to co-opt a phrase coined by Mark Twain, "Denial ain't just a river in Egypt." It's hard to imagine what city officials and even voters in Dallas were thinking when they approved an expenditure of $3-plus-million for improvements to the Cotton Bowl in an August 1967 bond referendum. That same measure allocated additional millions used to acquire land through the power of eminent domain, all for the purpose of expanding the parking area of Fair Park—even though the Cowboys would be in Irving in 1971.

Suddenly, the splintery wooden benches were gone, replaced, ironically, with uncomfortable metal seats painted blue and white—Cowboys colors! Unlike the wooden benches, the metal chairs had backs but created a new problem that no doubt padded the balance sheets of chiropractors. Folks in the rows behind them barely had room for their kneecaps, resulting in stiff backs all over Dallas on Monday morning.

And yes, well, the city threw in a few other modest improvements at the old bowl but too few to care about, launching a trend in Dallas that has sought to make repeated improvements to the ancient stadium despite its now hosting only one marquee game a year, that being Texas versus Oklahoma during the State Fair.

Disturbingly, the 1967 bond approval mandated the eviction of thousands of residents through eminent domain to create parking spaces that, with the Cowboys soon to be gone, would not be needed.

Robert Wilonsky, a former columnist for the *Dallas Morning News*, wrote a piece in late 2018 that revealed, sadly, how the city hoped to upgrade the Fair Park area, with or without the Cowboys. Wilonsky was writing about a new play staged in New York City, based on a book that chronicles an ugly chapter in Dallas history. The play, *Travisville*, was written by William Jackson Harper, who, Wilonsky writes, was inspired by a 1986 book written by Dallas journalist Jim Schutze called *The Accommodation: The Politics of Race in an American City.*

"The play tells how Dallas City Hall and the State Fair of Texas joined forces in the late 1960s to snatch the land beneath hundreds of South Dallas homeowners—a wound still tender," Wilonsky wrote. "The official line was that it was for parking. Bad enough. But the real truth resides in the pages of a 1966 report, which said that to improve the fairgrounds, the city must first disappear those 'poor Negroes in shacks' that were too close to Fair Park."[10]

This alone outraged Clint, and he said so in his 1970 book, *Clint's Corner,*[11] which he used to level a direct hit at the city of Dallas for using its power of eminent domain to displace the thousands of poor people who lived near Fair Park in exchange for improving a stadium, which the Dallas Cowboys had already announced they were leaving:

> The improvement of this area for the benefit of its residents should be our primary goal; it is a matter more important than museums, stadiums, or fairs. Obviously, no one disagrees with this. But there is disagreement as to the proper method by which we may attain this goal. I personally do not feel their homes, however humble, should be condemned until comparably priced homes are available to the dispossessed. What is often overlooked is that many of the dwellings being removed are owned by others, that the dispossessed are merely tenants. Specifically, one owner was awarded over $12,000, probably a fair, no pun intended, price; but the tenant was paying only $50 per month rent. Where is he to go? The creation of a parking lot is not the answer to urban renewal.

Cowboys fans had no way of knowing, of course, that 1966 would mark the first of twenty consecutive winning seasons, a feat no team has duplicated since. The Cowboys opened 1967 by beating the Cleveland Browns on the road, 21–14, then returning home to the Cotton Bowl to beat the Giants, 38–24.

Ready for a real distraction? One occurred on November 5, 1967, when just about everyone sitting in the crowd of 54,751 turned and looked at the hubbub occurring on the west side of the Cotton Bowl stands—the Cowboys' side.

Wearing a leopard-spotted miniskirt and carrying two cones of sticky cotton candy, a woman who turned out to be an exotic dancer—who had once worked for Jack Ruby—paraded down the stairs toward the field, greeted by guffaws and gales of laughter. Suddenly, just about everybody stopped paying attention to the Cowboys' 37–7 victory over the Atlanta Falcons—including the Cowboys, in particular quarterback Don Meredith. But for team executive Tex Schramm, the wheels had just begun to turn.

The blond interrupter turned out to be Dallas stripper Bubbles Cash, who inspired Schramm to utter a four-word declaration: "We could sell this." *This*, of course, turned out to be sex, resulting in the new incarnation of the internationally renowned Dallas Cowboys Cheerleaders, who still exist.

The Cowboys had cheerleaders as early as the team's inaugural season, but the squad was made up of local high school girls, with one male member, and were called CowBelles & Beaux. After Schramm's epiphany, they became the Dallas Cowboys Cheerleaders in 1969, and the rest, of course, is cash history. Sure, the cheerleaders made their debut in the Cotton Bowl, but they became a high-profile fixture in Texas Stadium, spawning movies, television appearances, and a worldwide profile. Heck, they even inspired the porno movie *Debbie Does Dallas*, all emanating from that one moment in the Cotton Bowl stands. In 2018, they also inspired a critically acclaimed documentary *Daughters of the Sexual Revolution*.

We should note, however, that Schramm's epiphany had more than a bit of help. Mitch Lewis was friends with Clint Murchison Jr., who regarded Lewis as a public-relations guru. In addition to that, Lewis was a friend, neighbor, and drinking buddy of Schramm's. Lewis's son, Mitch Jr., and others tell us that Lewis lobbied Schramm to use the Bubbles episode and create something new—which he did. So, what happened to Bubbles?

As we write this, we are told that Bubbles has retreated to the Texas Hill Country, where she's a proudly proselytizing born-again Christian and former pawnshop owner. It is no doubt safe to assume that Bubbles never received a dime in royalties for giving Schramm his epiphany. One more thing about seeing those photos of Bubbles in the 1967 Cotton Bowl—it's amazing how women and men alike were formally dressed, with the women wearing stylish overcoats and the men outfitted in coats, ties, and Stetsons, which many, in their pre-Bubbles moment, may have no doubt worn to church before heading to the stadium. The craze of fans wearing jerseys to the games obviously came later, no doubt thrilling NFL owners for fueling another *ka-ching* moment at cash registers.

The Cowboys ended the 1967 regular season with a win–loss record of 9–5. They opened the playoffs in the Cotton Bowl, beating their old nemesis, the Cleveland Browns, in a whopping 52–14 victory that won them the Eastern Conference.

No matter how cool that was, the game buried the lead, as they say in journalism. For Clint picked that day—December 24, 1967, Christmas Eve, no less—to officially announce that his beloved Cowboys were moving to a new stadium in Irving, Texas. He said the Cowboys' new home would have 58,000 seats and cost $15 million. It ended up being bigger and costing more than double that amount.

So, the 70,786 who sat on the splintery wooden benches in the Cotton Bowl cheered for a team that, incredibly, would soon be gone from Dallas.

Even so, there was serious football yet to be played.

Next up was the New Year's Eve match in chilly Green Bay, Wisconsin, for the NFL Championship, with the winner meeting the AFL champion in Super Bowl II.

With the temperature at Lambeau Field close to 15 degrees below zero at kickoff, and the wind chill hovering just above 50 below zero, the Ice Bowl, as it's now known in folklore, became what some consider the best game ever played, even better than the 1958 championship game between the New York Giants and Baltimore Colts that helped redefine professional football as America's true national pastime.

The Cowboys stunned the Packers at the start of the fourth quarter when Dan Reeves threw a 50-yard halfback pass for a touchdown to wide receiver Lance Rentzel, a 1967 acquisition, who, paired with Bob Hayes, gave the Cowboys the best wide receiver tandem in football—by far.

The Cowboys' 17–14 lead held until the final minutes, when Bart Starr demoralized Dallas on a quarterback sneak with 16 seconds left, giving the Packers their third straight championship and their second consecutive appearance in what is now known as the Super Bowl. Had 1966 and 1967 gone differently, it would have likely become the Landry trophy, *not* the Lombardi trophy.

Emotionally, the Ice Bowl was a killer for Cowboy fans, who longed for a championship they had patiently waited for through eight torturous seasons, which included a presidential assassination and their city being nicknamed the "city of hate." Dallas wanted a Cowboys' championship. It needed it. But it was not to be. Clint's mind was already moving a step ahead of the populace.

CHAPTER EIGHT

It's All in the Details

On the new home front in Irving, there was a lot going on.

With tax money off-limits, Irving officials ended up hiring a Murchison ally, a young, innovative attorney named Ray Hutchison, who would eventually marry Kay Bailey, a future US senator for whom the Kay Bailey Hutchison Convention Center is now named. Ironically, it sits on the very spot that Clint hoped to build his dream stadium in downtown Dallas.

Power and Ray Hutchison had gone to law school together. Power knew him as a skilled and reliable bond attorney. Then-Irving City Attorney John Boyle and Hutchison acquired the task of working with Clint's own high-powered attorney, Henry Gilchrist, who at the time headed up one of Dallas's most powerful and influential law firms.

Hutchison turned out to be what bosses would call a gargantuan hire. He alone hatched the financing plan, which as he put it years later was a no-brainer: "Texas Stadium ended up costing $31 million, but not a single dime of taxpayer money was involved," Hutchison said.[1]

"Irving had no money, so we needed to get creative," he told the *Dallas Morning News*.[2]

Boyle called Hutchison "the most innovative public finance lawyer to ever practice law."

Boyle noted that "Ray drafted a plan of financing from scratch, which is highly unusual because bond lawyers almost always rely on what's been done in the past. Clint Jr. and the city of Irving followed Ray's plan, and it worked exactly as he predicted."[3]

And yet, obstacles ensued. The US Securities and Exchange Commission had passed a rule that skeptics believed would derail Irving's seat option bond plan.

Hutchison and Boyle flew to Washington for a meeting with the SEC's general counsel.

"For one hour, Ray laid out his position for the general counsel on why the rule didn't apply to Texas Stadium," Boyle told the *News*. "It was some of the best lawyering I've ever seen."

When Hutchison finished, according to Boyle, the SEC's general counsel leaned forward and said, "We've worked on this rule for 10 years, but in 10 days, you've found a hole large enough to drive a truck through it."[4]

As the *News* noted in a 2012 article: "The SEC gave Irving its waiver and Texas Stadium became the first large sports complex to be built"[5] using seat option bonds.

And it was all because of Hutchison, whose reputation as a seat-option guru played crucial roles in later years for the creation and financing of Reunion Arena and American Airlines Center, the Ballpark in Arlington, AT&T Stadium, Texas Motor Speedway, and Gerald J. Ford Stadium at Southern Methodist University.

But Texas Stadium was Hutchison's first stadium financing success story.

The team had spent much of 1967 and would end up spending much of '68 working on ways of financing the Cowboys' new home, albeit quietly— privately. Power and his colleagues called an election for 1968, a nonbinding referendum, to ask Irving voters if they wanted their city to be the Cowboys' new home, albeit one that would not impose taxes. "Testing the water," as Matkin put it. It passed, by a wide margin. And then again, why wouldn't it?

Assuring the voters that there would be "no bonded expense" was, Matkin says, "a key ingredient. Bob as mayor kept beating that drum at every instance. No way would he be considering something that would be fully obligating the city of Irving with taxation."[6]

The eventual plan allowed for the creation of Texas Stadium bonds and Texas Stadium seat options, which Power called separate, written instruments. But here came hurdle No. 2. When you sell bonds, even today, they have to be approved by the state attorney general.

The Texas attorney general back then was Crawford Martin, whom Power described as "an old country boy from East Texas."[7] He wore a black patch over one eye. Martin became a potential new obstacle, whose power as a threat grew because of outrage brewing within the Dallas establishment that had rejected Clint's plea for a new stadium. They didn't want the stadium in downtown Dallas, but they didn't want it anywhere else, either.

"They were committed to doing whatever they could," Power says, "to kill the possibility of the stadium being built in Irving."[8] They lobbied newspaper and television stations and Crawford Martin, Power says, in seeking his disapproval of Irving issuing bonds.

"And these were people who could apply pressure," Power says. "When you think about who all was involved in those days with the Cotton Bowl . . ."[9]

He cites a Who's Who of Dallas power and influence, including such civic heavyweights as James Chambers, Robert Cullum, Joe Dealey, J. D. Francis, William Hawn, Erik Jonsson, Felix McKnight, John Stemmons, C. A. Tatum, R. L. Thornton Jr., and Angus Wynne. "Those were just a few of the people who were the board of directors of the State Fair."[10] And many of those were at the center of the Citizens Charter Association, which at the time "ran Dallas. That was Dallas," Power says. "Those were the people who were somewhat upset with us, feeling that we in Irving were usurping a position that rightfully belonged to them—to have the Dallas Cowboys."[11]

Shuler's mysterious manifesto offers a more tangible reason for why the Dallas elite was opposed to anything that threatened the Cotton Bowl and Fair Park. There was apprehension in Irving, Shuler writes in the documents found in the Irving archives, about the leaders of a sleepy little bedroom community being pitted against the powerful men of a powerful city.

"Neither did the city of Dallas want to give up the Cotton Bowl," he writes, "because so goes the Cotton Bowl, so goes Fair Park economically. The Cotton Bowl was the only thing that was making money for the State Fair."[12]

As Matkin says, Dallas's power brokers thought, "Clint could not pull off building the stadium somewhere else, so they were quite aggressive." They also had "a good hook," he says, on the Texas Highway Department, "which was vital to us getting roads around that teardrop. They had the Highway Department totally blocked out." For a long time, he says, the Highway Department "wouldn't even discuss roads around the stadium."[13]

Power says a Highway Department official was even quoted in the *Dallas Morning News* as saying that "many deaths would be caused" by Texas Stadium rising up in that location.[14]

Despite the rising cacophony from Dallas, little Irving trudged on, against the wind, focusing on how to pay for the stadium without a penny of tax money. A variation of the seat option bond concept had been used to fund new stadiums in prior decades at Baylor, Texas Christian University (TCU), and Texas A&M and—ironically—to add upper decks to the Cotton Bowl, thus creating "the house that Doak built," after the popularity of SMU running back Doak Walker fed the need for a bigger stadium in the late 1940s.

In the end, Murchison and Hutchison settled on interest-free bonds of $300, discounted at $250. It became a $250 purchase of a $300 face-value stadium bond. In other words, a football fan would buy an individual bond for $250 and redeem it years later for $300.

There was also a financing plan available, through the First National Bank of Dallas. For a $250 bond, it called for a down payment of $50 and monthly payments of $8 a month for 30 months.

The purchase gave the fan a bond and a separate piece of paper titled a Texas Stadium "seat option." That generated an option "to buy Cowboys season tickets for that seat," Power says. "The condition was, you had to buy the season tickets. You could only miss two years over the term of the life of the bond, or you would lose your option."[15]

For the Cowboys themselves, this meant selling season tickets only to those who had purchased seat option bonds, "which was a tremendous thing for them to do," Power says, "when they had the whole world out there to sell season tickets to. Clint agreed. That's the thing that really made it go."[16]

Those wishing to sit in the more desirable area between the 30-yard lines had to pay $1,000 for four $250 seat option bonds—for each seat—to allow them to sit there. In other words, a family wishing to purchase four seats inside the 30s would pay $4,000. Those wishing to sit outside the 30-yard lines had to pay $250 for each seat option bond, with in both cases, the fee for season tickets being added to the price.

To test the market, the city of Irving sent out a notice, asking for $50 deposits to give fans the right to purchase seat option bonds. "To our surprise," Power says, "the $50s started rolling in. It was amazing. We soon had enough deposits to total almost $7 million when the bonds were, in fact, purchased."[17]

Amid the craziness, there was still a football season that had to be played, and yes, in 1968, its home games would take place in the embattled Cotton Bowl.

The Cowboys of 1968 were truly amazing. Showing no signs of lingering grief over their crushing loss in the Ice Bowl, they finished the season with a 12–2 record, notching six straight victories to open the season, including a 59–13 win over the Detroit Lions in the season opener—which, maybe because of the announced defection to Texas Stadium, drew a surprisingly low crowd of 61,382. Attendance rose as the season progressed, with a near-sellout of 74,604 watching the Cowboys lose to, who else, the Green Bay Packers, 28–17. Even so, the Cowboys won six of their last seven, heading into the playoffs against the Cleveland Browns.

Stunningly, they lost in Cleveland, 31–20, suffering their third straight postseason collapse. The Cowboys would soon inherit the derisive mantle "Next Year Champions," with no one knowing which next year would end in a championship.

Just north and west of the Dallas city limits, Irving could not afford to suffer Cowboys' playoff fatigue. Irving was doing all it could to ensure its reputation as the little city that could, and for that matter, the Cowboys' owner was equally, feverishly preoccupied, having no time to indulge in grief over his team's latest on-field collapse.

The city of Irving agreed to issue the bonds by December 31, 1968, "and we said in writing," Power says, "that if we failed to do that, we'd send you your money back."[18]

Then came the next problem. On December 23, 1968, two days after the Cowboys' loss to Cleveland, Power was served with a lawsuit against the city of Irving, questioning the validity of the deal, the bonds, and so on. Texas law mandates that when there's a lawsuit over a city issuing bonds, the attorney general cannot approve bonds.

Power approached the plaintiff, hoping desperately to reach a compromise. The plaintiff agreed, with this condition: the city would host a second referendum, contending that during the first election, voters didn't fully understand the issues. "So, there we were," Power says. "On Dec. 26, 1968, the day after Christmas, we decided we would have to have another election"[19]—in January 1969.

"We had 20 days to hold an election on what had become a very complicated issue," Power says. They approached the Irving Jaycees, seeking their help in sending out fliers to voters to help answer questions. "They worked night and day literally to get it done," Power says. Every registered voter received a fact sheet within four days.[20]

On the day of the election, 68 percent voted in favor of Texas Stadium, ending the threat of the lawsuit and allowing the attorney general to approve the bonds.

The Cowboys agreed to assume the cost of operating the stadium, including police and fire protection. The Cowboys paid for traffic control. "The city of Irving was not out a quarter for the operation of Texas Stadium," Matkin says, "not at all like what you hear about other stadiums that are currently under construction. We tried to plug every potential hole that we could so that the citizens of Irving never had to pay a penny of taxpayer dollars for the stadium."[21]

The day after the election, the Irving City Council called a hastily arranged special meeting to approve all documents needed to build the stadium. They met Cowboys officials and "closed the deal," Power says, largely to avoid more litigation.

Power wrote Clint a city of Irving check for $3.2 million, the amount he had paid for the 85 acres of land on which the stadium would rise. "No interest, no nothing," Power says. "What he paid for it is all he got."[22]

All along, the city had remained steadfast in not asking taxpayers for a penny of revenue. Soon, however, it became painfully obvious that Irving officials had fallen short in raising the needed capital, limited as it was to the sale of seat option bonds. The tally added up to $7.5 million, leaving Clint and his checkbook to make up the difference. With no other choice, he *matched* the existing $7.5 million with his own purchase of bonds, doing so by writing a check. So, what did $15 million do? It gave a green light to construction of the stadium's shell.

Looking back, it offered yet another example of the risk-taking Clint Jr. inherited from Clint Sr. His ballsy decision to "let the dirt fly" at least fueled a sense of momentum, and sure enough, the city soon took in $5 million more in the sale of seat option bonds. Even then, still more was needed.

So, Clint got out his checkbook once again, matching *that* $5 million with a second purchase of seat option bonds, raising the bottom line in stadium capital to $25 million. It didn't stop there. He ponied up $6 million more on top of *that*, using a fresh outlay of revenue bonds to cover a wide range of mounting overruns, including a state-of-the art scoreboard.

At its highwater mark, Clint's own investment in Texas Stadium ended up approaching $20 million of the overall cost of $31 million. He eventually got back *some* of his money, through the ongoing sale of seat option bonds for reserved seats and luxury suites. But in the end, the Cowboys' owner was left holding $11 million in low-interest-bearing, illiquid revenue bonds.

So, yes, financially, how could you view it any other way? It was a setback, the sour end of risk-taking. Except for one very big thing: Clint had finally reached his dream of providing a state-of-the-art home for his beloved Dallas Cowboys. His only regret: it was in the quiet, quaint suburb of Irving and *not* downtown Dallas.

Veteran photographer David Woo captures the essence of Clint's persona by focusing on his signature look, including his penetrating eyes, dark suit and tie, brown-framed eyeglasses, perfectly trimmed crew cut, and, of course, his passion for football. (*Dallas Morning News.*)

Facing, Clint Jr.'s mother, Anne, died of hepatitis when he was only an infant. The terribly painful, irreplaceable loss of her maternal love left a lasting void in his psyche, with which he struggled for the rest of his life. (The Murchison Family Collection.)

Clint Sr. was a classic entrepreneur, who made a fortune as a successful pioneer in oil and gas, as well as in the pipeline industry. After World War II, he initiated a concentrated effort to transition control of his assets to his sons Clint and John by persuading them to return to Dallas to gradually take over day-to-day investment and management responsibilities. (Courtesy Ft. Worth Star-Telegram Collection, Special Collections, the University of Texas at Arlington Libraries.)

In the summer of 1941, Clint met Jane Katherine Coleman on a blind date in Dallas. She was beautiful, petite, and only 16 years old. The two fell head over heels in love and dated on a long-distance basis through the war years before marrying just as it was winding down. (The Murchison Family Collection.)

Facing, Weak and sickly as a child, Clint Murchison Jr. found his health during adolescence, but he always remained small in stature. His true strength lay in his extraordinary intellect, as confirmed in the caption accompanying his high school senior class yearbook photo. Appropriately, it took the form of a mathematical theorem: "The size of the body is inversely proportional to the size of the brain." (The Murchison Family Collection.)

Clint and Jane had four children. They and their children appear in this photo. Back row: Clint III, Jane, and Clint Jr; front row: Robert, Coke Anne, and Burk. In the background stands an early family home built by Clint in 1949. In addition to football, he also had a passion for architecture and design, which he actively pursued through his lifetime by immersing himself in designing and supervising the construction of several personal residences. His initial fledgling effort in 1949 would be followed by several much more ambitious world-class dwellings. He expended substantial time and energy in these projects and in so doing acquired the expertise and confidence to ultimately take on his final tour de force, Texas Stadium. (The Murchison Family Collection.)

Facing, After returning to Dallas to join their father in business, Clint and John formed a partnership, Murchison Brothers, through which to funnel their investments. In time they attained some singular successes, including the founding of the Dallas Cowboys, but they never approached Clint Sr.'s past achievements. Their partnership proved to be dysfunctional. John had no appetite for risk-taking, while his headstrong brother proved to be impulsive and lacked discipline in his investing. By the time of his tragic, premature death in 1979, John had initiated the dissolution of Murchison Brothers. (From TIME. © 1961 TIME USA LLC. All rights reserved. Used under license.)

TWENTY-FIVE CENTS

JUNE 16, 1961

MAKING MONEY WORK
A Texas Technique

TIME

THE NEWSMAGAZINE

CLINT & JOHN
MURCHISON

Bernard Safran

$7.00 A YEAR

(REG. U.S. PAT. OFF.)

VOL. LXXVII NO. 25

Above, Two of the Cowboys' original hires were head coach Tom Landry and future star quarterback "Dandy" Don Meredith standing left to right between Clint and an early Cowboys minority partner Bedford Wynne. (Courtesy Ft. Worth Star-Telegram Collection, Special Collections, the University of Texas at Arlington Libraries.)

Facing top, Clint was generally known as an intensely shy and introverted person, but beneath his stoic façade lurked a wild Mr. Hyde side. He could joke and party with the best of them and loved hanging out with a loud, funny, hard-drinking group of eccentrics known as the "Rover Boys." This photo captures a group of them at play. Top from left: Bob Thompson, Frank Northway, and Clint; bottom from left: Mitch Lewis's wife Marie, Gordon McLendon, and Jane. (The Murchison Family Collection.)

Facing bottom, Clint's periodic golf outings were all about having fun rather than keeping score. Here he hams it up with two of his buddies, DC lobbyist Tom Webb (L) and Jack Jones (R). (Dallas Cowboys Football Club.)

Clint's first hire in starting up the Cowboys was general manager Tex Schramm, whom he gave almost total autonomy in running the day-to-day football operations. Such was not the case with the development of Texas Stadium, which remained Clint's baby from the start. (Dallas Cowboys Football Club.)

Cartoonist Bill McClanahan created this wonderful rendering of football star Doak Walker, who in the late 1940s led the SMU Mustangs to years of phenomenal success. Ticket demand exploded, and SMU moved its home games from its small, on-campus facility Ownby Stadium to the Cotton Bowl, which underwent an expansion soon after. Upper decks were added first on its west side in 1948 and then on the east side in 1949, bringing its capacity to more than 75,000. In recognition of Walker's role as catalyst, a plaque was hung at the stadium's main entrance that reads: "The Cotton Bowl, the House that Doak Built." (SMU Alumni Association Directory 1966, DeGoyler Library, Southern Methodist University.)

For nearly 20 years commencing in the mid-1950s, Dallas artist Karl Hoefle created exquisite hand-rendered illustrations used on the covers of the Southwestern Bell Telephone's Yellow Pages. In this one, the artist focuses on Fair Park and the Cotton Bowl during the State Fair of Texas. In his highly detailed, miniaturized renderings, Hoefle created a magical fairy-tale quality by adding a plethora of tiny animals and other eccentric details. Grab a magnifying glass and check them out. (The Karl Hoefle Family Collection.)

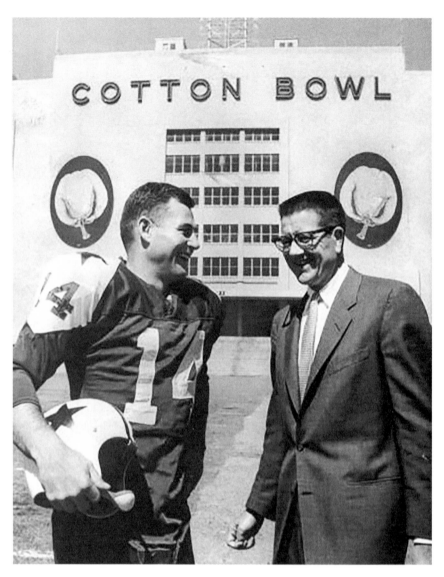

The Cowboys' first starting quarterback was Eddie LeBaron, who at 5 foot 7 was only an inch taller than Clint. As one of the shortest, if not the shortest, quarterbacks ever to play pro football, he quickly earned the nickname "the Little General." During the 1963 season, he was replaced permanently as the Cowboys starter by Don Meredith. (Dallas Cowboys Football Club.)

In the Cowboys' early years, Clint also happened to coach his three sons' YMCA six-man football teams. On many Saturdays after his YMCA games, he began calling Landry to playfully brag about his team's exploits and also to discuss the Cowboys' game scheduled for the following day. It grew into a running joke between the two and helped to enhance their rapport. Nowhere is this more apparent than in a brief, playful note Clint sent Landry on the eve of the Cowboys' first Super Bowl game: "Dear Tom, I have taught you all I can. From now on you're on your own." (The Murchison Family Collection.)

Even in the early years before the Cowboys began winning, Clint was thinking ahead and dreaming of a day when he might build a new stadium for them in Dallas. He almost never missed an away game and in attending them he always sat in regular seats in the midst of the home crowd so that he could experience the stadium to the fullest just as they did. While at the games, he took mental notes and critiqued every stadium, noting each of their assets and flaws. Eventually, he incorporated these observations in the design of Texas Stadium. (Lynn Pelham/The LIFE Picture Collection/Getty Images.)

All Pro defensive tackle Bob Lilly was one of the greatest players to ever play in the NFL. He played his entire career for the Dallas Cowboys and came to be known as "Mr. Cowboy." Of all of the players who played for the Cowboys during Clint's tenure as owner, Lilly was far and away Murchison's favorite. He most admired Lilly for his sportsmanship, stating that in all his years of watching the Cowboys play, he never witnessed Lilly take a cheap shot on an opponent. (Dallas Cowboys Football Club.)

1966 DALLAS COWBOYS

Despite the Cowboys' loss to Vince Lombardi's Green Bay Packers in the NFL championship game, Clint was proud of his '66 squad. FYI, he's the one in the dark suit. (Dallas Cowboys Football Club.)

Facing, Roy Hofheinz was an eccentric visionary on par in many respects with Clint. He led the effort to develop the Astrodome in Houston as the home for a major league expansion team first known as the Houston Colt .45s and later renamed the Houston Astros. Construction of the domed stadium began in 1962 and was completed in time for the 1965 baseball season. Hofheinz's accomplishment jump-started Clint's own long-held plans to build a new stadium in Dallas to replace the antiquated Cotton Bowl. (From the collections of the Dallas History & Archives Division, Dallas Public Library.)

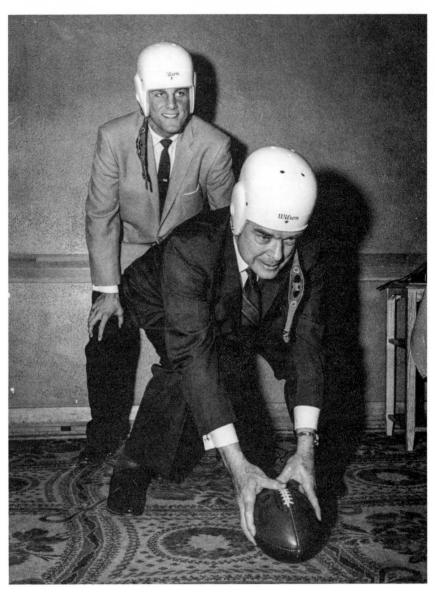

Erik Jonsson, pictured here playing center with Don Meredith at QB in a PR photograph, was the mayor of Dallas through the mid-1960s, when the Cowboys finally began winning and lifting the spirits of a city devastated by the assassination of President Kennedy. Jonsson was a brilliant, enormously generous man, but he wasn't a fan of football and remained clueless as to the role the Cowboys would play in rejuvenating the city's image and spirit. (The J. Erik Jonsson Collection, DeGoyler Library, Southern Methodist University.)

The opening of Texas Stadium in 1971 in Irving officially brought an end to the cold war that had existed between Clint and Erik Jonsson, who is pictured here. However, while the war was over, the healing would take time. On a brilliant spring day in 1974, Clint and the Boys Club of Dallas executive Ralph Pahel called on Jonsson in his Republic Bank Tower office, which had a stunning view to the north and west of downtown Dallas. As the two exited in the elevator after the meeting, Clint suddenly turned to Pahel and wisecracked, "Did you notice the great view Erik has of Texas Stadium?" (*Dallas Morning News.*)

The combination of Don Meredith throwing passes to Bob Hayes—who earned the nickname "World's Fastest Human" because of his record-setting performance in the 1964 Olympics—allowed the Cowboys during the 1966 season to wreak havoc on every team on the schedule. Here, Hayes catches a "bomb" from Meredith in a game against Washington in the Cotton Bowl. As a result, the 1966 season was the Cowboys' first winning season and the first of 20 consecutive winning seasons, a streak that continued even after Clint Jr. sold the team. Hayes' speed forced teams in the NFL to abandon "man-to-man" coverage and go with a "zone" defense, a practice that continues today. (From the collections of the Dallas History & Archives Division, Dallas Public Library.)

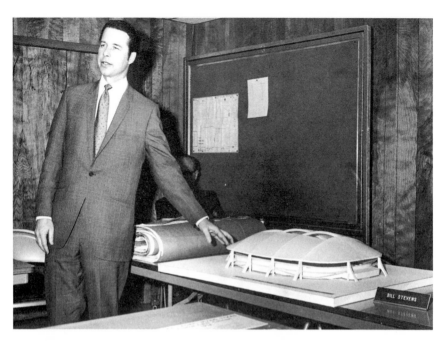

Robert Power stands next to an architectural model of Texas Stadium, which Clint had made and used as a display piece at many of the meetings he called to promote his vision for the stadium. Power's tenure as mayor was short-lived. Having accomplished his mission, he retired midway through his second 2-year term to return to his legal practice. At that time, he was retained by Clint as a consultant to Texas Stadium Corporation to troubleshoot issues as they arose with the city of Irving and other outside parties. It was a position he would hold through the time Texas Stadium was imploded in 2010. (From the Irving Archives and Museum.)

Contingent on finalizing a deal with the city of Irving, Clint officially announced his decision to build a new stadium in Irving on October 17, 1967. The *Dallas Morning News* memorialized it by publishing this amusing cartoon created by popular staff cartoonist Bill McClanahan. (The Murchison Family Collection.)

Facing, Warren Morey has long been recognized as the architect who collaborated with Clint in designing Texas Stadium. In fact, before officially commissioning Morey for the job, Clint worked with two other nationally recognized West Coast architects, Welton Becket and William Pereira, in developing conceptual renderings of the future home of the Cowboys. At the time Clint contractually finalized the stadium deal with the city of Irving, he released renderings produced by Pereira to the press. Morey later used them as a starting point in creating the final working drawings for the actual construction. (Courtesy Ft. Worth Star-Telegram Collection, Special Collections, the University of Texas at Arlington Libraries.)

Morey faced major engineering challenges in bringing Pereira's concept to life. He was forced to make certain compromises. If one compares Morey's rendering here with that of the California architect on the previous page, one can observe that it has lost some of the sleek, futuristic flair of Pereira's original design. Yet, it's still quite striking and its iconic hole-in-the-roof dome remains unchanged. (The Warren Morey Family Collection.)

Facing, In negotiating with Clint, city of Irving officials made things difficult by adamantly refusing to take on any municipal tax-based debt to build the stadium. Searching for a solution, Clint retained the services of the bright, young municipal finance consultant Ray Hutchison. Hutchison responded with an innovative plan that called for ticket buyers, and not taxpayers, to pay for the stadium. The key to his plan was restricting the sale of season tickets to only those willing to buy city of Irving Texas Stadium Revenue Bonds sufficient to pay for a specifically chosen seat in the stadium. The plan proved to be effective, but controversial. In the end, $31 million worth of the bonds were sold to finance the stadium. (Dallas Cowboys Football Club.)

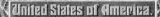

STATE OF TEXAS
COUNTY OF DALLAS

 **$300.00**

City of Irving Junior Lien Texas Stadium
Revenue Bond, First Series
(Non-Interest Bearing Seat Option Bond)

THE CITY OF IRVING (the "City"), operating under the general laws of the State of Texas and its duly adopted Home Rule Charter, for value received, hereby promises to pay to bearer, or, if this bond be registered to other than bearer, then to the registered owner hereof, on the 26th day of December, 2008, the principal sum of

THREE HUNDRED DOLLARS

without interest thereon. The principal hereof shall be payable at maturity at the principal office in Dallas, Texas, of the First National Bank in Dallas in lawful money of the United States of America.

THIS BOND IS ONE of a duly authorized issue of bonds of the City, dated December 26, 1968, and bearing the title aforesaid, all issued and to be issued for the purpose of providing funds to pay in part the costs of constructing and equipping a sports coliseum and related facilities of the City to be known as "Texas Stadium." Said issue, of which this bond is one, was issued and will be issued, along with other bonds of the City, under and pursuant to a certain Indenture of Mortgage and Deed of Trust (the "Indenture"), dated as of December 26, 1968, executed by the City to and with the First National Bank in Dallas, Dallas, Texas, as trustee (the "Trustee").

ALL BONDS ISSUED under the Indenture, subject to the priorities therein established, are secured by a lien upon certain rent and personal property of the City comprising Texas Stadium, and by a pledge solely of the net revenues thereof, as therein defined, and the holder hereof shall never have the right to demand payment hereof from any funds raised or to be raised from taxation.

THE INDENTURE SETS FORTH in detail the respective rights, duties, powers and privileges of the City, the holders of the bonds issued thereunder, and of the Trustee, all with respect to said security and to other matters relating to Texas Stadium. Among the rights reserved to the City therein are (a) the right to issue various types of bonds of various priorities, including bonds senior in right and lien to or on a parity with this bond; (b) the right to call and redeem this bond prior to maturity at the price therein stated and at any time without premium or penalty of any kind; and (c) the right to amend the Indenture under certain conditions and subject to certain restrictions. Reference is made to the Indenture for a complete statement of these and other rights of the City and to a description of the revenues pledged and properties mortgaged thereunder, the nature and extent of the security thereof, a description of the events of and remedies in case of default, this bond being strictly subject to all of the provisions thereof, to all of which the holder of this bond by his acceptance hereof agrees and assents.

THE INDENTURE PROVIDES THAT, after the payment of annual operating and maintenance expenses of Texas Stadium and after complying with the various fund requirements and bond priorities established therein, the Trustee shall utilize remaining available revenues for the purpose of mandatorily redeeming such number of bonds of this issue, and other issues on a parity herewith, for which revenues are available (as determined in accordance with the Indenture). The specific bonds to be thus redeemed each year shall be determined by the Trustee by lot at the times, in the manner, at the price and subject to the restrictions and other rights of the City specified in the Indenture. After mailing notice to the registered owners of any bonds thus selected for redemption prior to maturity, such bonds thereupon and forever shall be considered redeemed, paid and no longer outstanding and the holders thereof shall have only the right to receive the money thus set aside for the redemption of such bonds.

THE BONDS OF THIS ISSUE are registrable upon books kept for that purpose at the principal offices of the Trustee, as Registrar, such registrations to be noted on the reverse side hereof. The initial registration hereof will be made without cost to the bearer hereof. Subsequent registration of transfers will be made by the Registrar at the request of the then registered owner (or bearer, if not registered, or if subsequently registered in that manner) upon payment by the owner of the Registrar's charge for transfer from time to time in effect, and upon presentation of this bond together with due and proper proof of ownership by the owner in person or by his duly authorized attorney. Bonds of this issue as initially issued or if subsequently registered to bearer may be transferred by delivery only. All other bonds may be transferred only by the registered owner thereof with registration noted hereon as aforesaid, and neither the City nor the Trustee shall be bound otherwise. Bonds of this issue registered to bearer shall not be entitled to be included or considered in the selection of bonds for mandatory redemption as described elsewhere herein.

ALL THINGS NECESSARY to make this bond the valid, legally binding special revenue obligation of the City and to make the Indenture valid, binding and legal for the security hereof, have been done and performed and the issue of bonds of which this bond is one has been in all respects duly authorized.

IN WITNESS WHEREOF, THE CITY OF IRVING, TEXAS, has caused this bond to be executed and attested by the facsimile signatures of its Mayor and City Secretary, respectively, and its corporate seal to be hereunto affixed, and this bond to be approved as to form by its City Attorney, as evidenced by his facsimile signature affixed hereto, all as of the date of this bond as above written.

ATTEST:

CITY OF IRVING, TEXAS

Mary J. Gilleland
City Secretary

Robert Howie
Mayor

APPROVED AS TO FORM:

John F. Boyle
City Attorney

(SEAL) CITY OF IRVING · STATE OF TEXAS

CERTIFICATE

STATE OF TEXAS
COUNTY OF DALLAS
CITY OF IRVING

SECTION
ROW
SEAT

Texas Stadium

Seat and Ticket Option Certificate

THIS CERTIFICATE, when authenticated as herein required, shall evidence the right and option of the registered holder of this Certificate, as such registration appears on the reverse side hereof and on the Texas Stadium Seat and Ticket Option Registration Books, to purchase the season tickets, and the tickets for games not included in the season ticket package, applicable to the seat location noted hereon sold by the Dallas Cowboys Football Club, Inc., for all football games played in Texas Stadium by the professional football team known as the *"Dallas Cowboys."*

THE AFORESAID RIGHT AND OPTION was registered, and shall be held, administered, exercised, transferred, cancelled or forfeited, pursuant and subject at all times to the terms, provisions, conditions and limitations prescribed and provided in Ordinance No. 1705 of the City Council of the City of Irving, Texas. Among other things, said Ordinance, in part, provides (i) that, subject to the rights of the Trustee in the event of default under the Indenture of Mortgage and Deed of Trust of the City authorizing various series of Texas Stadium Revenue Bonds, said right and option shall be applicable and available for the initial period during which the *Dallas Cowboys* are required to conduct home football games in Texas Stadium (not less than 35 years); (ii) that the same shall be exercised at the times each year, and at the ticket prices from time to time established by the Dallas Cowboys Football Club, Inc.; (iii) that the standard of conduct applicable to all other occupants of Texas Stadium shall be applicable to the person occupying the above seat location pursuant thereto and at all times subject to the rights of the Dallas Cowboys Football Club, Inc., to maintain order in the routine and normal conduct of football events in Texas Stadium and to the police and governmental powers of the City; and each ticket thus purchased shall continue to be a revocable license for the event to which the same shall apply; (iv) that such right and option may be exercised with respect to the first applicable tickets sold for games in Texas Stadium, and must be exercised during the first year in which season tickets to *Dallas Cowboys* football team games are offered for sale for games to be played therein and additionally must be exercised in each year thereafter, in each instance by purchasing for the above seat season tickets to the games included by the Dallas Cowboys Football Club, Inc., in its annual season ticket package, as determined by it; and (v) that if the holder of said right and option shall decline, fail or refuse for any reason to exercise the same to the full extent required in clause (iv), next above, more frequently than one (1) time during each ten (10) year period beginning with the first year in which season ticket packages are sold, said right and option may be cancelled, terminated and declared void by the City without grace or notice of any kind by noting such fact on the registration books thereof; however, in such event, upon demand, the registered holder hereof shall surrender and deliver up this Certificate to the City, but such demand or surrender shall not be necessary to a complete, final and effective termination of such option. Reference is here made to said Ordinance for a complete statement of the foregoing and other provisions thereof.

THIS CERTIFICATE shall not be valid or effective for any purpose until and unless authenticated where indicated on the reverse side hereof by the First National Bank in Dallas, Dallas, Texas, and by initial registration by said Bank of the initial ownership of the option evidenced hereby on the registration form also appearing on the reverse side hereof. Subject to any applicable law, this Certificate and said right and option may be transferred by such initial owner and by successive owners by presentation hereof to the Seat Option Registrar from time to time designated as such by resolution of the City Council of the City, together with due and proper proof of such ownership and upon payment of such Registrar's charge for transfers from time to time in effect. Such Registrar shall be authorized from time to time to promulgate rules and regulations approved by the City relating to such transfers and to the time during, and circumstances and conditions under, which they shall be made, and the owner of such option shall be conclusively bound thereby. Such subsequent registrations shall be noted on the reverse side hereof and upon the aforesaid official registration books for Texas Stadium Seat and Ticket Options. This Certificate and the right and option it evidences may be transferred and assigned only in the manner thus provided, and otherwise shall be not negotiable, and neither the City, the Seat Option Registrar nor any other party interested herein or affected hereby shall be bound by any other transfer, and in any event in case of any dispute or difference between the registration hereof as the same appears on the reverse side hereof and as the same appears on said registration books, such books shall be final and conclusive except in the case of mistakes satisfactorily proven to the Registrar.

IT SHALL BE THE DUTY AND RESPONSIBILITY of each successive holder hereof to ascertain and determine from the Seat Option Registrar by reference to the aforesaid registration books whether or not the right and option evidenced by this Certificate is and remains outstanding and is effective or has been cancelled; whether this Certificate has been replaced because of alleged loss, destruction, mutilation or theft; and to determine the rules and regulations under, and the times during, which such transfers can be made and pursuant to which said option may be exercised.

IN WITNESS WHEREOF, THE CITY OF IRVING, TEXAS, by virtue of the Ordinance aforesaid adopted by its City Council, has caused this Certificate to be executed and attested by the facsimile signatures of its Mayor and City Secretary, respectively, and its corporate seal to be hereunto affixed, and this Certificate to be approved as to form by its City Attorney, as evidenced by his facsimile signature affixed hereto, all as of the day authenticated as shown on the reverse side hereof.

ATTEST:

Mary Gilliland
City Secretary

APPROVED AS TO FORM:

John F. Boyle Jr.
City Attorney

CITY OF IRVING, TEXAS

Robert H. Power
Mayor

CITY COUNCIL
ROBERT H. POWER, Mayor
R. DAN MATKIN, Mayor Pro Tem
BOB HALEY
JOE G. JETER
KENNETH REYNOLDS
CLIFF SHASTEEN
JIM WILCOX

In addition to securing Seat Option Bond rights for season tickets in the stands, fans could also do the same for a luxury suite with seating for twelve spectators. The cost was $50,000. A standard suite came unfinished and consisted of a 12' × 16' bare space with a concrete floor and Sheetrock walls. Cost of interior decoration was borne by the buyer. Of all the 178 Circle Suites, the most outlandish and expensive of all was the "Let Them Eat Cake" suite, which had a Louis XIV motif, including a vaulted ceiling, an ornate fine crystal chandelier, velvet tufted chairs, antique oil paintings, and a fully equipped bar staffed by a tuxedo-clad butler with white gloves. (John G. Zimmerman/Sports Illustrated Classic/Getty Images.)

Facing, Upon securing their seats through the purchase of revenue bonds, each bondholder was issued another legal instrument know as a Texas Stadium Seat and Ticket Option Certificate. It came free of charge and provided bondholders the right to buy the season tickets for their specific seats, as long as the bonds were outstanding. The seat option certificate was severable from the revenue bond and could be transferred/sold to others. In fact, as the Cowboys' popularity escalated, the value of the seat options appreciated enormously, far exceeding that of the revenue bonds themselves. (Dallas Cowboys Football Club.)

How it feels to be the 7ᵗʰ sardine in a size 6 can!

For three hours, Stanley feels like a middle-guard during a goal-line stand. His eyeballs could see better if they were mounted in each knee. He practices "alternate breathing" — when his seat mates inhale, Stanley exhales. He'd like to pull up his socks but he's afraid he'll grab the wrong leg. Go for a hot-dog? It would be easier to run solo through the Viking defense. Poor Stanley!

Above and facing, In order to raise money by selling Seat Option Bonds, Clint targeted ticket-buying Cowboys fans, who regularly attended their games at the Cotton Bowl. One marketing effort was composed of a series of amusing, cartoon-styled print ads, which ran in the Cowboys' game programs. Created by Clint's friend and PR guru Mitch Lewis, the ads contrasted the current experience of a typical spectator named Stanley Mudge at the Cotton Bowl versus what could be expected in the future at the new improved Texas Stadium. (The Mitch Lewis Family Collection.)

Hang in there, Stanley! The great day is coming!

Next year, the age of the [elbow-room] Texas Stadium

At last. The end of the pre-pressed seat. Away with cardboard shin-guards. No 12-hour after-game hunched-back hangover. Stretch out, Stanley, loll. Theatre-type seats (even the end zone) 21 inches wide, 31 inches deep, back-to-back. Rows wide enough to let people by without dislocating hips. A stadium people-engineered for fans like Stanley who like live action with living room comfort. It's no dream, Stanley, you'll be sitting pretty — pretty soon.

HAVE YOU YOUR TEXAS STADIUM SEATS? (Stanley has!)
For seat information, call Texas Stadium Corporation: 363-3923

Before breaking ground on Texas Stadium, Clint and the city of Irving faced many obstacles, including a last-minute lawsuit brought by an irate Irving citizen, which threatened to derail the stadium's funding. A settlement was quickly reached, but it called for a citywide referendum to approve the project a second time with little advance notice. Anxiety ran high as city officials mounted an intense grassroots campaign to get out the vote. From the look of things, they left no stone unturned in accomplishing their goal. (From the Irving Archives and Museum.)

Facing top, The official groundbreaking of the Texas Stadium was held shortly after the successful referendum. Clint and Mayor Robert Power served as official spokespersons. After overcoming so many obstacles in getting the ball across the goal line, their spirits were running high. Clint brought the house down when he playfully opened the event by unveiling what he referred to as an official rendering of the future stadium. To everyone's surprise, it turned out to be an enlarged photo of the current day Roman Colosseum with a blue and silver Cowboys decal stuck to it. (The Murchison Family Collection.)

Facing bottom, Texas Stadium was located on a teardrop-shaped parcel of land at the confluence of Highways 183, Loop 12, and 114. This aerial photo of the stadium site clearly delineates the boundaries of the property on which it was located. Clint believed it to be the best location for a stadium in the entire Dallas–Fort Worth metropolitan area. (Dallas Cowboys Football Club.)

As unlikely as it may sound, the inaugural event featured at Texas Stadium was a 10-day-long Billy Graham Crusade, which ran from September 17–26, 1971, even though the stadium was far from complete. The Graham crusade drew an estimated 500,000 people over its 10 days in spite of stormy weather and largely unpaved and muddy parking lots. Coach Landry, who was a close friend of Graham, chaired the event and also was a featured speaker just as he would be over fifty times at other Billy Graham–sponsored Crusades during his lifetime. (The Murchison Family Collection.)

Facing top, The giant buttresses positioned around the circumference of the stadium supported the weight of its famous roof. Constructed of reinforced concrete and poured in place, they were sunk an incredible 90' deep in the ground and rose 80' above it. When the stadium was imploded, three of them actually withstood the series of blasts and defiantly remained standing. (Courtesy Ft. Worth-Star Telegram Collection, Special Collections, the University of Texas at Arlington Libraries.)

Facing bottom, The Cowboys actually played and lost to the Baltimore Colts in Super Bowl V to cap off their final full season at the Cotton Bowl. It was a frustrating, mistake-filled game for Dallas and quickly was christened the "Blunder Bowl." The disappointment ran high, but the city of Dallas helped relieve some of it by sponsoring a downtown parade to show its appreciation. Given his low-key, behind-the-scenes management style, Clint made an unlikely leader of the Cowboys caravan as he quietly but proudly made his feelings known. (Courtesy Ft. Worth-Star Telegram Collection, Special Collections, the University of Texas at Arlington Libraries.)

The Landry-led Cowboys capped off their first season at Texas Stadium by crushing the Miami Dolphins in Super Bowl VI in New Orleans. After the season, one extremely enthusiastic fan, who also happened to be a master woodworker, demonstrated his appreciation by giving the head coach a hand-carved mahogany door, which contains three panels each with its own distinct Cowboys motif. The beautiful, oversized door first hung at Landry's office at Expressway Tower and later at Valley Ranch. In 1989 when he was replaced as coach, he removed it from the doorway of his office once and for all and took it home with him. (Dallas Cowboys Football Club.)

During a home game in 1967, Bubbles Cash, a stripper who had once worked for Jack Ruby, made an unannounced appearance at the Cotton Bowl. The crowd's reaction was electric and enthusiastic. Even Dandy Don and his teammates stared up from their huddle on the field. Clint's friend and PR executive Mitch Lewis took note of the sensation incited by Bubbles. Later he spoke to his neighbor and drinking buddy Tex Schramm and recommended that he should try to use the energy to launch a makeover of the Cowboys' cheerleading squad. Tex went to work and eventually developed the perfect formula, one based on dance and showmanship. (*Dallas Morning News.*)

Another carryover from the Cotton Bowl was trumpeter Tommy Loy, who played the "Star-Spangled Banner" as a soloist before every Cowboys home game from the time of his original commission on Thanksgiving Day in 1966 until the final one of the 1988 season, which coincidentally also happened to be Tom Landry's final game as the Cowboys coach. Loy was selected after a brief audition by Clint personally just hours before the Thanksgiving Day game commenced. The owner, who was a patriotic ex-marine, would later confide his decision to go with a trumpet soloist was inspired by Montgomery Clift's heroic role in the movie classic *From Here to Eternity*. (Dallas Cowboys Football Club.)

Clint believed in the old adage "If it ain't broke, don't fix it." His loyalty to people in the Cowboys organization served him well during his tenure as owner. Such was certainly the case even with Wilford Jones, otherwise known as Crazy Ray, the team's unofficial mascot beginning in 1962 at the Cotton Bowl and transitioning to Texas Stadium through his death in 2007. Everyone, especially Clint, loved Crazy Ray and his laugh-inducing slapstick. Here he is photographed with the Washington Redskins' legendary mascot Chief Zee, Bum Bright's minority partner Ed Smith, and Smith's two sons. (The Ed Smith Family Collection.)

Drew Pearson, left, and quarterback Clint Longley chiseled their way into Cowboys' folklore on Thanksgiving Day, 1974, when Longley replaced an injured Roger Staubach at quarterback—and led a come-from-behind rally that resulted in a game-winning touchdown pass to Pearson. Longley and the Cowboys would, however, eventually part ways, after he "sucker-punched" Staubach, forcing the Cowboys to get rid of him via a trade. The ensuing parlay of draft picks led to the Cowboys picking college sensation Tony Dorsett as their new running back—a franchise-changing move that soon led to a championship. (From the collections of the Dallas History & Archives Division, Dallas Public Library.)

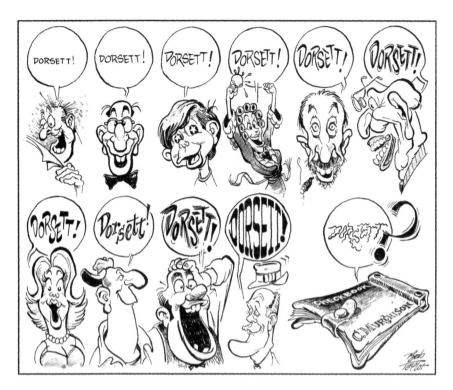

In the spring of 1977, the Cowboys struck gold when they traded up to acquire the No. 2 draft choice in the entire NFL and selected future Hall of Fame running back Tony Dorsett. Enthusiasm ran high in Dallas when the team later successfully signed Dorsett to a contract, which made him the team's first million-dollar player in history. Even though his signing came at a cost for Clint, it was an epic moment for the Cowboys and their fans. Cartoonist Bob Taylor captures the moment perfectly in his cartoon. (The Murchison Family Collection.)

Roger Staubach, left, and Tom Landry would eventually become a matchless combination of quarterback and coach. Here, the two are pictured in a game in the Cotton Bowl during the 1969 season, which happened to be Staubach's first. He left the US Naval Academy after the 1963 season, during which he won the Heisman Trophy as the best college player in the country. As per Navy rules, he then spent five years as an active-duty member of the military, including service in the Vietnam War. He joined the Cowboys as a rookie in 1969, despite being 27. He did not become the Cowboys' starting quarterback until 1971, when he was 29. (From the collections of the Dallas History & Archives Division, Dallas Public Library.)

Facing top, In 1983, beleaguered by financial setbacks and failing health, Clint was forced to do the unthinkable and put the Cowboys up for sale. At the top of the owner's shortlist was H. R. "Bum" Bright, a wealthy, self-made local businessman who also happened to be the chairman and largest single shareholder of RepublicBank. After Bright rejected Murchison's initial overture, RepublicBank CEO Charles Pistor, who was interested in capturing the Cowboys as a high-profile client, jumped into action and convinced him to pursue the purchase. In the photo, Bum Bright, Charles Pistor, and Tex Schramm appear from left to right. (The Charles Pistor Family Collection.)

Facing bottom, Through Clint's 24-season span as owner of the Cowboys, no one in the organization benefitted more from his unwavering, unconditional support than his three key executives: Head Coach Tom Landry, GM Tex Schramm, and Director of Player Personnel Gil Brandt. After personally hand-picking Landry and Schramm for their respective positions, he later had the prescience to authorize Schramm to hire Brandt to ferret out talent in the college ranks. Incredibly, their tenure with the Cowboys exceeded that of his own. Subsequent to his sale of the franchise to Bum Bright, they continued to carry out their duties for an additional five seasons until Jerry Jones acquired the team in 1989. (Walter Looss Jr/Sports Illustrated Classic/Getty Images.)

Clint Jr. and his first wife, Jane Murchison—with whom
he shared four children—were divorced in the early 1970s.
Years later, after selling the Cowboys, Clint was forced into
bankruptcy and suffered the ravages of a terminal neuro-
logical disease that led to his death on March 31, 1987. His
second wife, Anne, stood by him during these challenging
times. Her support along with the comfort afforded him
by his newfound faith helped him accept his fate with
strength and dignity. Here he is pictured with Anne at his
last family Christmas celebration mere months before his
death. (The Murchison Family Collection)

Facing top, Bum Bright's ownership of the Cowboys was
short-lived. At the press conference at which he announced
the sale of the team to Jerry Jones, a humiliated Schramm is
shown brooding in the background. In teeing up the sale to
Jones, Bright left both Schramm and Landry completely in
the dark. He was well aware of Jones's plans to replace them
both and was fearful they might disrupt the sale through
their influence with their friend and ally NFL Commissioner
Pete Rozelle. (Courtesy Ft. Worth-Star Telegram Collection,
Special Collections, the University of Texas at Arlington
Libraries.)

Above, At the same press conference announcing the sale of the franchise to Jones, Bright and Jones are pictured heartily shaking hands in a symbolic confirmation of their deal. In fact, at the time they had only made a deal in principle. Weeks upon weeks of tough, hard-nosed negotiations would follow before the transaction was finally signed, sealed, and delivered. (Courtesy Ft. Worth-Star Telegram Collection, Special Collections, the University of Texas at Arlington Libraries.)

Only months after acquiring the Cowboys, Jerry Jones and new Cowboys coach Jimmy Johnson are seen hustling off a Valley Ranch practice field. They were under a great deal of pressure at the time and showed it. As the Cowboys' caliber of play deteriorated dramatically in the last years of Bright's ownership, its financial performance of the franchise along with that of Texas Stadium hit the skids. Jones knew he had to turn things around quickly and he did. Coach Jimmy Johnson contributed to the cause by bringing the team back to the playoffs in only three seasons and winning a Super Bowl to cap off the fourth. As the popularity of the team surged, a driven Jones had the moxie and know-how to translate its success on the field into profitability at all levels of the organization. (Courtesy Ft. Worth-Star Telegram Collection, Special Collections, the University of Texas at Arlington Libraries.)

Jones decided to build a gigantic new home for the Cowboys in Arlington several years before the Cowboys ceased playing their games at Texas Stadium. His decision precipitated the need for the Cowboys and the city of Irving to negotiate an exit plan in order to guarantee a smooth transition. The wish lists of each party were highlighted by one major, all-important priority. In the case of the city, it was the overriding need to repaint (at Jones's expense) the stadium's roof, which through years of neglect had become an eyesore and a major embarrassment for the city. For Jones, it was demolishing Texas Stadium after his team left for Arlington. After much wrangling, both of them got their big wishes met. (From the Irving Archives and Museum.)

CHAPTER NINE

Getting It Built

T HE NEXT STEP was the one Clint had dreamed of for years—designing and building the darn thing.

When it came to design, Clint had his own ideas. He had spent 10 years—indeed, a full decade—building his own private Xanadu, a 25-acre estate on Forest Lane in Far North Dallas that also fell prey to the ongoing pettiness being hurled at him by the Dallas establishment.

As it became increasingly clear that Clint and the Cowboys would not be staying in the modestly renovated Cotton Bowl, city officials upped their retaliation, and it got petty. The esteemed, he-can-do-no-wrong Mayor Jonsson refused to widen the road in front of Clint's new home on Forest Lane—despite the rest of the street being widened—and Bob Cullum put up signs in Simon David, a chic gourmet food store owned by the Tom Thumb chain, that credit would not be extended to members of the Murchison family under any circumstances. Signs, for everyone to see.

But long before that, Clint had in his mind's eye exactly the kind of home he wanted for the Cowboys.

During the early 1960s, the wannabe architect summoned to his office Cowboys' scouting director Gil Brandt and gave him an assignment: tour the country looking at new, state-of-the-art stadiums.

"I remember noting that the new stadium at the University of Oregon was situated so that the press box looked directly into the sun. No good," Brandt told his boss. "At the University of Indiana, every seat faced in toward the field; seems obvious these days, but back then there were often seats with poor sight lines. This stadium, in many ways, turned out to be a good model for the design of Texas Stadium."[1]

Clint also liked the design of Rice Stadium in Houston, whose sterling example of modern architecture offered simple lines and unadorned functionality. Its sight lines benefited from the simple reality that it was built solely for football, which Clint proclaimed a necessity in creating the best possible experience for the fans.

During the late 1960s, the new-stadium trend took the opposite (wrong) turn. New facilities being prepared in Oakland, San Diego, Cincinnati, Philadelphia, and other cities were all about pleasing two constituencies, leaving neither sport satisfied. To this day, the foul lines in Oakland, where baseball's Oakland A's still play, are a joke. Because the stands are so far back—to accommodate the grid of a football field—pitchers benefit from the easy outs they can get from popups that, in most stadiums, would land in the tenth row or higher.

Having to accommodate baseball and football both would, Clint believed, lead only to flaws. And again, time proved him right. By the early 1990s, the opening of Camden Yards in Baltimore ignited a trend of "retro" baseball parks popping up all over the country, while the football stadiums that followed were, finally, made only for football.

Sight lines were just the starting point. For the design-minded Clint, comfort and style trumped everything. He marveled, for instance, at the magnificent Aztec Stadium (Estadio Azteca) in Mexico City. Opened in May 1966 and designed by architects Pedro Ramirez Vazquez and Rafael Mijares, the Mexican soccer palace offered luxury suites or "skyboxes" that were far more desirable than the cramped versions at the tippy top of the Houston Astrodome. They would serve as a model for those constructed at Texas Stadium, which spawned a trend now followed by every new stadium in the country, including in some cases, high school stadiums.

Clint was forever on the hunt for more enduring quality. As he told Gary Cartwright in 1965:

Everyone in sports is complaining that television is hurting their attendance . . . which it is, but that's shutting the barn door after all the animals are out. Promoters have got to restyle their product to the times, and that means ultra-luxury stadiums, weather conditioning, theater-style seats, private clubs, maybe even a night club atmosphere where people watch the ball game while waiters in tuxedos serve champagne and lobster. It's not a civic responsibility for people to come out and watch us play. It's our responsibility to get them out.[2]

He also wanted a stadium that in no way resembled the Cotton Bowl (except for sight lines). As a cost-saving measure, the original plans for Texas Stadium called for benches in the end zones, but when Jonsson and Cullum allocated Cotton Bowl improvements in the 1967 bond referendum, removing any and all bench seating from the Fair Park stadium, Clint ordered an immediate change. Some would argue that Jonsson and Cullum were behaving in a mean-spirited manner, simply as part of their game of one-upping Clint Jr. In other words, the Dallas duo made the change only to hurt Clint.

So, in January 1969, the city of Irving signed off on "substituting 30,000 stadium chairs in lieu of wooden benches,"[3] elevating the price tag of Texas Stadium another $443,000.

On January 25, 1969, Clint and the Irving brain trust convened the official groundbreaking of the Cowboys' new home. Clint surprised everybody by pulling back a curtain and unveiling a photograph of the Roman Colosseum, with a Cowboys sticker on one of the windows. "Your Bond Money in Action . . . Texas Stadium," the caption read.

Appearing with Clint was Cowboys president and general manager Tex Schramm and quarterback Don Meredith, then only six months away from announcing his retirement. His last game ended up being the heartbreaking 1968 playoff loss to Cleveland, which devastated Meredith, partly because Tom Landry benched him in favor of Craig Morton. The grief extended to Clint and his Irving conspirators, who feared that the team's third straight postseason collapse could potentially deal a fatal blow to their still-fragile dreams.

As he scooped up the first shovelful of dirt during the groundbreaking, Clint laughed and said, "OK, where's Howard Currens?"

His question was, of course, born of contempt. Currens's lawsuit ended up forcing the second approval of a referendum by Irving voters—weeks before the groundbreaking. It passed by a 2-to-1 margin. And had it failed, who knows?

Meredith's appearance did much to lighten the mood. Irving residents besieged him for autographs. Irving mayor Robert Power introduced Dandy Don by saying, "Here's the man who's going to lead us to the Super Bowl!" Knowing more at that point about his future plans than Power did, Meredith replied, "Are you sure?"

Bob St. John, then the Cowboys beat writer for the *Dallas Morning News*, described the austere surroundings as being "comparable to a vacant lot, a cow pasture with chug holes, dead grass and all the trimmings. When Meredith arrived, he looked around and quipped, 'Yes, yes, the turf is definitely going to be a factor.'"

"Well," Clint said, "we had to cut costs somewhere."[4]

The statement was truer than anyone imagined. For on the day of the groundbreaking, Clint had not yet hired an architect. He had, however, already consulted a pair of prominent West Coast architects to amplify his vision for the stadium.

To create precisely the stadium he wanted, he needed someone local and on the ground that he could trust implicitly.

And then finally, he found him.

A. Warren Morey's big break came about, as many do, by happenstance. He had designed the Dallas Gun Club, which ended up playing a pivotal role in the history of Texas Stadium. The gun club job gave him the entrée to Clint's friend Max Thomas, for whom Morey would design a house, which Thomas loved. In biblical terms, it was gun club begets Max's casa, which begets Texas Stadium.

Clint had interviewed Morey months earlier and told him he would call him when he needed him. So, in the early days of 1969, Morey found himself waiting by the phone a lot. And then one day, it rang.

"Clint said, 'Do you want to come over and talk about the stadium?'" Morey recalls. "I said, 'Yes sir, I'll be right there!' I was there in nothin' flat. He gave me the contract, even though I'd never designed a stadium in my life. But most architects think they can design anything."[5]

Morey signed the contract in February 1969, a month after the groundbreaking, but soon learned that it was only a starting point. Before he ever put pencil to pad, he served as a sounding board for a client whose ideas were often presented in microscopic detail.

The Cowboys owner envisioned an open-air structure, the roof of which would cover its 65,000 seats but leave the playing field exposed to the elements. His lieutenant, Tex Schramm, had argued that maybe they should go even further and build an air-conditioned domed stadium, à la the Astrodome, which would have lured the Super Bowl to Irving. But Murchison stuck to his guns, believing all along that whatever the weather happened to be that day needed to be a part of the game.

And so was born the famous hole in the roof that emerged as the stadium's most enduring symbol. But Clint's imprimatur reached well beyond the roof. He demanded another first for football stadiums, that being luxury suites between the upper and lower decks, which affluent fans could purchase for $50,000 each (or 200 seat option bonds at $250 each).

That was the big stuff. But Clint's ideas went way beyond that. A letter from Morey to Clint, dated June 26, 1969, shows what we're talking about. We quote from it here, and yes, you're right, it's all about . . . where people would do their business:

A) You want ceiling hung toilet compartments in the concourse restrooms.

B) You want wall hung water closets throughout.

C) You want flush, stainless steel towel dispensers throughout, and we will use plastic waste containers for used towels throughout.

D) You want the ceramic tile floors and walls in the concourse restrooms to be similar to that in the new American Airlines restrooms at Love Field.

E) You want the lavatory units to be similar to AA Love Field only without the automatic water control feature.

F) You want the individual urinals to be equal to or similar to those on the typical office floors in the First National Bank.

G) The soap dispensers are to be integrated into the lavatories throughout the project.

That wasn't the only memo Morey got that radiated Clint. In one, dated March 28, 1969, Clint playfully wrote:

Items which I wish to approve: All restroom fixtures, restroom tile, restroom partitions as to type and color; all light fixtures, both as to type and location; radiant heat fixtures to as to type and location; loudspeakers as to location; all paint as to color; all railing; all exposed hardware; carpeting as to type and color; all wall cover [and finally] security dog as to breed.

The Cowboys owner wanted a lot for $31 million. Morey is most proud of having fulfilled his client's wishes for even less than the budget Clint imposed. His design also included two bridges (one for cars, one for pedestrians) that spanned State Highway 114.

The idea of permanently enclosing the stadium, a la the Astrodome, "was never discussed," says Morey, noting that the maverick owner had no desire to mimic the air-conditioned Astrodome, which had opened to great fanfare in 1965. The only regret he expressed to Morey was not getting to build in downtown Dallas.

Soon after Morey was hired, however, Clint was still toying with the idea of a sliding plastic bubble that would serve as a retractable roof. Not that he didn't want it. He particularly liked the idea of having it for off-season events, such as rodeos and concerts. He was still thinking about it even during construction but in the end had to face the fact that it would fail, based on engineering tests conducted at the time.

In January 1968, he'd wishfully hoped for exactly that, "a sliding plastic bubble" that would cover the playing surface of what was then envisioned as a $15 million stadium, with barely more than 50,000 seats. Its cost, of course, would double, and the seating capacity would exceed 65,000, making it the fourth-largest stadium in the NFL.

In a 1991 letter to a columnist for the *Dallas Morning News*, Morey elaborates on why the sliding plastic bubble became a casualty: "The structural engineers for the manufacturing company realized that the later loads which would be imposed on the arches by a flexible fabric could not be accommodated and the idea was abandoned."[6]

More than anything, Morey admired what he calls Clint's quiet chutzpah and to this day marvels at Texas Stadium's financing plan, which above all protected the taxpayers of Irving from even a penny of financial liability.

"I thought it was a very fair way of doing it," says Morey, who laughs about the fact that he bought four of the $250 seat option bonds and before AT&T Stadium opened in Arlington in 2009 got a check in the mail for $1,200 when they fully vested. When Morey agreed to a lengthy interview with Michael Granberry of the *Dallas Morning News* in 2008, he said he hadn't used the tickets in years. (A friend bought them.)

Morey's design, which followed to the letter Clint's instructions, lives on as a model for the twenty-first century.

Bryan Trubey, formerly a design principal with Dallas-based architecture firm HKS and the "design lead" of the Cowboys' showplace in Arlington—a role he also played with downtown stadiums in Indianapolis and Minneapolis *and* the Texas Rangers' new $1.2 billion ballpark in Arlington, Texas— admits there were elements of Texas Stadium he chose to emulate, the hole in the roof chief among them.

"Our opening is shaped a bit differently but still sends the same kind of trademark message," Trubey says.

Morey's design "set up a lot of great things to occur and not just the unique cutout in the roof or the fact that it had two levels of luxury suites for the first time, although those were two big things," Trubey says. "That made it an iconic structure or recognizable structure, as compared to any other stadium at the time. It's as indelible a part of the history of the Cowboys as any particular play or owner or anything."[7]

Design gurus have seized on what it was that made Texas Stadium different—and long after the fact, dynamic. Mark Lamster, the esteemed architecture critic of the *Dallas Morning News* and author of *The Man in the Glass House: Philip Johnson, Architect of the Modern Century*, which won raves from the *New York Times*, had this to say about Clint's creation, 11 years after its demolition:

> Traditionally, the American football stadium did not put much emphasis on comfort. Early stadiums like the Harvard Bowl or Soldier Field in Chicago, aimed for a classical monumentality, reflecting the gladiatorial spirit of the game and an architectural tradition dating to the Roman Colosseum. Within, the grandeur gave way to compact bleacher seating, mostly general admission, and with few concessions. Texas Stadium took that model and flipped it, transforming the stadium from a place to simply watch a game, into a genuine hospitality environment, with luxury boxes and hierarchical seating.

Before he got to that point, however, Warren Morey had his work cut out for him. And how. His biggest task? Pleasing Clint.

Six months after meeting the Cowboys owner, Morey produced his first set of drawings, drawing only a deafening silence from Clint. Though those ended up being *the* plans for the stadium of his dreams, the one he had staked a career, a reputation, and even a legacy on, Clint never said a word about them. The Cowboys owner was, Morey says, easily the most eccentric person he ever met. "He was a very quiet man but a very interesting person. He had gone to MIT. He was a bit of an egghead in some ways and a little stubborn in some ways."[8]

He never shook Clint's hand—nor was it offered—until, one afternoon, when Morey arranged a meeting in the owner's office. He was astonished, he says, to see the owner shake the hand of each person who entered. But he never again saw him shake anyone's hand.

Morey calls his project his most daunting for reasons that exceeded even Clint's eccentricity. Until Texas Stadium, he had never had to satisfy multiple bosses. Because the city of Irving owned the land and the stadium, he had to answer to the mayor. He ended up working with two—and a pesky city council that in the beginning felt compelled to let him know who the real boss was.

"The client is always the supreme actor on the stage," Morey says. "You do what the client wants, because he's paying the bills."[9]

Born in Wichita Falls, Texas, Morey moved with his family to Tulsa, Oklahoma, before he was 5. He began college at what is now Oklahoma State University by taking courses in chemical engineering. But one night, he dropped in on a fellow student and saw architectural drawings all over the wall. He soon switched majors.

He met his wife, Jozelle, during his army days at Fort Sill, Oklahoma. They were married in 1947 and had a son and a daughter. By the time Morey died in Plano, Texas, in February 2021, at age 99, he had multiple grandchildren and great-grandchildren.

The tall, professorial Morey opened his own firm in Dallas in 1957. He designed the arts and sciences building at Stephen F. Austin State University in Nacogdoches, Texas, a parking garage and Sunday school for First Presbyterian Church of Dallas, and a Holiday Inn hotel complex in downtown Dallas.

Texas Stadium, of course, remains his legacy, with the hole in the roof having long ago chiseled itself into the folklore of sports history.

"I feel rather sad about it," Morey said not long before the stadium's implosion on April 11, 2010. "So much of my energy was tied up in that project."[10]

He hoped, at least, that his design will be remembered. He never really got the strokes from Clint that he deserved, or at least didn't get them verbally. He remembers Clint's reaction to a dedicatory plaque Morey added on his own, as part of the design, etching in bronze a torrent of glowing words, carved in tribute to the Cowboys' owner.

"Clint just stood there, staring at it for the longest time," the architect says with a laugh. "And then he walked away, not saying a word. I'm just guessing he liked the design, because he never said. Then again, that was Clint."[11]

Talk about lame ducks!

So, the Cowboys announce on December 24, 1967, that they're leaving Dallas and the Cotton Bowl and moving to the grasslands of a bedroom community named after writer Washington Irving, who wrote *The Legend of Sleepy Hollow*. Its central character is the Headless Horseman, which offered all kinds of ironies for the kinds of risks the owner of the Dallas Cowboys was taking in moving to Irving.

But in 1969, the Cowboys were still playing football, and for the first time ever, in their tenth season, they were doing so without Don Meredith. They were also still confined to the Cotton Bowl, where they operated as tenants with landlords who bordered on the hostile, who at this point made no secret of hiding their disdain for the Irving Defectors. If anyone thought the Jonsson–Cullum coalition was a classy bunch, their treatment of the Cowboys in the final days at the Cotton Bowl should dispose of that illusion forever. The truth is, they blew it, and on some level, they must have known it, especially as the Cowboys' national profile rose dramatically after they left the Cotton Bowl.

Let's start with the mayor.

J. Erik Jonsson became mayor of Dallas in 1964, in the tender aftermath of the Kennedy assassination. He won reelection three times, and each time, decisively. He served 7 years and chose not to run for reelection, ironically, in the same year—1971—that Clint's Cowboys said goodbye to Dallas and the Cotton Bowl, which Jonsson had fiercely defended. As mayor, the native New Yorker presided over the most austere accomplishments in the history of Dallas. He pushed through a $175 million bond program that financed the opulent city hall, designed by I. M. Pei; the Dallas Convention Center; and the Dallas Central Library, now the J. Erik Jonsson Central Library. Most important of all, he spearheaded the development of Dallas/Fort Worth International Airport, which did nothing less than transform the region. Dramatically. The airport alone is largely responsible for Dallas–Fort Worth becoming, by 2021, the nation's fourth-largest metro region, trailing only New York, Los Angeles, and Chicago.

But did Jonsson miss the point of what the Cowboys could have meant—and ended up meaning, despite being in Irving—to a city deeply wounded by being branded as the "city of hate" in the wake of President Kennedy's assassination? We the authors contend that, yes, he very much missed the point. Having the Cowboys in downtown Dallas in a new stadium might well have prevented downtown from being the ghost town it became in the 50 years, and more, after Kennedy's death.

As Gail Thomas, then president and executive officer of the Trinity Trust, said at a symposium days before the fiftieth anniversary of the president's death, Dallas missed out on the emotional healing the city so desperately needed. "We have not wanted to own the shadow of the assassination," Thomas said at the event hosted by the *Dallas Morning News* and the Dallas Institute of Humanities and Culture. "In a sense, we've been a city without a shadow. There was that sense that the heaviness was not acceptable. We had to build and soar and achieve and be a powerful city."

Before the symposium, a close friend advised her, Thomas said: "Don't talk about the darkness. Don't talk about the shame." That, she said, "has been our problem. We must own the shadow of the assassination. In psychology, the shadow is what carries the soul of the place."[12]

There is one man who made sure that post-assassination Dallas built, soared, and achieved everything it took to become "a powerful city"—Erik Jonsson.

And he was, of course, the mayor of Dallas when the Cowboys said goodbye to Dallas. He could even be described as the architect of Dallas losing the Cowboys. Granted, he was never a sports fan, but did he harbor any regret about Dallas losing the Cowboys? Maybe.

After he left as mayor, he occupied a suite near the top of the Republic National Bank building. He could look out the window and see the west side of downtown Dallas, where Clint hoped to build his dream stadium in the city he loved, and with its hole in the roof shimmering in the distance, he could see Clint Murchison Jr.'s Plan B—Texas Stadium.

As Bruce Tomaso wrote in his obituary for Jonsson in the *Dallas Morning News* in 1995, the former mayor, gazing out his expansive window, said he could "see all the mistakes I made."

But in the autumn of 1969, there was still a season to play, and the Cowboys did so as part of a United States that appeared to be courting a nervous breakdown inflamed by dizzying highs and lows. In July 1969, Senator Edward Kennedy, the political heir to the legacy of brothers John and Robert Kennedy, drove his car off a bridge in New England, killing his only passenger, a young woman, shattering forever his presidential dreams.

Two days later, men walked on the moon and planted the American flag in its gray dust, fulfilling the we-were-first dream of President Kennedy. In August 1969, a band of killers known as the Manson Family invaded the home of actress Sharon Tate, brutally slaying Tate, who was eight months pregnant, and four other people. The next night, the Manson Family staged a brutal encore by murdering an older couple that lived in Los Angeles, not far from the Benedict Canyon home Tate shared with Hollywood director Roman Polanski.

Less than a week later, almost half a million young people flocked to the Catskill Mountains in upstate New York for the Woodstock music extravaganza. They were their own kind of blissful army, matching numbers with the more than half a million US troops still fighting the Vietnam War in 1969, with many never making it home.

With Craig Morton replacing Meredith at quarterback, and a promising rookie on the roster named Roger Staubach, who, after spending five years in the navy, including his own stint in Vietnam, offered the Cowboys staggering depth at quarterback and more hope for the future than the team ever dreamed of having. On November 16, 1969, the Cowboys played the Redskins at the newly renamed RFK Stadium (in honor of Robert F. Kennedy, who'd been assassinated a year earlier), and the new president, Richard M. Nixon, was in attendance. He got to watch the Cowboys beat the Redskins easily, 41–28. Rookie running back Calvin Hill, who as a graduate of Yale University symbolized the Cowboys' yen for intelligent players, rushed for 150 yards. Hill would finish the season as the NFL's offensive rookie of the year.

The Cowboys ended up winning eight of their first ten games and found themselves in the playoffs once again against, who else, the Cleveland Browns. And, of course, the Browns provided yet another Cowboys crusher, beating Dallas in the Cotton Bowl 38–14, stunning everybody, who thought the 11–2–1 Cowboys were Super Bowl bound for sure. Would Dandy Don have made a difference? Who knows? Dandy had something even bigger waiting for him.

The lame-duck blues melted into the 1970 season, which represented the Cowboys' Cotton Bowl swan song. Talk about the best of times and the worst of times. The 1970 season was truly one of the most bizarre and easily the most manic. On November 16, 1970, the Cowboys had won five and lost three when they met the St. Louis Cardinals as characters in a hot new television show called *Monday Night Football*. The popularity of the show was already soaring, due mainly to the unexpected crazy chemistry of its two "color" announcers, the irascible Howard Cosell and, yes, Dandy Don Meredith. The Cowboys welcomed the First Cowboy and their national television audience with one of their worst performances ever, getting throttled 38–0 by the St. Louis Cardinals.

As the fans shouted, "We want Meredith!"—a sweetly ironic twist to all the times Meredith had heard "We want Morton!"—Meredith quipped, "I'm not about to go in there." But the 1970 season would offer a lot more than that.

Four days after a 16–3 victory over the Green Bay Packers on Thanksgiving Day, Cowboys wide receiver Lance Rentzel was arrested in the posh suburb of Highland Park for exposing himself to a 10-year-old girl. That ended Rentzel's Cowboys career, not to mention his marriage to Hollywood starlet Joey Heatherton.

In retrospect, it's amazing that the Cowboys failed to suffer any more fallout from Rentzel's arrest than they did. Rentzel was an All-Pro receiver and not easily replaced. After all, he caught what should have been the winning touchdown pass in the Ice Bowl.

Even so, after being shut out by the Cardinals, the otherwise stoic, unemotional Tom Landry broke down in front of his team, a moment of unexpected bonding that All-Pro defensive tackle Bob Lilly credited for the Cowboys winning five straight to close the season en route to their first Super Bowl.

As the luck of "Next Year's Champions" would have it, however, the Cowboys lost one of the strangest Super Bowls ever—later dubbed the Blunder Bowl—falling 16–13 to the Baltimore Colts on a last-second field goal, in a game marred by goofy tipped passes, fumbles that didn't really occur, and other ghastly calls in the pre-video replay era. One of those happened when the Cowboys' hot new rookie, running back Duane Thomas, appeared to fumble before crossing the goal line. A twenty-first-century replay would have shown that, no, Thomas was already down, his knee touching the Orange Bowl turf when the ball squirted out. Even so, Cowboys center Dave Manders appeared to recover the fumble. But the refs ruled otherwise. Instead of the Colts getting the ball, the Cowboys should have been allowed to keep it, and no doubt, would have scored.

In what became a fitting symbol of the Cowboys' 11 years of frustration, an angry Lilly took off his helmet when the game ended and hurled it skyward, a moment that even in January of 1971 went viral. It summed up more than anything the emotion of spending 5 straight years as "Next Year's Champions." It made it even worse for the fans, especially young ones, who so hoped the Cowboys would repair the image of the "city of hate" in the aftermath of President Kennedy's assassination.

So, what did it mean? The Cowboys had spent eleven full seasons in the Cotton Bowl, giving the old girl some of her richest memories but failing to win a championship for the people of Dallas, who nonetheless had fallen deeply in love with the football team that Clint Murchison Jr. always wanted to own.

For Clint, it soon became a case of have team, will travel. He only hoped that all those loyal fans, who deserved so much more, would make the ride with him.

CHAPTER TEN

The Beginning

A T TIMES, HOWEVER, vindication felt like a distant fantasy. A document signed by architect A. Warren Morey on August 11, 1971, little more than a month before the Cowboys' Irving debut, noted that construction had slowed due to "the unseasonably wet weather and the plumbers' strike"[1] wreaking its own havoc. The *New York Times* reported that the Cowboys' Irving debut was thrice delayed because of heavy later summer rain that stopped work on the parking lots.

That led to an almost biblical situation the night the stadium opened, when the 10-day Billy Graham crusade christened the stadium, albeit without a single paved parking lot.

The crusade lasted from September 17 to September 26, 1971, welcoming such dignitaries to its 178 luxury suites as former President Lyndon B. Johnson and wife Lady Bird and country music icons Johnny Cash and June Carter Cash. Sharing the stage with the Reverend Graham was a Cowboys triumvirate of Roger Staubach, Rayfield Wright, and Dan Reeves.

Graham rivaled Woodstock in drawing more than half a million during his 10-day visit, with more than 42,000 showing up the first night, muddy parking and all.

Given that Graham was preaching in what was then professional football's most luxurious sanctuary, the text of his sermon sounds more than a tad ironic more than half a century later.

In her story in the *Dallas Morning News*, Parmley noted that Graham "took the wisdom, pleasures, wealth and power of the august King Solomon Monday night at Texas Stadium and rendered them all 'The Bubbles That Burst.'" Graham's comments, seen through the lens of the twenty-first century, feel eerily prophetic.

"Throughout the nation," the preacher intoned, "people are trying to find amusement, pleasure, knowledge, security and love. Solomon had it all and said it is not worth it."[2]

"Are you ready for some football?" In the case of Texas Stadium in the late summer of 1971, the answer was no.

Clint's palace may have been ready for Reverend Graham and his band of believers, but it was nowhere near ready for football when the '71 season kicked off. Dallas opened with two straight road games, victories over Buffalo and Philadelphia, but delays exacerbated by rain and the plumbers' strike forced Clint's Cowboys to endure two more games in Fair Park, the first coming on October 3, 1971, in a game won by the Redskins, 20–16. The next week, the Cowboys defeated the New York Giants, 20–13, on a Monday night, in what became the Cowboys' last appearance in the Cotton Bowl—or the city of Dallas, for that matter. And let's be honest, who would have ever thought *that*? Irony of ironies, the game was carried on *Monday Night Football*, with Don Meredith being one of three calling the game in the TV booth in the press box upstairs.

Meredith wasn't the only one who showed up.

A near-capacity crowd of 68,378 came to Fair Park to deliver a warm Dallas goodbye to the Cotton Bowl Cowboys.

But the drama wasn't ending. It was only beginning.

Stadium issues were not the only thing going on. Coach Landry made sure of that. Before the Cowboys unveiled their new home, a bizarre, post-Meredith quarterback controversy engulfed the start of the new season. Landry began the season by alternating Craig Morton and Roger Staubach at quarterback. Morton would play one game, Staubach the next, regardless of the score. Morton started the season-opening victory at Buffalo but presided over the first two losses of the season, in the Cotton Bowl against Washington and on the road two weeks later in New Orleans.

So, it was fitting, perhaps, that Roger Staubach, who later earned the nickname "Captain America" as he cruised to the Pro Football Hall of Fame, got the starting call for the team's first-ever game in its one-of-a-kind new home.

Finally, the day arrived. Texas Stadium ushered in the Cowboys' first of nearly 40 years in their new home on a gorgeous fall afternoon on October 24, 1971. Under a cloudless sky, the temperature never went above 74. As Chris Berman said at the demolition years later, there was magic from the start.

It took four plays—2 minutes 16 seconds.

Running back Duane Thomas, who over a contract dispute had taken a vow of silence, refusing to talk to teammates, coaches, or the news media, took the handoff from quarterback Roger Staubach and swept right, making his own lasting statement. With future Hall of Fame inductee Rayfield Wright leading the way, sweeping right from his left tackle position, Thomas scored on a poetic 56-yard touchdown run—the inaugural Cowboys' score in Clint's dream home.

It served as an omen.

Landry had still not settled on a starting quarterback, alternating games between Morton and Staubach, who played the entire opener at Texas Stadium, defeating the New England Patriots, 44–21. Staubach's making Texas Stadium's debut so memorable made Landry's decision the next week all the more bewildering.

For the road game in Chicago, he actually resorted to playing Staubach and Morton on alternating *plays*, in what came to be known as his infamous "quarterback shuttle." (True Cowboy historians know he had done this before, however, imposing the shuttle on Meredith and veteran Eddie LeBaron and other quarterback pairings.) The Bears responded to Landry's strategy by beating the Cowboys, 23–19, forcing Staubach before the next game to request a private meeting with the coach, during which he gave Landry a me-or-Morton ultimatum.

With Staubach as the newly named starter, a job he would not relinquish until his 1979 retirement, the Cowboys won seven in a row, finishing with a win–loss record of 11–3. They defeated the Minnesota Vikings in the first round of the playoffs, and on January 2, 1972, they beat the San Francisco 49ers, 14–3, in the NFC Championship Game, the first of many played at Texas Stadium.

Two Sundays later, the Cowboys played in their second Super Bowl and steamrolled to their first championship, beating the Miami Dolphins 24–3 at Tulane Stadium in New Orleans. Like the Chicago Cubs ending the Curse of the Billy Goat, or the Boston vanquishing the Curse of the Bambino, the Cowboys had finally torpedoed the "Next Year's Champions" insult.

For Clint's band of coconspirators in sleepy little Irving, the glee was almost indescribable.

"It was such a good feeling to see a Dallas Cowboys playoff game in Texas Stadium," says Robert Power, as though a part of him still can't believe it. "It was an *awesome* feeling."[3]

His stadium triumph complete, Power had resigned as mayor, turning over the job to Dan Matkin.

Getting past seemingly insoluble problems, such as never really having the money to build the stadium, then fending off two lawsuits, one of which (temporarily) tied the hands of the Texas attorney general, Power says the ultimate victory "had a tremendous impact on the people of Irving. There we were, a little bedroom community. We took on an awesome project. Nobody thought we could do it. The leadership of a whole area was fighting to stop us any way they could."

From the start, Irving and even Clint were underdogs, engaged in a fierce battle with the power elite of neighboring Dallas. "And that's why we were successful," Power says. "The people of Irving got tired of these outsiders trying to tell us what we could do as a city."[4]

Power says the feeling of vindication was never greater than when he and his colleagues discovered exactly *who* was shelling out the $50,000 for Texas Stadium luxury suites.

The names included members of the R. L. Thornton family. It doesn't get any more establishment Dallas than that. But then Power learned that the unyielding guardians of Fair Park—yes, even Bob Cullum—had each forked over 50 grand for their own suites.

There was nothing better, Power says, than seeing "their big fat selves sitting in those boxes to watch the Cowboys."

It's worth taking a long look back at Texas Stadium with its first season having the happiest possible ending. Much of it had to feel like justice for Clint, who must have smiled when told about this:

Even Bob Cullum, one of his fiercest critics, was among those willing to shell out five figures for the best seat in the house—at Texas Stadium.

Cullum was indeed among the overflow crowd of 65,708 that made the trek to Irving to watch Cowboys history change right in front of him. Clint told the *Dallas Morning News*: "As far as I can tell everything worked out, except we hadn't figured it would rain from August to the first of November."[5]

Overall, the stadium got rave reviews, especially when compared to the Cotton Bowl.

Texas Stadium drew favorable first impressions for having its first row of seats only 40 feet from the sidelines and perched 7 to 12 feet above the playing field, whereas at the Cotton Bowl, fans on the first row often had to stand to peer over the hulking players standing in front of them.

Critics saluted the 115 clean drinking fountains, 565 public address speakers, 86 new restrooms, the more than 1.4 million watts in the lighting system (perfectly suited to color television), and the gleaming green Tartan Turf.

That last one did not exactly thrill the players.

"The turf was extremely hard," Lee Roy Jordan is quoted as saying in the book *Remembering Texas Stadium: Cowboy Greats Recall the Blood, Sweat and Pride of Playing in the NFL's Most Unique Home*, co-written by Cowboys great Drew Pearson and the late Frank Luksa.

"Roger Staubach and almost every quarterback who played there had some concussions," Jordan said. "That got to be a real question mark after we'd played there a while and saw the results."[6]

Tartan Turf, Jordan said, left players with an immediate, negative impression. "I saw guys tear up their knees because the turf would grab and didn't give like the ground would or like some of the newer turf they have now."

Jordan said he suffered "a contusion on my hip from hitting the ground. I had to have it drained several weeks in a row. That turf wasn't a favorite surface for anyone."

Running back Walt Garrison, who played with the Cowboys from 1966 to 1974, calls the field "one of the worst in the league. I don't know what kind of turf it was but if you slid it would cut the hell out of you. There was also very little padding under it. That stuff was harder than Chinese arithmetic. If you landed on it, it would jar you."[7]

Linebacker Thomas "Hollywood" Henderson, who played with the Cowboys from 1975 to 1979, had this to say:

> Texas Stadium to me was like landing on the moon. The artificial turf, the speed of it, I had a sense that I could do well on it because I was faster than anyone. But I also had a sort of fear of what I'd considered a parking lot . . . this hard surface. It was more like concrete than grass. But I soon learned how to navigate it to my advantage.

The feeling in the stands channeled an entirely different world from that of the Cotton Bowl. It took a while, but the suites, which were sold as stark concrete shells of 16 square feet, began to resemble something never before seen in a football stadium. Sales literature for Texas Stadium advertised "your personalized penthouse . . . similar to a second residence, like a lake home or a ranch."[8]

Each cost $50,000, not counting the annual purchase of a dozen season tickets, the combination of which, according to the book *The Big Rich* by Bryan Burrough, "became a massive source of revenue for the Cowboys, one that over the next three decades led to the demolition and construction of scores of stadiums across America as owners in every American team sport began demanding stadiums with luxury suites of their own." As the book notes, "Some fans took to calling it 'Millionaires' Meadows.'" As *Esquire* magazine quipped: "Wanna buy two tickets to the Dallas Cowboys? Struck oil lately?"[9]

In August 1972, Clint's old friend, former *Morning News* sports columnist Edwin "Bud" Shrake, wrote a piece about the suites for *Sports Illustrated*. Shrake touched on another Clint invention, the Stadium Club, which pulled in a new source of revenue now duplicated in stadiums and arenas all over America.

In the "dry" confines of Protestant-heavy Irving, only the suites and the Stadium Club permitted alcohol, a reality that lingered until the Jerry Jones era.

That appealed greatly to suite holders, who began to outfit their $50,000 concrete shells in elaborate Corinthian detail. One of them, Shrake wrote, hired a decorator and spent close to $40,000 on what came to be known as the "Let Them Eat Cake" suite.

It was "a Louis XIV outfit with a vaulted ceiling, a chandelier with 1,000 prisms, velvet tufted chairs, oil paintings, a refrigerator, sink, icemaker, freezer, telephone, television and a bar staffed by a butler in white gloves. The décor of the other suites varies from Spartan simplicity to cubicles that are fixed up in Ranch-house Plush, Neiman-Marcus Mod, Las Vegas Traditional, Psychedelic Flash, Molded Plastic Futurama, Tahitian Fantasy, and so forth."

Clint shared with Shrake his rationale:

"There was a time when you could subject sports fans to any indignity, but that day is past, although most promoters don't yet realize it. The Dallas City Council had their heads in the sand," the owner said, taking one more shot at the Cotton Bowl–or–nothing crowd.

Shrake asked about the Astrodome, drawing this Clint response: "We could easily have closed up the hole in the roof, but I don't like watching football in the Astrodome. Our fans are protected but can still see the sky. We haven't totally ruled out the elements. Because of the competition of television, you have to cater to the customers as they have never been catered to in the past."[10]

And that's the main thing Clint wanted—the right to give the fans what they deserved. And how was he able to do that? By negotiating the right to control Texas Stadium Corp., which he believed all along could become even more valuable than the team itself, a truism that the Cowboys' future owners came to realize themselves.

Let's face it, Clint had next to no leverage in negotiating the deal with the city of Irving. He never challenged them on not taking money from taxpayers, but he did push back hard on their insistence to own the stadium and the land on which it sat. Ultimately, he caved on that point as well.

What he did want, however, was something he considered even more valuable—the right to *manage* the stadium throughout the Cowboys' long-term lease. His eyes lit up when he spoke about what he saw as the stadium's vast profit potential. (Jerry Jones has proven to be a master at underscoring this point.) Clint did manage to gain control of architectural design and construction. But again, the big baby was management of the stadium. He even gave it a name—Texas Stadium Corp. The Shakespearean rub, however, came in the form of unforeseen construction costs, which ballooned the price tag to $31 million, meaning that, in 2008, when the stadium's lease expired, all of that would have to be repaid—plus interest—to those who had financed its construction through the purchase of seat option bonds. What effect did that have? It gutted the potential upside of Texas Stadium Corp., all but erasing any hope of profitability for Clint.

CHAPTER ELEVEN

The Beginning of the End

CLINT WAS RIGHT: Texas Stadium did mark the beginning of the end—of the past.

Newcomers reveled in how it differed from the Cotton Bowl, in the safe walk to and from automobiles (although it could be a bit far to the outer reaches of the Red Lot), clean concession stands and restrooms, comfortable seats with armrests, ample leg room, and the most watchable vantage points of any venue in the country.

And yet, something was gone, maybe forever. No longer did millionaires from the Park Cities sit among Blacks from South Dallas and blue-collar whites from Pleasant Grove and Mesquite. Egalitarianism—which defined the Cotton Bowl crowd, emulating the feeling of Ebbets Field in Brooklyn, New York, where Jackie Robinson played from 1947 to 1957—was dying a slow death, not just in Irving but all over the country.

And the players, who were lucky back then to make what first-round draft choice Duane Thomas made during his 1970 rookie season—$20,000—felt the economic disparity as much as the fans did.

In Pearson and Luksa's book *Remembering Texas Stadium*, defensive end Larry Cole, who played with the Cowboys from 1968 to 1980, delivered an indictment of the sweeping change, saying that "old school guys—Lee Roy [Jordan] and guys like that, they hated that stadium. We used to talk about the Christians, lions and gladiators in the context that there were all those fat cats up in the luxury boxes drinking Scotches and we were the peons down there getting paid very little to entertain them. Our concept of football was more like the Cotton Bowl with the crowd sitting outside and involved. You didn't watch a football game with a coat and tie on from a box."[1]

Future Hall of Famer Bob Lilly, who excelled at defensive tackle for the Cowboys from 1961 to 1974, noticed the difference in the crowd immediately, as he shared with Pearson and Luksa:

> We came from the Cotton Bowl, where we'd developed a robust, rowdy fan base. We got to Texas Stadium and it never occurred to me that there was a different type fan . . . people who bought bonds. I thought Texas Stadium would be louder because it was enclosed. When we were on the road in New York, Washington and Philadelphia and our offense was on the field, their fans were so loud our receivers, quarterbacks and running backs had trouble hearing the snap count.
>
> We had the same type fan base at the Cotton Bowl. At Texas Stadium, we didn't have that. It was a big thing. We had it at the Cotton Bowl and at Texas Stadium the next week we didn't. It was pretty obvious. This was a different fan base.[2]

Jethro Pugh, who played defensive tackle for the Cowboys from 1965 to 1978, echoed Lilly's comments, telling Pearson and Luksa that the atmosphere at Texas Stadium felt like that of "a tennis match. I mean, people even wore mink coats there. At the Cotton Bowl, you had the shoeshine guy there. You'd see him on Main Street and then at football games. People like that. When the game was over, you'd go across the field to shake hands and because of lack of crowd noise the other team would say, 'What is going on here?' To be honest, it got to the point where we enjoyed going out of town. You go to Washington and all hell breaks loose. Other places were like that, too."[3]

Yale-educated Calvin Hill, who played running back for the Cowboys from 1969 to 1974, laughs about other first impressions, such as those of Lilly, who noticed the "pristine" atmosphere, prompting him to ask: "Can we spit out here?"

Hill contends it remains one of the best places ever to watch a football game, though the players were always aware of an us-versus-them dichotomy.

In *Remembering Texas Stadium*, Hill recalled a practice at Texas Stadium "when it started raining. I mean it poured on the field. Tex [Schramm] was watching from the stands, which were dry. Lilly, who was always coming up with something, said, yeah, that's the way it's supposed to be—we're getting wet and the power positions are dry."[4]

As time wore on, however, Larry Cole said players began to see that this was "a pretty nice place . . . nice locker rooms. What really was nice was when we started playing games there late in the year. Hey, that cold wind didn't blow in through the hole in the roof. I loved playing there during the playoffs."[5]

Future Hall of Famer Randy White, who played with the Cowboys from 1975 to 1988, "most remembers coming down that tunnel before a game. That's what I remember. I don't remember a game. I don't remember a play. I remember coming out on the field, that feeling I had before a game. Walking out of that tunnel . . . going on the field . . . the fans . . . the stadium . . . the excitement . . . every emotion inside of you was alive. Being able to go out there and compete. That's my fondest memory of Texas Stadium."[6]

And of course, no one will ever forget the hole in the roof. Linebacker D. D. Lewis is now most widely credited for coming up with the line that the hole existed "so that God can watch his favorite team."

Staubach tells one of the best stories about the hole and how it chiseled itself into his own memory, recalling a moment he shared with Coach Landry, whose stoic personality seemed perfectly suited to Texas Stadium.

"We were driving," Staubach says, "and I went to the sideline during a timeout to get the play. I was standing with him, waiting, and waiting, while he looked up through that hole in the roof. Finally, he looked back at me and told me the play. As I started back on the field, I said, 'Coach, I always wondered where you got those plays.' I know he heard me. The other coaches were laughing. But he never changed expression. He didn't miss a beat."[7]

Perhaps more than any other Cowboy, Staubach left a lasting imprint on Texas Stadium—except for the 1972 season. He was injured during a pre-season game and did not resurface until the playoffs. Morton stepped in and led the Cowboys to a 10–4 win–loss record with no Duane Thomas in the backfield. Thomas had worn out his welcome with the Cowboys and ended up being traded to the San Diego Chargers.

The Cowboys made the playoffs, facing the San Francisco 49ers at Candlestick Park two days before Christmas in 1972. Staubach had not played a down, until the Cowboys trailed by 15 points late in the second half. Think about that—15 points was a major deficit, since the NFL had not yet adopted the two-point conversion rule. But in what remains one of the greatest Cowboys comebacks ever, Staubach led the Cowboys to an utterly improbable 30–28 victory, only to lose to the Redskins 26–3 a week later in the NFC Championship Game.

In 1973, the Cowboys matched their 10–4 record from the previous season and qualified for the playoffs for the eighth straight season, only to lose to once again in the NFC Championship Game. Even so, they had forcefully established themselves as a member of the NFL elite and had by far the League's best stadium. Imitation is the highest form of flattery, they say, and other NFL teams had begun to imitate the trend spearheaded by Texas Stadium. Football-only stadiums opened in Kansas City in 1972 (Arrowhead Stadium, owned by the Cowboys' Dallas Texans rival, Lamar Hunt) and in Buffalo in 1973 (Rich Stadium). The Pontiac Silverdome, where the Detroit Lions would play, opened in 1975 as part of the same sweeping trend.

As evidence of the League saluting Texas Stadium, for the first and only time ever, the NFL Pro Bowl took place in Irving, before a crowd of 47,879.

In yet another Clint invention, one designed to pull revenue from an otherwise empty parking lot, Texas Stadium launched a three-screen drive-in movie theater in 1973.

Clint got credit for inventing collapsible screens, "where each night," the *Dallas Morning News* reported, "the theater manager pushes a button and hydraulic jacks lay the screen towers down on pillars. The screen towers can be raised by the same jacks prior to theater time each evening."[8]

In the shared partnership between Texas Stadium Corp., Gordon McLendon's McLendon Corp. and McLendon Theaters, Texas Stadium Drive-In debuted with the triple-header of *Deliverance, The New Centurions,* and *The Valachi Papers.* Former mayor Robert Power remembers marveling at the Oscar-winning film *The Godfather* from a seat in his car at the Texas Stadium parking lot.

Richard Peterson, the CEO of McLendon's drive-in movie operation, which at one time marshaled drive-ins across the Southwest, told us the McLendon Companies started with a 10-year lease on the Texas Stadium experiment, but alas, "the theater did not perform well." Texas Stadium Drive-In began at a time when drive-ins were headed for a down-and-out status anyway. But that wasn't all. "More devastating," Peterson writes, "was the fact the screens were flooded with massive lights from the highways surrounding the stadium."

And then he laid this one on us: "After the McLendon lease had run out, another operator took over the operation. The name was [the late] Jim Gallagher, who began showing porno films." He did so, Peterson says, in a futile attempt to salvage the business. Forgive us making the joke, but would there have been any better place to show *Debbie Does Dallas*?

Clint was doing whatever he could to maximize profit, and throughout its history, that also extended to rock 'n' roll.

The stadium's debut show happened on June 28, 1974, in the midst of a searing Texas heat wave, when the legendary Allman Brothers Band seized the stage as headliners. The Marshall Tucker Band and Joe Walsh and Barnstorm also appeared, giving Clint's baby a healthy dose of snappy rock. And for years, Texas Stadium lingered as *the* outdoor venue for rock music in the Dallas–Fort Worth area. There would be thirty-six concerts in all at Texas Stadium, with the last one occurring on May 29, 2004, when Jimmy Buffett, George Strait, and Alan Jackson commandeered the stage. But during the nearly 30-year history of concerts at Texas Stadium, the venue would host a musical Who's Who: Crosby, Stills, Nash & Young and the Beach Boys (1974), as well as Michael Jackson and his family band, the Jacksons, which in 1984 became the first concert staged during Bum Bright's ownership of the Cowboys. Clint admitted having gone to the concert but was forced to experience the strange sensation of sitting in someone else's suite—as a guest.

Concerts continued after Clint, however, adding up to a total of thirty-six staged during the history of Texas Stadium. They included Madonna (1987); Pink Floyd (1988); Guns N' Roses and Ziggy Marley (1988); Kenny Loggins (1989); New Kids on the Block (1990); Genesis (1992); Guns N' Roses and Metallica (1992); U2 (1992); Garth Brooks (1993); Pink Floyd (1994); the Eagles (1994); Billy Joel and Elton John (1995); and the finale, Jimmy Buffett, George Strait, and Alan Jackson (2004).

The 1974 season was among the Cowboys' twenty consecutive winning seasons, but that was it. For the first time in 9 years, the Cowboys did not make the playoffs, finishing with a win–loss record of 8–6. Even so, one of the more delicious moments unfolded on Thanksgiving Day, 1974, when an injured Roger Staubach left the game with the Cowboys trailing the Washington Redskins 16–3 in the third quarter.

Rookie quarterback Clint Longley, forced into the backup role after longtime Cowboy Craig Morton had been traded to the New York Giants, was about to insinuate himself into the annals of Texas Stadium history and Cowboys folklore.

He hits tight end Billy Joe Dupree with a 35-yard touchdown pass. Moments later, he led the Cowboys on a 70-yard drive culminating in a 1-yard touchdown run by Walt Garrison.

But with 28 seconds left and no time-outs, the Cowboys were losing 23–17. Longley faded back to pass and connected with Drew Pearson down the middle for a 50-yard touchdown pass. At that moment, the Texas Stadium crowd may have reached its loudest moment ever. Cowboys won, 24–23.

Given the immediate nickname "the Mad Bomber," Longley unwittingly provoked what may be the best postgame quote ever. It came from offensive lineman and Stanford University graduate Blaine Nye, who called Longley's performance "a triumph of the uncluttered mind." In 2008, ESPN named the Longley game the second best in the history of Texas Stadium.

Longley's career did not have a happy ending. He managed to last two seasons on the Cowboys roster (1974 and 1975), but in 1976, he sucker-punched Cowboys icon Roger Staubach in the locker room during the preseason, provoking a suspension and then a trade to the Chargers, who, incredibly, gave the Cowboys their first- and second-round draft choices—an insanely lucrative parlay that Dallas used to obtain from the Seattle Seahawks what became the draft rights to Heisman Trophy winner Tony Dorsett. So, maybe Longley did the Cowboys a favor? How can you look at it any other way? Just more of the drama that unfolded at Texas Stadium during Clint's long ownership.

Years later, Longley apparently had no desire to reminisce about his Cowboy days. Seeking an interview, coauthor Michael Granberry sent him a letter via FedEx. Longley refused to accept the package.

Granberry's friend, sports journalist Matt Mosley, fared even worse. He drove to the Gulf Coast of South Texas to try to interview Longley but had a door slammed in his face. It didn't stop there.

Mosley waited in his car until Longley and his wife left the house in their big ol' pickup truck, which in Mosley's words "was headed toward the ocean." Mosley followed the truck, "at a safe distance, just to see where they were going."

But then the Mad Bomber spotted him.

"He turned around, and he was coming at me head-on. I swerved off the road and veered hard to my right. It was like playing chicken or something. He was coming right at me."

Mosley narrowly escaped but credits Longley with giving him a serious Mad Bomber scare.

In 1975, the Cowboys entered their fifth season in Texas Stadium. At the start, it looked anything but promising, with such luminaries as Bob Lilly,

Bob Hayes, Cornell Green, Walt Garrison, Dave Manders, John Niland, and Calvin Hill suddenly missing from the roster. Coming off an 8–6 season, the Cowboys appeared to be nothing more than a rebuilding experiment.

But 1975 would soon prove to be noteworthy for Dallas, producing one of the best draft classes in the history of the NFL. Picks included future starters Randy White (soon to be heralded as the best defensive lineman in the game), Thomas Henderson, Burton Lawless, Bob Breunig, Pat Donovan, Randy Hughes, and Kyle Davis. In all, the Cowboys assembled twelve picks, and all twelve made the roster, becoming "the Dirty Dozen."

The Cowboys surprised everybody by opening with four straight victories, and despite finishing second in the NFC East, behind the St. Louis Cardinals, they made the playoffs, traveling to Minnesota as a wild card team to face the Vikings.

During their 38 years in Texas Stadium, the Cowboys produced so many unforgettable moments, and 1975 was second to none.

Oh, sure, it came on the road, but Staubach's most defining play unfolded on December 28, 1975, in Bloomington, Minnesota, when, with 24 seconds remaining, he threw what became his immortal "Hail Mary" touchdown pass, as the Cowboys stunned the Vikings, 17–14, to advance to the next round of the playoffs. Call it a pivotal chapter in the making of a legend. And give Staubach pop-culture credit: Until he used the term *Hail Mary* to describe a desperation moment, it was a term used solely in the Catholic Church. It came to define far more than a touch of magic in a football game.

Staubach described the play by saying, "I closed my eyes and said a Hail Mary." But by 2015, on the fortieth anniversary of his invoking the term, Staubach gets the credit for *Hail Mary* having entered the nomenclature in all sorts of ways. In 2015, the CBS series *The Good Wife* titled one of its episodes "The Hail Mary." Showtime's *Homeland* concluded its tenth episode in its fifth season with star Claire Danes's Carrie alluding to another character's "Hail Mary" attempt to avoid being caught for teaming up with the Russians. Or consider this 2015 headline in the *Dallas Morning News*: WILL OBAMA'S "HAIL MARY" AGAINST COLLEGE COSTS BE A WIN FOR STUDENTS?

And then there's this: Perhaps more than any other moment, Staubach's "Hail Mary" continues to resonate deep in the heart of Cowboys Nation. Coauthor Michael Granberry remembers watching the game on his crummy 8-inch black-and-white television with broken rabbit ears in his Ratso Rizzo–like apartment in Anchorage, Alaska—a modest living unit that his friend Paul Nussbaum referred to as Swamp II, given that it was only slightly better than his previous grim domicile, Swamp I. Nussbaum also watched the game with him, rooting mightily against the Cowboys and feeling quite smug until Staubach heaved back and threw the Hail Mary. It was oh-so-sweet when Pearson caught the ball but even more so when the black rotary-dial phone rang loudly in Swamp II. It was Granberry's dad on the line, calling from Dallas, overjoyed at what Staubach and Pearson had managed to pull off and wanting to share it with his oldest child.

It got even better the next week, with the Cowboys crushing the Rams in sunny Los Angeles, 37–7, advancing to their third Super Bowl.

Cast as colossal underdogs, they took the Pittsburgh Steelers to the wire, losing 21–17. But two things had been established: they were arguably the NFL's most exciting team, and they played in the League's best stadium, by far.

The Cowboys opened the 1976 season by winning five straight games on their way to an 11–3 record and yet another NFC East title. But in the first round of the playoffs, they surprised everybody by losing to the Los Angeles Rams, 14–12.

But then came 1977, when the Cowboys anointed Tony Dorsett, the best player in college football, as their first-round draft choice. Dorsett ended up the second overall pick. The terms? Dallas gave Seattle, where Dorsett said he did *not* want to play, their own (later) first-round pick and three second-round choices—a package made possible only by the Clint Longley trade to San Diego. And that was possible only because Longley, the Mad Bomber, sucker-punched Staubach.

Dorsett signed a 5-year contract for $1.1 million, becoming the first player in franchise history to reach such a lofty figure, although it was the second largest contract signed by a rookie, with running back Ricky Bell edging out Dorsett with his own $1.2 million contract. Bell was never even remotely close to the back Dorsett became. In 1994, Tony D. landed the trifecta—he was inducted into the Pro Football Hall of Fame, the College Football Hall of Fame, and the Dallas Cowboys' Ring of Honor.

From the moment he donned No. 33 (Duane Thomas's old number), Dorsett was a stunner. Name any other back who showed the explosion he did blowing through the line. We don't think you can. On December 4, 1976, he became the first player in franchise history to rush for more than 200 yards in a single game. The Cowboys finished with a 12–2 record and two *Monday Night Football* appearances, which elevated their reputation and that of their stadium even more.

In what became one of the most dominant Cowboys seasons ever, they hammered Chicago (37–7) and Minnesota (23–6) in the playoffs (both games being played at Texas Stadium) and blasted the Denver Broncos in the Super Bowl in New Orleans, winning 27–10 and solidifying their reputation as the League's showiest team. At that point, the Cowboys under Tom Landry had played in four Super Bowls, winning twice.

Dorsett made a huge difference. He ended up playing with the Cowboys from 1977 to 1988, helping lead the team to two Super Bowl appearances and one of its two championships in the Clint era. Dorsett has his own Super Bowl memories, waxing eloquent about "the silhouette of Coach Landry walking the sideline . . . the hole in the roof so God could watch his favorite team play. It's also a landmark for the city of Irving . . . lots of wonderful memories of great games won and lost, great rivalries."[9]

It is easy to make the case that, when it came to the teams Clint Murchison presided over, the 1977 edition was undoubtedly the best.

If anything, the 1978 season proved to the city of Irving what a sweetheart deal it got from Clint Murchison Jr. The Cowboys were on one serious roll. For the third consecutive year, they finished in first place in the NFC East. And they closed out the season by appearing in their fifth Super Bowl.

Staubach finished the '78 season as the top-rated passer in the League. Drew Pearson and Tony Hill qualified as the best wide receiver combo in the League, and, of course, who could forget the one and only Dorsett at running back? The defense hummed under linemen Ed "Too Tall" Jones, Harvey Martin, and Randy White, and the secondary had Cliff "Captain Crash" Harris, Charlie Waters, and Benny Barnes. It was quite the assemblage of talent, and it showed. In a rematch of an earlier Super Bowl, Dallas fully expected to win this time against the Pittsburgh Steelers. Fourteen players from the game would end up in the Hall of Fame, nine from Pittsburgh, five from Dallas.

The Cowboys shut out the Los Angeles Rams in the NFC Championship Game in the LA Coliseum 28–0 and headed to the Orange Bowl to face the Steelers. And yes, they should have won. With Dallas trailing 21–14 in the third quarter, tight end Jackie Smith dropped what should have been an easy touchdown pass from Staubach, who grimaced when it happened. Smith ended up in the Hall of Fame, but the poor guy never recovered from his infamous drop—which, frankly, did as much as anything to help the Steelers win, 35–31. It was, however, one crazy-wild game.

Two curious footnotes to the 1978 season that added their own complement to the legacy of Texas Stadium: in April, before the season started, the TV show *Dallas* debuted on CBS. It became a monster hit, dominating the US market and most of the world. British actress Julie Graham, growing up in Scotland, admitted being obsessed with *Dallas*.

"Obsessed," she once told Michael Granberry and the *Dallas Morning News*. "Everybody in the UK was obsessed with it. 'Who Shot J.R.?' may still be the biggest show ever in the history of British television."[10]

Graham's obsession extended even to clothing.

"I've still got a fantastic T-shirt that says, 'I Love Sue Ellen.' It remains one of my favorite possessions."[11]

Dallas endured until 1991, paying homage to Texas Stadium for more than a decade by showing an aerial shot of the hole in the roof for 13 years. Remember what we said in the intro? The shot became so iconic, it provoked a question from the ringleader of the 9/11 terrorists, who apparently fantasized about flying a plane through the hole.

Speaking of iconography, the season may have ended on a down note, but in preparing the 1978 highlight film, NFL Films gave the Cowboys a whole new problem, albeit in the form of a compliment. They titled the year's recap *America's Team*, a label that in the 40 years since seemed to have done as much harm as good. As much as anything, it made the Cowboys perpetual targets.

In the last year of the Texas Stadium decade, one event stood out more than any other: Roger Staubach retired. He'd been a fixture since the opening whistle on October 24, 1971, when the Cowboys christened the stadium by crushing the Patriots.

Maybe his leaving was an omen, because the rest of the Clint-Tex-Tom era just never felt the same.

Before Roger's tearful goodbye speech, the Cowboys still had to play the 1979 season. And it, too, was a good one, though nowhere near as good as those that came before it. Yes, the Cowboys won their division, but Charlie Waters got hurt, Thomas "Hollywood" Henderson ended up flaming out, and Too Tall Jones left to pursue, of all things, a boxing career. The Cowboys lost in the first round of the playoffs with Staubach throwing his final pass to offensive lineman Herb Scott, which was, of course, a penalty, as the Cowboys fell to the Rams, a team they had always throttled in the past.

But in one way, 1979 stood out more than any other season because of Staubach and what he did in the final seconds of a late-season game against the Washington Redskins. To this day, many call it Texas Stadium's high point.

The late Frank Luksa had this to say about the game:

> This was Staubach's last hurrah, his 21st fourth-quarter comeback and one of 14 in the final two minutes. His second touchdown pass in the last four minutes—an 8-yard fade route to Tony Hill with 39 seconds left—supplied a he's-done-it-again climax.
>
> The game featured a series of wild surges. Washington scored the first 17 points, Dallas the next 21, Washington 17 more in succession and Dallas the final 14. The game included the most famous tackle in Texas Stadium history—defensive lineman Larry Cole's third-down stop of John Riggins to prevent the Redskins from deep-freezing their 34–28 lead . . . All-in stakes rode with the outcome, another reason even Hail Mary author Staubach described it as "absolutely the most thrilling 60 minutes I ever spent on a football field." Bitter rival Washington drew a playoff blank. The Cowboys won the NFC East title, their last hurrah under Staubach. Staubach's Hall of Fame career ended a week later on an incongruous note during a 21–19 playoff loss to the Los Angeles Rams. He completed his last NFL pass to guard Herb Scott, an ineligible receiver.

Staubach said goodbye soon afterward, citing repeated concussions in an emotional press conference at Texas Stadium, where, his voice breaking, he paid tribute to Landry, "the man in the funny hat." Staubach had hammered out a legacy during a remarkable period in Cowboys' history. From 1970 through the playoff loss in 1979, the Cowboys won 105 regular season games, more than any other franchise.

So, what did 1979 mean? One door closed and another opened.

One more thing about 1979: Texas Stadium took on a new tenant, Southern Methodist University, which, like the Cowboys in 1971, moved its rapidly rising football team from Fair Park to Irving. SMU's inaugural season in Texas Stadium introduced the football world to running back Eric Dickerson, who spent 4 years at SMU and then rushed for more than 13,000 yards in the NFL. He still holds the NFL's single season rushing record with 2,105 yards. Dickerson and the 8 years the Mustangs played in the stadium only added to its already rich legacy.

SMU remained in Texas Stadium through the 1986 season, after which they were assessed the "death penalty" by the National Collegiate Athletic Association (NCAA), which determined, among other things, that the Mustangs were paying some of their players. It is the only time in the history of college football that any team has been given the death penalty. SMU was prevented from playing its 1987 season and chose on its own not to play in 1988. When the school resumed playing football in 1989, it did so in Ownby Stadium, on the SMU campus. In 2000, the on-campus Ownby site morphed into the $42 million Gerald J. Ford Stadium, which, following the example Clint had set, included its own gleaming bank of luxury suites.

The best evidence of the Cowboys beginning to unravel was their 1980 draft. They drafted twelve players, but this was hardly the Dirty Dozen. Only quarterback Gary Hogeboom, taken in the fifth round, stands out as a player anyone would remember.

Even so, the season went well. Landry radiated hubris in praising what he called "the system," and Danny White enabled the feeling by having a very good year in the wake of Staubach's retirement. QB White guided the Cowboys to a 12–4 regular season record (one win better than Staubach's last season) and a wild card playoff berth. The Cowboys played that one on December 28, 1980, dousing the Los Angeles Rams at home, 34–13.

The next week defined the season as being forever memorable and had people wondering if White had inherited the DNA of Staubach's late-game karma. Uncannily, he brought the Cowboys from behind, throwing a late-game, 23-yard touchdown pass to Drew Pearson with 47 seconds left that eked out a thrilling win over the Falcons in Atlanta, 30–27. When the fourth quarter began, Dallas trailed 24–10.

That put the Cowboys in the NFC Championship Game in Philadelphia against the Eagles, who won 20–7. (As it turns out, it would be the first of three straight Cowboys appearances in the NFC title game—and they lost all three, giving Staubach's successor the mixed feeling of taking the Cowboys to three straight NFC Championship Games, and losing them all.)

Once again, in 1981, the Cowboys proved their endurance, their reliability. Strange new foes dotted the landscape, but Dallas remained Dallas under the stoic Landry.

The Cowboys finished with a typically dominant 12–4 record and an NFC East title, their fifth in six seasons.

But 1981 was also noteworthy for the Cowboys, producing a second straight draft that reeked of mediocrity. Yes, they drafted twelve players, but none made a mark in creating anything that added up to a lasting memory. (You wouldn't be out of line by calling this draft its own version of a "Dirty Dozen.") As critics would say later, in analyzing the Cowboys' approaching fall, bad drafts were stacking up like mounds of fetid trash, and sooner rather than later, Dallas's collective drafts would trigger a devastating collapse.

Even so, the Cowboys opened the playoffs with a resounding 38–0 victory over the Tampa Bay Buccaneers at Texas Stadium.

It was easily one of the most convincing Cowboys playoff wins ever.

So, once again, the Cowboys headed to the NFC Championship Game—this time in San Francisco. The 49ers had beaten Dallas in week six, 45–14, but with less than a minute to play, Dallas clung to a 27–21 lead. So why would Landry do anything different? And yet, he did. He often had the tendency to change, at the oddest moment, this time by putting in his highly suspect prevent defense (only three linemen rushing, eight men playing back), when up to that point, Dallas's regular configuration on defense had been terrific, rising to every moment and raising the question: *Why* make a change . . . now? The problem with a prevent defense in such a situation is that it opens the door to a good quarterback shredding the opposition with a stunning series of short passes. It also makes sacking the QB almost impossible. Second-guessers say Landry lost the Ice Bowl Game in 1967 for the same reason. So, why fix it if it ain't broken? Sad to say, but the prevent defense was Landry's fatal flaw. Otherwise, he's the one they talk about now, with Vince Lombardi and Bill Walsh being those who came in second to the Great Landry. As the legendary Blackie Sherrod was fond of saying, "All the Prevent Defense does is prevent you from winning!" Indeed.

Landry's lust for the prevent defense did nothing more than allow a new legend to rear his head sooner than he would have otherwise. Methodically, quarterback Joe Montana led the Niners all the way down the field, shredding the Cowboys' defense with short passes, capped off by a desperation pass to Dwight Clark that chiseled itself into football folklore as the Catch. To this day, it remains one of the most memorable moments in the history of San Francisco sports.

Few remember this, but dammit, we do. Dallas took the ensuing kickoff, and with seconds remaining, White hit Drew Pearson with a slant pass that *almost* went for a touchdown. San Francisco defensive back Eric Wright was able to grasp only the thread of Pearson's jersey. Otherwise, Pearson was *gone*, and would have given Danny White his own Hail Mary moment. (By today's rules, it would have also resulted in a "horse-collar" penalty, moving Dallas 15 yards deeper into San Francisco territory and putting them within easy range of a game-winning field goal.)

Even then, the Cowboys were not quite doomed. Remember they needed only a field goal, and Dallas had the best kicker in the game at that point in Rafael Septién. But on the next play, White fumbled the snap. Game over.

So, Dallas lost, 28–27, in the second-most crushing loss in the history of the franchise, exceeded only by the Ice Bowl. Sure, hindsight is 20–20, but looking at it now, Montana and the Catch hastened the Cowboys' fall as much as any other single moment. To see Montana complete that pass over the outstretched hands of Too Tall Jones marked nothing less than the end of one era (the Cowboys) and the launch of another (the 49ers). And for the Niners, it truly was the beginning of a dynasty. Montana soon won kudos as the game's best-ever quarterback, until, that is, a sixth-round draft pick from Michigan named Tom Brady began playing for the Patriots in the year 2000.

The 1982 season was bizarre, to say the least. For one, the NFL Players Association called a strike against ownership, reducing the season to nine games. The Cowboys finished with a 6–3 record but still managed to produce Cowboys magic along the way—the kind of magic that distinguished Clint's 24-year ownership and the team's entire tenure at Texas Stadium.

No one should be surprised that it was Tony Dorsett who wrote the chapter. He stamped into his autobiography his most meaningful career moment in the last regular-season game, at Minnesota against the Vikings, when he took the ball from the Cowboys' 1-inch line and ran like a quarterhorse for a 99-yard touchdown, which, of course, remains to this day the longest scoring run from scrimmage in the history of the League. It is perhaps symbolic of what a weird year it was that Dallas lost the game anyway. Adding further to the strangeness of the moment was that Dallas had only ten men on the field when the Cowboys' center snapped the ball. For whatever reason, Dorsett ran through a hole the size of Waco, but did so on what was essentially a busted play.

The Cowboys won a first- and second-round playoff game at Texas Stadium, easily, but then flew to Washington to meet the dreaded Redskins. And of course, the Redskins won, 31–17, giving Dallas its third straight loss in the NFC Championship Game. It became a sad trifecta that haunted quarterback Danny White, who, the naysayers said, was no Staubach and never would be. This makes us laugh, though, considering the Cowboys' 26-year Super Bowl drought that began in 1996. Three straight conference championship appearances? The twenty-first-century Cowboys would take that in a heartbeat, baby.

Poor White got injured in the Redskins game and ended up sobbing on the bench, for all to see on national television. Landry replaced him with backup Gary Hogeboom, and for a while, it looked like Hogeboom might pull it off. No such luck, and the coach never looked back at White, whose career began a slow, sad decline.

From the hindsight-is-20-20 department: before the season began, the Cowboys drafted fifteen players in the 1982 draft, which many contend was the all-time worst in franchise history—fifteen players and not a single keeper. In other words, *bad*.

Who could have possibly guessed that 1983 would be Clint's swan song as Cowboys owner? Just the thought of Clint selling the team was enough to make Cowboys fans shudder with fear, not to mention Tex and Tom, who very much wanted to stay employed.

But before we knew such a thing could even happen, the Cowboys began the season with more Cowboys magic, which for one game made White look like Staubach. Before a national television audience on *Monday Night Football*, Dallas fell behind by 20 points at halftime but rallied with a crazy comeback to win, 31–30. They cruised to a 12–4 record, despite finishing second in the NFC East. Even so, they broke an NFL record by making the playoffs for the *ninth straight year*.

It was precisely that kind of quality and longevity that left Clint with a legacy that, until Robert Kraft and the Patriots, no one came close to matching. Tom Brady led the Pats to a nineteenth consecutive winning season in 2019, but in 2020, he stunned the football world by defecting to the Tampa Bay Buccaneers—who won their first Super Bowl with Brady as QB. With a win–loss record of 7–9, New England fell one season shy of matching the Cowboys' twenty-season streak.

The Cowboys logged another bad draft in 1983—they were stacking up like entrees at the Original Pancake House at this point—but did manage to snare one player you'll remember when they grabbed defensive end Jim Jeffcoat in the first round. Jeffcoat was not Hall of Fame material, but he was damn good. Too bad that good Cowboys teams were about to disappear right in front of him.

Give credit where credit is due, however. Schramm and scouting director Gil Brandt had long been among the best ever in signing undrafted free agents who could actually play. Drew Pearson was such a player, and so were safety Bill Bates and offensive lineman Mark Tuinei, who made the team as unsigned free agents in 1983 and played great for years.

Speaking of Pearson, 1983 was the year he passed Bob Hayes as the franchise leader in receptions. So, he was very much part of the Cowboy mojo when the team showed up at Texas Stadium on December 26, 1983. Yes, the Cowboys were once again in the playoffs, despite it being a first-round, no-bye-for-us wild card game. And who else but Pat Summerall and John Madden were there to broadcast the game for CBS, which Cowboy haters in those days believed was an acronym for Cowboys Broadcasting System. During Clint's years of owning the Cowboys, the team became a ratings juggernaut, a fixture on national television. Make no mistake, it did not come later. It started with Clint. Period.

And one more thing.

We feel compelled to say something here that resonates deeply with Dallas natives who lived out of state but who always came home at Christmas to a team they could count on for being there when it came to the playoffs. Clint had created precisely that kind of team, that kind of hometown exuberance. For 20 straight years, it was nothing less than Dallas's collective celebration at Christmas. It felt exactly like the line from the Gordon Lightfoot song, "Did She Mention My Name?"

Is the home team still on fire, do they still win all the games?

Damn right. At least it felt that way.

And on the day after Christmas, 1983, we got to celebrate the fact that the Cowboys were playing a playoff game at home, in Texas Stadium. For many fans, it meant taking a Cowboys Flyer to the game, a special $5 round-trip fare on a Dallas Area Rapid Transit bus—a price and a privilege that Clint preserved the entire time he owned the team. (DART, as it came to be known, was actually founded in 1983.) For anyone who thinks Texas Stadium was designed only for the wealthy, they're wrong. You could catch the Cowboys Flyer at a shopping mall parking lot near your house and have your own onboard tailgate party with fellow Cowboys fans. It was damn near as much fun as the game. You didn't pay a penny for parking, and you parked in the Blue Lot, next to the stadium entrance. The Cowboys Flyer experience lasted until Jerry Jones bought the team. He maintained it until Texas Stadium closed, but soon after buying the team—and in need of additional VIP parking spaces—he moved the lot more than a mile away, near the University of Dallas campus, which made the walk to the stadium on a cold or icy day almost unbearable, not to mention dangerous. He canceled the Flyer option altogether when he moved the team to Cowboys Stadium, where he charged $75 for parking—yes, $75.

As co-author Burk Murchison notes, the Cowboys' Flyer was merely one example of his dad's effort to make the experience of going to a game as pleasurable *and* affordable as possible. He cites reasonable ticket prices and concessions, with volunteers from local charities manning the concession booths *and* taking home a percentage of the profits. And most of all, he says, reserved parking was low, as in nowhere near the $75 Jerry Jones charges.

The Clint philosophy was much in evidence on the day after Christmas, 1983, when the good vibes were still hummin'. The Cowboys' playoff experience remained a sweet component of Dallas's yuletide bliss, even for families that didn't celebrate Christmas, and there were plenty of Jewish and Muslim Cowboys fans. If you don't believe us, we'd be happy to introduce you. And on the day after Christmas, 1983, we were even playing at home—which, alas, didn't matter. We lost to the Rams, 24–17, with no one except Clint having the remotest clue about the sad, sad story about to be written, one that would change the Cowboys forever.

And not for the better.

Clint was in far worse shape than anyone knew. As his son, coauthor Burk Murchison later wrote in a personal essay about his dad:

> In the early 1980s, Dad's health deteriorated dramatically, and he suffered significant financial setbacks stemming from a collapsing real estate market, historically high interest rates and general mismanagement. In 1984, under tremendous financial stress, he was forced to do the unthinkable and sell his beloved Cowboys to a partnership headed by a local Dallas businessman, Bum Bright. A short while afterwards he had to file for personal bankruptcy protection. He lived the remainder of his life confined to a wheelchair and largely unable to speak.

Even his beloved Xanadu, Texas Stadium, would soon become the province of a rascal named Bum.

CHAPTER TWELVE

Clint's Fall from Grace

HE WAS SHORT, and shy, and lived in an era long before email or the internet or social media. He thrived in an age when letter-writing was an art, and in that respect, he was Matisse, Picasso, and Jackson Pollock rolled into one.

He was also a relentless practical joker, for whom no one escaped the wrath of his razor wit. At times, his cartoonish attacks extended even to Cowboys players, and yes, even to the great Tom Landry.

We have told you all about his tireless, shameless assault on Washington's racist owner George Preston Marshall, and yet, there are so many more examples.

Part of the reason he excelled as a prankster was that he *was* short and shy. No one expected such a little guy to be so cunning. But this was a guy you didn't want to cross, or else he would punk you. It was like having Sacha Baron Cohen as the owner of the Dallas Cowboys.

His humor excelled because few of the Cowboys' players had any idea who he was. The unsuspecting included blond wide receiver Golden Richards, who loves to tell the story about mistaking Clint for someone he wasn't. Richards says:

> We were on the plane returning from a game my rookie year. And this little guy with a flat-top and one of those awful thin ties came back into the players' area. I thought he was a sportswriter and began to give him a really hard

time. I was popping off my best one-liners; things like, "I bet that tie was really something back when it was in style," and "Does your personal barber travel with you?" The guy laughed about it and proceeded down the aisle. When he was out of earshot, [quarterback] Craig Morton, who was seated next to me, says, "Golden, do you have any idea who that guy is?" He quickly informed me that it was Clint Murchison. I can't tell you how badly I wished for a parachute. It was over a year later when we happened to be at a party at Lee Roy Jordan's house. Clint was mingling with the players and not really saying much. After a while he went over to Lee Roy's gun cabinet and got his rifle out and came over to where I was sitting and pointed it right at me. "I just wanted you to know that I haven't forgotten what you said about my tie."

Those who knew him well say Clint's exotic sense of humor compensated for perceived shortcomings that sprang from social awkwardness and what they called extreme introversion. He expressed his gift through jokes and well-conceived pranks that targeted friends and acquaintances for decades. In the process, no one was spared.

One of Clint's earliest recorded examples of prankish behavior came when he was a youngster and vacationing with friends on Matagorda Island, a hunting and fishing retreat owned by Clint Murchison Sr. and his business partner, Toddie Lee Wynne Sr.

Clint Jr.'s guests included Toddie Lee Wynne Jr., who later became a 5 percent owner of Clint's Cowboys. Clint and the other boys were fed up with Toddie Lee Jr. sleeping in late every morning, so he was soon made the object of a devilish prank, which in retrospect feels almost as dangerous as Clint's having pointed a gun at Golden Richards.

Toddie Lee Jr. loved his morning pancakes, especially if they were smothered in tablespoons of thick, dark maple syrup. Well, Clint decided to teach him a lesson one morning by dousing his pancakes in motor oil. Toddie Lee Jr. took a bite, chewed briefly, and then, staring each boy in the eye, proceeded to pour more motor oil on his pancakes and gobble down the whole pile. Needless to say, Clint Jr. and his buddies were mighty impressed.

One of his best stunts came before the Cowboys' 1977 season, but to place it in context and fully appreciate it, you have to go back to midseason, 1971.

Coming off an excruciatingly painful loss to the Baltimore Colts in Super Bowl V at the end of the 1970 season, the Cowboys were not playing well and had fallen two games behind Washington with seven left to play. To make matters worse, All-Pro tackle Ralph Neely dislocated his ankle and broke his leg in a freak accident while motorcycling with teammates on a lakefront property near Dallas.

Coach Tom Landry was, in a word, pissed.

"I didn't know anybody was riding motorcycles, but you can't have rules for everything. I'm not going to have one now. If a guy is stupid enough to jeopardize his whole career that way, a new rule isn't going to protect him."[1]

Landry filled the gaping hole on the Cowboys' offensive line by persuading retired Cowboy Tony Liscio to replace Neely. With Liscio filling in for "Easy Rider" Ralph, the Cowboys caught a tailwind in the second half of the 1971 season and finished by winning their first Super Bowl.

That's only the preface to the story. Fast-forward to May 5, 1977, when the Cowboys traded up to acquire the No. 2 overall selection in the NFL draft from the Seattle Seahawks. The price was steep—the fourteenth pick in the first round plus three in the second—but Dallas parlayed the trade into picking Heisman Trophy–winning running back Tony Dorsett. Less than a month later, Dorsett would become the Cowboys' first million-dollar player.

Clint Jr. was writing the checks, of course, but otherwise remaining silent, as was his wont. Little did Landry know, but the owner was plotting his next prank. One day, Landry arrived at the practice facility, only to find that his reserved parking space was occupied by a motorcycle. And it was quite the dazzling machine, painted in bright Cowboys colors of metallic blue and silver, with the words *Property of Tony Dorsett* etched in bold letters on each side of the bike's spherical gas tank. The machine also carried a personalized license plate: TD-33. Landry's reaction? The look on his face, players said, made it all worthwhile.

Of course, those who prank will soon be pranked themselves, a fate Clint narrowly escaped before the Cowboys' debut at Texas Stadium on October 24, 1971.

Clint was a proud member of the Rover Boys, who were known for the hardest of hard partying and also for orchestrating funny and often shocking pranks targeting one another or some unsuspecting outsider that they deemed worthy of abuse. The Rover Boys' jokes were not idly planned. And they often involved a supporting cast of turkeys, leopards, goats, chickens, baby alligators, racehorses, and black bears.

Radio czar and fellow Rover Boy Gordon McLendon decided to shock the world and of course Clint by making him the object of this ultimate prank moments before the Cowboys took the field at their new home. McLendon had arranged for a circus elephant to be led onto the field and then to be seated and remain seated in the very middle of the Cowboys' star on the 50-yard line, moments before kickoff. It was a ballsy, hilarious scheme that would have disrupted the game, and of course, Clint's big day. In the end, only a day or so before the game, McLendon thought better of it and pulled the plug. Maybe he chose not to do it because it would have made King Erik and State Fair Cullum endlessly happy.

In an age when sports owners kept the media as far removed from themselves and the players as possible, Clint was the opposite. He reveled in the writing and prank-playing of such austere members of the Fourth Estate as the legendary sportswriters who peopled Dallas's media ranks in the 1960s— Blackie Sherrod, Dan Jenkins, Edwin "Bud" Shrake, and Gary Cartwright, who for quite a long time served as Cowboys' beat writer. He dug them, and they dug him. But they, too, were wild. At the time Jack Ruby gunned down Lee Harvey Oswald, Shrake was dating Jada, Ruby's lead stripper at the Carousel Club. The fact that Shrake later fell in love with former Texas governor Ann Richards, who became his life partner, only shows you how much a man can change. And change would later happen to Clint Jr., some good, but much of it awful.

At his peak, Clint Jr. was a wildly successful businessman and sports owner, a prank player extraordinaire, but in the end, the joke was on him. We asked Robert Murchison, Clint Jr.'s youngest of four children (who include two brothers and a sister), to share with us his thoughts about his dad. He did so in an incredibly moving essay.

As Robert wrote about his father, "He ended his career in bankruptcy and is considered a failure. He destroyed one of the great American fortunes. What happened?"[2]

In comparing his dad to his grandfather, whom he knew as "Pop," Robert wrote:

> How did he fail where his father succeeded? His character failed him. Dad was brilliant, but his problem was that he knew he was the smartest guy in the room. This hubris led him to believe that he was always right and everyone else, wrong. Unlike his father, he did not know when to surrender to economic forces working against him. His obstinance drove Pop and [brother] John to distraction and eventually led John to decide to liquidate Murchison Brothers.

While his obstinance was a weakness, it paid off, Robert wrote, "when he engaged with top level executives like Frank Crossen and Paul Seegers at Centex, Tex Schramm and Tom Landry at the Cowboys and Paul Trousdale in Hawaii. But otherwise his obstinance was a liability and it cost him dearly and was a factor in his bankruptcy."

In conclusion, Robert writes that "the success of the Cowboys raised Dad's profile. Unsavory characters that normally would not be attracted to him fawned on him and his wealth. His personal lifestyle became reckless. Dad befriended many of these characters. They took advantage of their friendship and his generosity. He employed them, lent them money and invested in their businesses though few were astute businessmen nor had any intention of paying him back much less making him money."

Like his father before him, Robert writes, Clint Jr. "had to sell good assets to pay for bad ones. But too many bad ones caused the financial tightrope to begin to sway. This problem was compounded in the early 1980s by a collapse in oil prices" that led to oil being priced below $10 a barrel, "thus reducing the value of his oil and gas assets which in turn caused a collapse in Texas real estate, thus reducing the collateral value of the assets he had pledged to the banks."

There was also a dramatic rise in interest rates. "Around this time," Robert writes, "the family did a major refinancing and borrowed $52 million from a consortium of banks. It was priced at 110 percent of prime plus 1.5. With the prime rate at 21.5 percent, the effective interest rate was 25.15 percent!"

In the same way that oil—black gold, Texas tea—would play such a vital role in the creation of the Dallas Cowboys, so too did it underscore its demise.

As Clint Jr.'s youngest child concludes, his financial empire had fallen headlong into a haymaker. "With an incredibly high cost of capital," Robert writes, "Dad's debt-ridden, far-flung investment empire could not support itself, forcing Dad to declare bankruptcy in 1985 and bring to an end one of America's storied financial empires."

Even so, Clint Jr.—confined to a wheelchair and barely able to speak, and now a self-professed born-again Christian in love with a new wife, who would soon be a widow—had one more trick up his sleeve. It, too, involved its own Big D, which did nothing less than secure the long-term future of his beloved Dallas Cowboys.

CHAPTER THIRTEEN

A Rascal Named Bum

F OR CLINT MURCHISON Jr. to even think of selling the Cowboys had to be torture. He was losing a chunk of his heart, his soul. But stuck in a wheelchair and wallowing in debt, he had no way out. What he didn't want was for someone to buy the Cowboys and *move* them. The very thought of it was like sticking needles in the eyes.

Jack O'Connell, a business associate and trusted friend appointed by Clint and Tex Schramm to find a buyer, knew the criteria he had to meet. He had to make sure the man (or woman) had the money and could be counted on to keep them as what they were: the *Dallas* Cowboys. O'Connell began scouring the *Forbes* magazine list of the 400 richest people in America. And, oh my, look who might have bought them.

"I could have bought an NFL team," future president Donald J. Trump told reporter Ira Berkow in 1984. "There were three or four available—that still are available, including, of course, the Dallas Cowboys."

Trump said no, despite admitting that the Cowboys had a "bigly" reputation.

"I feel sorry for the poor guy who is going to buy the Dallas Cowboys," Trump told Berkow. "It's a no-win situation for him, because if he wins, well, so what, they've won through the years, and if he loses, which seems likely because they're having troubles, he'll be known to the world as a loser."[1]

At the risk of leapfrogging too far ahead, let's examine Mr. Trump's "hot sports opinion." Texas billionaire Harvey Roberts "Bum" Bright was, to use Trump's word, the "loser" who ended up buying the Cowboys.

Bright paid $55 million for the Cowboys in 1984 and agreed to assume $22.5 million in additional debt associated with the team. And in addition to *that*, he paid Clint Murchison Jr. $21.5 million for Texas Stadium Corp., which Murchison owned individually. But between the time he bought the team and sold it, he'd also invested an additional $40 million for the installation of his Crown Suites I and a pair of state-of-the-art video scoreboards that hung from the ceiling of the stadium. Not to mention incurring millions in operating losses.

Five years after buying the Cowboys, Bright sold to Jerry Jones for $140 million.

Forbes reported in 2021 that Jones's Cowboys had ascended to a staggering value of $5.7 *billion*, making them the world's most valuable sports franchise for the sixth consecutive year. Losers? Really? What would they be worth if they were winners?

The truth is, in the spring of 1984, the words—*the Cowboys might be for sale*—was enough to send the sports world into spasms of shock and awe.

That spring, the Cowboys were gearing up for their annual pilgrimage to balmy Thousand Oaks, California, for training camp. The team had concluded its eighteenth straight winning season in 1983. Its profile had never been higher. The same could be said for its iconic home, whose hole in the roof was a staple of the opening credits of *Dallas*. As the city prepared to host the 1984 Republican Convention, which would nominate the wildly popular Ronald Reagan to a second term, everything seemed to be going swimmingly in the town sports columnist Blackie Sherrod loved to call "Large D."

But beyond the veneer, fault lines were cracking. The secret would soon skitter out, like a fourth-quarter fumble by Tony Dorsett.

Jim Dent, then the Cowboys beat writer for the *Dallas Times Herald*, was left scratching his head by the call he got from the personal assistant of Tex Schramm.

"Can you come over?" she said quietly. "Mr. Schramm needs to see you—privately."

Dent surmised correctly that Schramm was sitting on a scoop.

"Tex was usually in a good mood," Dent said. "But this time, he was sitting in his office, crying. He's not bawling, but tears are rolling down his cheeks. I thought maybe he had cancer, or his wife had cancer. 'Tex,' I said, 'what is it?'"[2]

Schramm stunned Dent by saying:

"Clint has to sell. He's broke."

Dent knew why Schramm was crying.

"The ride was over," he said. "It would never be the same, and he knew it. And it wasn't."

What few people knew is that, months earlier, in late 1983, Jack O'Connell was already on the job, having secretly approached Bright, for one, to see if he might be interested in buying the team. It's important to note that O'Connell approached Bright—not the other way around. Bright appealed to the Cowboys more, say, than Donald Trump or any other potential owner who lived out of town. Bright was local—and enormously wealthy. Plus, he was almost certain to leave the Cowboys in Irving, which for Clint mattered as much as the sale price.

Unbeknownst to anyone but O'Connell, Clint had spelled out four conditions in advance of quietly seeking a buyer: the Cowboys had to remain local, local, local, but there was more, and each condition mattered deeply to Clint. They were, in order:

1. The management rights of the stadium held by Texas Stadium Corp. were to be sold with the team.
2. There would be no price set in advance for the team/stadium package.
3. Schramm and Landry were to be part of the sale and remain with the team *after* the sale.
4. Despite his rapidly failing health, which included not being able to walk or speak coherently, Clint Murchison Jr. *must* be apprised of every step in the upcoming negotiations.

All of which led O'Connell straight to a Bum.

The effort soon went into overdrive, in the person of intermediary Charles H. Pistor Jr., who, on behalf of RepublicBank—where Pistor served as chairman and CEO—worked hard to persuade Bright to become the second owner of the Dallas Cowboys.

Bum was gangly tall and wore thick black glasses, his teeth yellowed by decades of chain-smoking. Business associates said in the aftermath of his death that they could not remember seeing him without a cigarette stuck to his lips or dressed in something other than a don't-screw-with-me business suit. He wore a military-style "burr" and had a habit of peering at a rival or colleague with such icy blue eyes that it sent a chilling message to the guy on the other end: "I am *not* to be messed with."

H. R. "Bum" Bright had made his fortune in oil and gas before expanding his portfolio to include investments in trucking, banking, real estate, and what would become his financial Achilles' heel, the savings and loan industry. He was, by most accounts, a risk-taking millionaire by his early 30s. A graduate of Texas A&M University, he was a wildcatting, chain-smoking Aggie and proud of it—and for O'Connell, a strange choice from the word *go*.

Bright openly admitted he'd never attended even one Cowboys game. Nor did he seem interested in watching them on television. He was, however, a crazed fan of the team of his alma mater, the Texas A&M Aggies. Every time they played a home game in College Station, Texas, he made the 3-hour, 181-mile trek from Dallas and back to see his beloved Aggies tee it up. If no one else went with him, he made the trip by himself.

Despite his antipathy with the Cowboys, the more O'Connell and Pistor lobbied Bright, the more the old Aggie dug the idea of assuming the mantle from a wounded Clint. For if there was one thing Bum dug, really dug, it was deals.

As his friends say, he was, in fact, "addicted" to deals. The only thing he loved more than deal-making was smoking, though the two often happily intersected.

Bright was well known in Dallas, and in some circles, had a ghastly reputation. His right-wing politics made national news in 1963, Dallas's darkest year. Elected in 1960, President John F. Kennedy found some of his fiercest critics in Dallas. They included the irascible Bright, who with other like-minded businessmen, namely Nelson Bunker Hunt, purchased for $1,465 a hostile full-page ad that appeared in the *Dallas Morning News* on November 22, 1963, the day Kennedy landed at Love Field—and flew out hours later in a body bag.

Although Bright and Hunt conceived the ad and paid for it, it was signed by only one individual—Bernard Weissman, a right-wing crusader, who, according to the Sixth Floor Museum at Dealey Plaza, was a member of the John Birch Society. When it came to the ad, Weissman soon became the scapegoat. The Warren Commission summoned him to testify about it. And because Weissman was Jewish, Jack Ruby later told investigators that he feared a fellow Jew signing his name to the ad might lead to an anti-Semitic backlash in Dallas. Whether that became even part of his motive, no one will ever know. But Ruby gunned down the only suspect being held for the assassination, Lee Harvey Oswald, in the Dallas police station 2 days after Kennedy was killed.

It's worth noting that making someone else take the heat became a pattern for Bright. Knowing the ad would be politically radioactive—even without Kennedy being gunned down on Elm Street—Bright made sure to keep his name nowhere near the ad. But it didn't stop there.

You can draw a sharp parallel to Bright selling the Cowboys to Jerry Jones in 1989. Rather than inform beloved coach Tom Landry that his tenure was up after 29 years, Bright relegated the dirty deed to Jones, making it look like Jones had *fired* Landry, when in fact, all he wanted was to partner with his own coach (Jimmy Johnson, his former teammate at Arkansas) in shaping a bold new era for the Cowboys. As it was, Jones took *all* the heat. To this day, he continues to be known as "the man who fired Tom Landry." Bright didn't like Landry and had wanted him gone for quite some time but never had the guts to fire him.

Hours before his death, President Kennedy saw the ad, paid for by Bum Bright and Nelson Bunker Hunt. It happened at the Hotel Texas in Fort Worth, where top aide Kenneth O'Donnell showed it to the US president during breakfast.

"We're heading into nut country today," Kennedy said. Hour later, he was dead, his brain blown out by a sniper. He was 46 and the married father of two children, ages 5 and 2. The ad and the crime that followed ignited Dallas's ignominious new brand: "city of hate."

Years later, the *Dallas Morning News* interviewed Bright, who was finally ready to retire. Robert A. "Bob" Miller, who worked for the *News* until he was 91, and who worked on the city desk at the time of Kennedy's assassination, saved his powder for the final question. (Miller shared his recollections in an interview for this book not long before he retired in 2015.)

Given what happened on November 22, 1963, did Bright harbor regret about paying for the ad?

Bum leaned forward in his chair and gave Miller *the look*, and with a voice so angry it sounded like a roar, all but screamed his reply:

"I'd do it again tomorrow!"

When it mattered most, Bright had Jack O'Connell right where he wanted him. He figured out fast that O'Connell was every bit the chain smoker he was. And when it came to a deal, Bright let it all ooze out like the long, slow drag of a smelly Camel.

After 10:00 one night, in the closing stretch of selling the Cowboys, O'Connell ran out of smokes—which Bright was hoping for.

As O'Connell wrote later, "He would only give me some of his at a price— ONE DOLLAR PER CIGARETTE. Fortunately, I had money! And that story made the front page of the *Wall Street Journal*."[3]

Exhausted from Bright and an endless stream of picayune detail, O'Connell ran headlong into a stalemate. Problem was, he and Bright were still short of reaching a deal by $100,000.

"To break the deadlock," O'Connell wrote, Bright "finally offered to flip a coin for double or nothing! That means he would pay $200,000 for the debated receivable. We flipped MY QUARTER! I lost and Bum grabbed the quarter to boot!"[4]

So, who was Jack O'Connell?

He had been affiliated with the Cowboys since 1973, when his company, O'Connell and Co. Inc. was contracted to manage Clint's baby, Texas Stadium. He would hold that position until 1984, when the Cowboys and the Stadium Operating Contract passed officially from Murchison to Bright.

O'Connell admitted being surprised, even stunned, when Clint summoned him to his office in the early 1980s to tell him he wanted to sell.

"What I'm about to tell you," O'Connell said Clint told him, "only Pete Rozelle, Tex and I know at this time. You must keep it between the four of us . . . I'm going to sell the Cowboys."

Clint assigned O'Connell "to handle the whole thing. By that time, he had begun to lose his health, his ability to walk and talk. Clint set no price. Of course, he wanted the most he could get . . . Of course, I was proud of his confidence and this new assignment. I knew this would be the most ever paid for any kind of sports franchise; I knew it would be a historic sale and one that would capture international attention. AMERICA'S TEAM!"[5]

Once word got out that America's Team was for sale, "would-be buyers came out of the woodwork from all over the world," O'Connell said, including, as we now know, Donald Trump.

> The job of determining whether or not they had the financial ability to make perhaps a $100 million purchase and to determine whether or not they would be approved by the NFL was up to Tex and me exclusively. We talked to scores of buyers and reported to each other daily. We wore out the *Forbes* list of the 400 Richest People in America! We tried to first check out everyone from the greater Dallas-Fort Worth area and worked on other Texans because we didn't want the new owner to move the team.

Of course, Clint himself got many, many calls and told them they would hear from Tex or me. His callers included people from the Middle East, Saudi Arabia in particular! There would be would-be buyers with every kind of financial plan you can imagine! And many of those people were highly aggressive and demanding—almost as if they had some divine right to buy the team.[6]

The overall process, O'Connell said, took almost 2 years. Unbeknownst to Cowboys fans, Clint had begun shopping the team as far back as 1982, when the fissures in his empire began to widen. He and Schramm considered Richard Rainwater of Fort Worth. He showed only mild interest. They considered Philip Anschutz of Denver, who years later underwent the scrutiny of a profile in the *Los Angeles Times*. Once, at a championship soccer match in Europe, a friend puzzled over Anschutz's downcast demeanor, finally asking the reclusive billionaire why he appeared that way.

"Well, it's tough for me," he said. "I own both teams."

Schramm later said that "15 to 20" parties made "serious inquiries" about owning the Cowboys. In addition to Trump, they included Florida real estate developer George Barbar. Cowboy's management considered Barbar "highly motivated," but Barbar lived in Boca Raton, Florida, not Texas, so a red flag went up immediately. They wanted no one who might flirt with the idea of moving the team. The Boca Raton Cowboys sent a chill down everyone's spine.

O'Connell gave serious thought to Dallas auto executive W. O. Bankston and Vance Miller, a close friend of Clint's and arguably the boss's favorite for becoming the next Cowboys owner. But as O'Connell wrote: "I just didn't believe Vance could put together the money." Miller said he hoped to get the money via a loan from RepublicBank, whose chairman and chief executive officer Charles H. Pistor Jr. was simultaneously lobbying for one H. R. "Bum" Bright to buy the team via financing from Republic. Bright served as the largest shareholder of Republic and chairman of its loan committee.

"I liked his chances of getting the money!" O'Connell wrote. "I learned that he could borrow 100 percent of the money from the bank at 'LIBOR plus 3.8 percent.' Until I was told that, I didn't know what 'LIBOR' even meant! [It means 'London Inter Bank Overnight Rate,' the interest rate loaned overnight by one bank to another. We're talking big banks!]"[7]

Initially, Bright appeared to have no interest and reminded everyone within earshot that he was an Aggies fan, not a Cowboys fan. He also openly resented Cowboys coach Tom Landry for being an alumnus of the University of Texas, the Aggies' bitter archrival. In Texas, such ludicrous nonsense actually matters.

Upon learning of Bright's purchase of the team, Landry joked about it with his usual dry wit. As he quipped to his longtime barber Truman Wolf, "I always knew I'd end up working for an Aggie."[8] But for Bum, it was no laughing matter. *Seriously.* Only in Texas.

Enter Pistor, the head honcho at RepublicBank, where Bum was Customer No. 1. Pistor rang Bum at home wanting to talk about "a highly confidential opportunity." Bad timing. Bum was pissed. Pistor called on a Sunday. As O'Connell wrote, for "every Sunday of his adult life, Bum brings together his children and grandchildren for Sunday dinner. The family was due at Bum's house in 30 minutes, so Bum wanted to hear the deal on the phone. Pistor resisted for fear someone would overhear them. Bum would not change his family dinner, so on the phone it was."[9]

Pistor pleaded with him to buy the Cowboys, telling him how fantastic an opportunity it would be. Yeah, yeah, Bum said. Besides, he'd already heard about the deal and, frankly, had zero interest. "Pistor persisted in telling Bum that in his [Pistor's] international banking work when he would go to Tokyo, for example, the only thing Japanese bankers wanted to hear about was the Dallas Cowboys. It would be good for Dallas, good for RepublicBank, good for Bum to be the owner of the Dallas Cowboys."[10]

Evidently, Pistor played the right notes. Negotiations went into overdrive, with Schramm being recruited to proceed to the next step. "Clint had lost much of his ability to talk," O'Connell wrote. "His wife, his children, the household help and I were about the only people that could understand him, so all communication with Bum on the deal was through me."[11]

O'Connell describes Bum circa 1984 as "a self-made man worth hundreds of millions. He was not active in many publicly owned businesses; he owned 100 percent of whatever he owned. He was a tough and tireless negotiator about 10 years older than I."[12]

Soon, however, Clint laid the offer on the table. He would sell the Cowboys for $60 million, plus the assumption of debt related to the development of the Dallas Cowboys Training Center—Valley Ranch in Irving—and $25 million for Texas Stadium Corp., which O'Connell said was "close to double the sales price of any other sports franchise up to that time in history."[13]

Bright and O'Connell met in the law offices of Jenkins & Gilchrist in downtown Dallas on a Sunday afternoon and chain-smoked and yakked until the wee hours of a Monday morning.

"There was no food, no restaurants open in downtown Dallas," O'Connell said. "I looked through the offices of a few lawyers whom I knew well and finally found a few boxes of Girl Scout cookies. That was it for all of us for 'dinner.'"[14]

Girl Scout cookies and, of course, smokes. O'Connell was a three-to-four-pack-a-day guy, which was mild compared to Bum. Paying for cigarettes and losing a coin clip for $100 grand was, as it turns out, not the worst of it. For O'Connell and the Cowboys, an unexpected and unpleasant chapter reared its head amid acrid cigarette smoke and the sticky aftertaste of Girl Scout cookies.

With minority partners Toddie Lee Wynne Jr. and Fritz Hawn owning 5 percent each, Clint and brother John Murchison split evenly the controlling 90 percent. As we mentioned earlier, John was so incredibly low-profile, virtually no one knew he was even involved, much less an equal partner with the head guy. Which became fully, shockingly apparent after he died, when his estate suddenly got motivated to make its own bid for owning the Cowboys.

Before Bright surfaced as the likely buyer, John Murchison's heirs made their interest known, albeit privately. But when Cowboys great Roger Staubach balked at the idea of managing a limited partnership on their behalf, John's family turned its attention to what it could get through the sale of the team, and before too long, here came World War III.

John had actually died years earlier. His widow, Lucille Gannon "Lupe" Murchison, had, O'Connell wrote, "agreed to sell the Cowboys for anything above $50 million." But days before the closing with Bright, John's son and daughters threatened to sue Clint, "alleging that more than had been agreed upon should be paid" for the team "and less for Texas Stadium Corp., which Clint owned exclusively."[15]

O'Connell called the episode "tense" and "unpleasant," made even more so by the fact that it may have done lasting damage to the relationship of the Murchison brothers' extended family. Brother John's family had initially demanded an additional $2 million in the purchase price—to be shared proportionally among all four shareholders of the Cowboys' franchise. O'Connell said: "In the final analysis, Bright offered $900,000 to break the impasse and get John's family to drop all claims against Clint and the other sellers. Lupe's lawyers wouldn't accept that, but when Clint [and the other owners, Wynne and Hawn] all said they would forego any part of the new $900,000, give it all to John's heirs just to get the deal done, it was accepted."[16] The agreed-upon $900,000 in the end represented 45 percent of the $2 million demand—which was commensurate with the portion of the team owned by brother John's estate.

Again, as broadcaster Don Ohlmeyer once told broadcaster Tony Kornheiser about such matters: "The answer to all your questions is money."

Finally, the long-awaited closing was set for Friday, May 18, 1984, at RepublicBank. The entire second floor was reserved for what amounted to a chapter in sports history. The end of an era. But, "sure enough," O'Connell wrote, "a roadblock came up. Part of what Clint had to deliver at closing were certain Texas Stadium bonds held at Vernon Savings & Loan as collateral for some loan. Vernon Savings had agreed to release the bonds, then reneged at closing. They insisted on $1.38 million in cash to release those bonds!"[17]

There was, O'Connell wrote, "only one place I could get $1.38 million at that time and that was from my new best friend, H. R. 'Bum' Bright. He and I talked out the deal. He finally said he would pay $1.38 million more for Texas Stadium Corp. to get this thing closed, provided Clint would give up the 'profits interest' but have the right to buy back that 'profits interest' anytime within three years at $1.38 million plus accrued interest at prime. I got Clint to agree."

And then, yet another drama ensued.

"By this time," O'Connell wrote, "the bank wire via which all funds in this transaction were to be sent around the country was about to close! The interest people would lose on this $80 million over the weekend was alarming! Bum Bright called the chairman of the Federal Reserve Bank to get him to keep the wire open for another half hour!!!"[18]

Finally, it was done.

At 3:17 p.m. on May 18, 1984, at RepublicBank in Dallas, ownership of the Dallas Cowboys Football Club, Inc., and Texas Stadium Corp. officially transferred from Clint Murchison Jr. to H. R. "Bum" Bright and his "limited" partners for what O'Connell called "the highest price ever paid for any sports franchise anywhere."[19]

Emotionally spent, O'Connell retreated to Dallas's elite restaurant the Palm "and had two quiet drinks all by myself."[20] Preparing to leave, he noticed in the booth next to him Lamar Hunt, the owner of the Kansas City Chiefs, née Dallas Texans, Clint's archrival with whom he shared the Cotton Bowl from 1960 through 1962, when the two were competing like hell to seize the loyalty of Dallas sports fans.

"I gave him the news," O'Connell said, "and flew home to Houston after one of the most challenging and emotional days of my life."[21]

For Bright, the "challenging and emotional" part underscored an old cliché: the devil was in the details, which in this case were hellish. And lying at the bottom of the detail bin was Texas Stadium Corp.'s daunting obligation to redeem the $31 million in revenue bonds (plus interest) needed to build Texas Stadium.

To help with that, Bright appointed the super-capable James B. Francis Jr.

The product of a wealthy Dallas family, Francis was stocky and tough in appearance. He had a piercing stare and a deep, gravelly voice, not unlike the linebackers whose checks would soon be signed by Bright.

Francis brought a powerful cachet. By the year 2000, he and his wife counted as two of their closest friends outgoing Texas governor George W. Bush and wife, Laura. With an arm-twisting power known only to a few, Francis spearheaded Bush's fundraising efforts during two runs for the White House as head of the "Pioneers."

Francis became the confidante of a president. Even so, he said he'd never met anyone quite like Clint Murchison Jr.

His speech badly distorted, Murchison was confined to a wheelchair with an illness eerily similar to Lou Gehrig's disease. Even so, he managed to convey to Francis that he cared more about *where* the Cowboys played than he did the Cowboys themselves.

He harbored an almost-maniacal passion for Texas Stadium, which remained his legacy, his achievement, which Schramm and Landry could never touch.

Murchison showed Francis how he'd created not just a stadium but also a prototype for generations to come, one that reached a zenith in the Cowboys' $1.2 billion AT&T Stadium, which opened in 2009. Jerry World, as it came to be known, was Texas Stadium on steroids.

"My eyes were opened," Francis said, "and Clint is the one who did it."

Murchison had figured out as far back as the 1960s, Francis said, that a stadium could be a whole lot more than a stiff seat, exposed to the elements, where you could gulp down a stale hot dog and a Dr Pepper and risk infection by peeing in a public restroom barely fit for animals, much less human beings. For decades, that was the model in most cities, but Murchison, unlike other owners, saw the stadium, far more than the team, as sitting on a treasure trove of untapped potential.

"He singlehandedly had the vision when he created Texas Stadium to create the first of what has now become a huge business that every team in sports—not just professional football, but sports as a whole—has followed," Francis said. "And that is that the stadium as an entity is as valuable as your television contract, that it can pay for itself *and* generate tremendous ongoing revenue. Before Clint, nobody knew that."[22]

Initially, Francis said, boss man Bum was not at all aware of how lucrative the stadium could be even when the chance to buy the Cowboys was put in front of him on a blue and silver platter. But Murchison *schooled* him, whetting his appetite for a deal he couldn't pass up. Even so, when Bum heard the figure of how much debt was still hovering like a vulture over Texas Stadium Corp., he damn near choked.

So, what was the debt? The $35 million in principal and interest owed to bondholders whose purchase of seat option bonds had built the stadium. The return on the bonds came due in 2008, which happened to be the final year of the Cowboys' lease at Texas Stadium.

Getting rid of the debt required a stroke of genius, which Francis said even a physically impaired Clint Murchison Jr. managed to summon. It came in the form of a rare financial concept offering its own Big D—"Defeasement."

In the era of double-digit inflation that bedeviled Jimmy Carter's single presidential term and Reagan's first, interest rates hovered near a crushing 18 percent. Today, they're in the low single digits. In order to solve the debt debacle, Murchison zeroed in on US government securities—"Zero coupon US Treasury bonds"—that at the time carried interest rates of 13.5 percent. They would soon emerge as the secret weapon that vanquished the Texas Stadium debt. Francis said:

> He came up with the idea, and we implemented it. He had no money, but we did. As the new owners of Texas Stadium Corp., we would buy zero-coupon US Treasury bonds that would mature on Dec. 15, 2008, which was exactly two weeks before the debt on the stadium was due.
>
> We would donate—in other words, we would give those [US Treasury] bonds to the City of Irving—to hold as collateral to pay off the debt. So, we bought $35 million worth of [seat option] bonds for $2.3 million and then gave them to the City of Irving. The interest would accrue on a tax-free basis, because a municipality owned the bonds. That made it a tax-free transaction. Totally. So, from June 1, 1984, we got to operate the stadium as if all the bondholders were paid off and the stadium was debt free. It's called *defeasing*. It's the practice of substituting collateral. We "defeased" the debt.

What defeasing allowed, according to coauthor Burk Murchison, was "the ability to convert the operations of Texas Stadium Corp. from an operating agreement where most available revenues were dedicated to retiring the seat option debt to a lease with the city of Irving, which paid the city of Irving 8 percent in revenue, thereby opening up the profit potential for the owners of Texas Stadium Corp."[23]

As Francis says, "We paid off a $35 million debt at Texas Stadium for $2.3 million. It was brilliant. It was a function of the high interest rates, which Clint and only Clint knew how to manipulate.

"I want to stress the absolute novelty, revelation and revolution of his thought process back in the late 1960s and how it related to stadiums, vis-à-vis their financial viability and profitability," Francis said. "Nobody else saw what that man saw, even in his condition."

And just as Clint told Francis it would, Texas Stadium emerged as the prototype for all modern stadiums, which between 1984—when Bum bought the team—and now have thrived, like a virus.

"At one point, it was actually laughed at around the league as Clint's folly," Francis said. "That changed, however, and when it changed, it changed dramatically."

The deal Clint and Francis arranged took the ball to the 10-yard line. It was then up to Bum and O'Connell to take it across the goal line.

What heightened the complexity, Francis said, was that the deal involved the team *and* Texas Stadium Corp., which Clint owned outright and which in some respects he cared much more about. Incredibly, in retrospect, Francis said, "none of Bum's partners wanted involvement in the stadium. They saw it as a loser. They wanted to buy the team and wanted nothing to do with the stadium. And they were *wrong*."[24]

But the reality is, his partners were never offered it, because Bum was shrewd enough to realize its profit potential. And given that, he wanted it for himself.

So, it came down to this: the team awash in charisma offered next to nothing in cash flow, while Texas Stadium was now positioned to be a major cash cow—for Bum and Bum alone. Fast-forward to 1989, when Bright sold to Jerry Jones, who also, at least initially, longed for the team while caring nothing about the stadium.

"It was me who convinced Jerry that that was the stupidest position he could take," Francis said. "Because I had been taught by Clint to believe otherwise. And now," as the proprietor of a stadium that cost more than $1 billion, "he gets it," Francis said with a laugh. "But at the time, he didn't either."[25]

Which is why Francis calls Clint a visionary. What was "counterintuitive" to most people, he said, was second nature to the Cowboys' founder.

During the team's early days, Murchison made lease payments on the Cowboys' original, aging home, the Cotton Bowl, but soon realized that if *he* controlled the stadium and its revenue, leaving money on the table would no longer happen.

"When you look at the results years later," Francis said, "you realize that this wasn't an accident. This was planned and had logic behind it. He set it up perfectly."[26]

And yet, during early negotiations, Francis and O'Connell focused first on the team. O'Connell, he said, "was very knowledgeable about the football side of it. He was less knowledgeable as to why everything was set up the way it was with Texas Stadium Corp." Which posed a problem. For a while, "no one could verify key details," Francis said, "because Mr. Murchison had lost the ability to communicate. His speech was horribly impaired. He was deathly ill."[27]

Francis would eventually negotiate directly with Clint, though never with ease.

"It was, I would say, rudimentary. I had to get close to him to hear him. I got little bits and pieces of sentences. It was very labored on his part."[28]

After months of immersing himself in seemingly endless particulars and trying to understand Murchison's mind, Francis figured it out, which he said only enhanced his respect for Clint. For instance, it was illegal to sell liquor in the Bible-heavy hamlet of Irving, Texas, which inspired Clint to craft yet another end-around. He created the Texas Stadium Club, which as a private entity allowed him to bypass local laws and give himself another revenue stream, one he didn't have to share in the socialistic world of NFL ownership.

"You had to pay huge dues to join the private club," Francis said. Just to sit in the stadium club was $1,000 a year per suite holder. "It's the same thing that Jerry does with these pavilions now. More bells and whistles, but again, it was started by Mr. Murchison."[29]

The negotiation for the team was simple, straightforward, and, Francis said, fair. O'Connell was a shrewd but principled negotiator. Negotiations for the stadium corporation and stadium club were far more complicated.

"And the reason was, Mr. Murchison was much more interested in that. He had it in his head that the stadium was his baby. He turned the team over to Tex and Tom, but no one but him handled the stadium. Tex had no authority over the stadium. None. Zero."[30]

Murchison was, for lack of a better word, Francis said, "*picky* as to what was going to happen at that stadium after the sale. He wanted to know in detail what we were thinking."[31]

To produce even more revenue, Francis and Bright wanted to build a ring of 114 new luxury suites above the upper deck, just below the roof of the stadium.

"They were called Crown Suites, because they were around the top of the stadium, like a crown," Francis says. "And then we were going to put in Diamond Vision, state of the art video screens as dramatic to 1984 as Jerry's monstrosity was to 2009."[32]

Each screen weighed 50,000 pounds, provoking no small measure of worry from the dying Cowboys owner. "Mr. Murchison was convinced that we were going to crash the stadium in. And let me tell you, there was some justification for it."[33]

When the first screen was lifted, Francis was horrified to see "that it literally lifted a half-inch. We lifted it a bit higher, and it held. So, we took it on up."

In closing the deal in 1984, Bright formed a limited partnership, with Bright as general partner, Tex Schramm as managing partner, and nine other limited partners as an added vehicle to purchase the Cowboys. In a separate transaction, Bright alone acquired Texas Stadium Corp. for $21.5 million, with a percentage of future profits added in.

And yet, another major hurdle remained. The sale required the approval of all the owners in the League, which had never before permitted a limited partnership.

"We went to Hawaii, we met with [Commissioner Paul] Tagliabue, but it was a big deal," Francis said. "They acted like they were moving mountains. Really, they were so snobby."[34]

And yet, it happened.

"Clint really opened our eyes," Francis said, "to the potential of the stadium as a revenue source. It's amazing how many of his fellow owners just didn't get it. Of course, they all do now, and he's the reason why. And I don't think he gets nearly enough credit for it."[35]

But not even Clint had answers for the Cowboys on the field. The long, slow slide had begun.

The first Cowboys team owned by Bright finished the 1984 season with a win–loss record of 9–7 but missed the playoffs. They won four of the first five and went 5–5 over the final ten games.

A season-long quarterback controversy, like those of earlier eras, bedeviled the team, with Landry unable to settle on the latest shiny new thing, Gary Hogeboom, or veteran Danny White, who took over for Captain America, Roger Staubach.

The Cowboys were slipping. White had taken them to three NFC Championship games in 1980, 1981, and 1982—all losses—and in 1983, Dallas had finished 12–4 before losing in the first round of the playoffs.

The 1984 season was the Cowboys' twenty-fifth, the team's silver anniversary, so it felt peculiar having Bright as owner, and the team courting mediocrity for the first time since the 1960s. And in every way possible, Bum was Bum.

Years before buying the Cowboys, Bright needed to have his gall bladder removed. The doctor ordered a 10-day hospital stay. Nope, Bright said. Ain't gonna do it. So, he got a new doctor, refused to be put to sleep, talked throughout the surgery, and checked out that night. Two days later, he was back at work.

"A man has to do what he's got to do," he often said.

In keeping with the mantra, Bright loved the idea of pulling money from Texas Stadium, which, à la Clint, *he* envisioned as a serious cash cow. From the moment he bought the team, Bright instructed his team to go as heavy as possible on luxury suites.

In January 1985, David Casstevens, then a columnist for the *Dallas Morning News*, outlined Bright's newest proposal: "If you're wondering how lunch with J. R. Ewing has any relevance to sports, then maybe you haven't seen the newspaper ads. Next season, the Circle Suites no longer will be the place for Dallas' high rollers to wine and dine their friends and clientele. As part of a $40 million project, Texas Stadium Corp. is constructing 114 Crown Suites. 'A new level of luxury,' the ad calls them. The Crown Suites will offer 'all the excitement of spectator events' in the privacy and 'exclusive ambiance of your own luxurious space.'"[36]

Those who paid the price rode inside glass-enclosed elevators to the lofty Crown Suites, which peered down from Texas Stadium in an ornamental ring just beneath its famous roof, which, of course, had a hole in it. "We're talking lush pile carpet, tilt lounge chairs, refrigerators, private phones, mirrored walls, dimmer switches, drop-leaf buffet tables and a bar," Casstevens wrote.[37]

Never mind that the players looked like ants from that far away. Each Crown Suite came equipped with a computer terminal. "Push one button and scores from around the NFL will pop onto the screen," Casstevens wrote. "Push another and get Tony Dorsett's statistics. The computer will do everything but mix you a martini and fetch your slippers."[38]

The price? For suites between the 35-yard lines, Bright charged $125,000 per year or a purchase price of $1.5 million. End-zone suites leased for $30,000, with a purchase price of $300,000. Whether it was the daunting sales price or the fact that the Cowboys were slipping in the standings, Bright sold only a handful. Clint's initial price for a suite was $50,000.

In 1985, Bright's second year, the Cowboys made the playoffs with a 10–6 record but lost in the first round. The Los Angeles Rams, now playing their home games in the Big A, a converted baseball stadium in suburban Anaheim, cruised to a 20–0 shutout.

But that was nowhere close to the moment that symbolized the Cowboys' onrushing demise or the flat line of Bright's tenure as owner.

On November 17, 1985, the 7–3 Cowboys welcomed to Texas Stadium Mike Ditka's Chicago Bears. The Bears were a perfect 10–0, and they annihilated the Cowboys, who looked sadly overmatched.

A single play symbolized the game, the season, and the Cowboys' fall from grace. Quarterback Danny White, who doubled as the team's punter, decided on his own to initiate a fake punt. From the moment it unfolded, it reeked of failure. White came nowhere close to running for a first down, and as he tried in vain, futility dogging his every step, Landry was seen yelling on national television, "No, Danny, no!"

Indeed, no, Danny, no.

Bright was picking up the vibe.

In their good news–bad news netherworld, the Cowboys had at least finished the season with a winning record, giving them a distinction no team has equaled since: twenty consecutive winning seasons, all with Tom Landry as coach.

But by the end of the '85 season, rumors began to circulate that Bright wanted out with this condition: the team was for sale but not the stadium, which is precisely what Clint predicted would happen.

Even esteemed insider Blackie Sherrod opined in his column for the *Dallas Morning News*: "At the risk of seeming tabloidish, let us report the wildest rumor of the week was that the Cowboys again are for sale. That some Bum Bright partners have lost enthusiasm for the project and that confidential offers are being sought. Presumably the deal would not include Texas Stadium lease and new luxury suites and resulting income, which are Bright's personal projects. But it's probably pure gossip, so don't tell a soul."[39]

By 1986, the cracks were big enough to drive a truck through.

In what would serve as a foreshadowing of future financial woes encircling the team as a whole, minority owner Craig Hall—who purchased a 10 percent stake in the Cowboys when Bright bought the team—was forced into bankruptcy, because of mounting problems related to the savings and loan industry. His 10 percent stake in the Cowboys was bought by Bright and minority partner Ed Smith, a Houston businessman.

A native of Ann Arbor, Michigan, who owned a building by his eighteenth birthday, Hall overcame a childhood complicated by epilepsy to join the ranks of the city's multimillionaires after moving to Dallas in 1979.

In the go-go era of the decade that followed, he made even more money. Finally, in the real estate crash that swallowed up so many of the city's heavyweights, he lost it all. He declared bankruptcy and settled with the Resolution Trust Corporation for $102 million, part of which covered a failed S&L in Denison.

But when it came to the Cowboys, Hall escaped at the perfect time.

For the first time since 1965, they failed to close with a winning record, ending the team's and Tom Landry's matchless streak of twenty consecutive winning seasons.

Emboldened by the off-season acquisition of running back Herschel Walker, the Cowboys won six of their first eight games. But Danny White broke his wrist in a road game against the New York Giants, and backup quarterback Steve Pelluer managed only a 1–7 record. Pelluer would have been shut out completely, had he failed to muster a narrow 24–21 win over the Chargers in San Diego.

On December 7, 1986, the forty-fifth anniversary of the Japanese attack on Pearl Harbor, the season fell prey to a truly bizarre milestone.

Coach Landry—a highly decorated World War II bomber pilot—was forced to leave the game because of death threats phoned in to the stadium.

Soon after the third quarter expired in the Rams' 29–10 victory, Landry was escorted into the tunnel that led to the Cowboys' dressing room. He returned with 12:15 remaining, wearing under his trademark sports coat a bulletproof vest.

By early 1987, Blackie Sherrod was back to writing about a looming Cowboys sale.

"It wouldn't surprise some if Bum Bright sold the Cowboys one of these days. There were some real estate holdings around Valley Ranch that made the purchase attractive, and the real estate economy is rather ill. Bum's new skyboxes at Texas Stadium, thought to be a lucrative fringe income, haven't exactly sold like pancakes. Bright's image is not of one who suffers losses patiently."[40]

By 1987, it got even worse. The Cowboys finished with their second straight losing season (7–8), and off the field, Bright got a heavy helping of the dark side of being an NFL owner. The players declared a strike for the second time in six seasons, walking out after the second week of the season. Unlike the first strike, the League replaced the strikers with veterans and free agents who were willing to cross the picket line, several notable Cowboys among them, including Danny White, Randy White, Tony Dorsett, and Ed "Too Tall" Jones—each of whom was contractually obligated to play. Replacement players participated in three weeks' worth of games.

In December, after a home loss to the Atlanta Falcons, Bright spoke out publicly against Landry for the first time, foreshadowing what would come in 1989. He said the team's play calls had left him "horrified."

He added *on the record*: "It doesn't seem like we've got anybody in charge who knows what he's doing other than Tex."[41]

The low point, of course, was 1988, which left the Cowboys with a 3–13 record. Soon after the season started, Bright gave Schramm 90 days to find a buyer for the team. Schramm enlisted the aid of New York–based investment banking firm Salomon Brothers.

The Bright timeline offers a compelling look at what went wrong with his own career and by extension how that affected the Cowboys.

In the early 1970s, Bright acquired Trinity Savings Bank, a small thrift based in Dallas. In 1974, Bright joined the board of directors of RepublicBank and by the early 1980s had become one of its largest shareholders.

In 1984, Trinity Savings bought Texas Federal Savings for $88 million. Together, the thrifts held $2.3 billion in assets and were renamed Bright Banc Savings Association. Near the end of his life, Clint Jr. joked that he knew Bright was an Aggie, because he couldn't spell the word *bank*.

In 1985, for the price of $107 million, Bright Banc bought Dallas Federal Savings and Loan Association, which held $2.2 billion in assets.

In 1986, Bright formed "Vulture I," an investment fund designed to buy repossessed real estate from his Bright Banc and other institutions.

In 1987, RepublicBank and InterFirst Corp. agreed to merge as First RepublicBank Corporation in a deal engineered by Bright.

In 1988, with the Cowboys enduring their third straight losing season, Bright faced staggering losses of his own. First Republic collapsed. Its banks were sold to NCNB Corporation. Bright lost an estimated $29 million on his First Republic stock, which he had used in part to capitalize Bright Banc.

In 1989, the coup d'état—federal regulators seized Bright Banc over mounting real estate losses.

Even with his empire crumbling, Bum remained, well, Bum. He had suitors wanting to buy the Cowboys. They included Los Angeles Lakers owner Jerry Buss. But the most promising potential buyer was former Hollywood executive Marvin Davis, who from 1981 to 1984 headed up one of the world's biggest studios, 20th Century Fox.

The sale appeared so certain that Bright flew to Los Angeles to close what Salomon Brothers executive Jack Veatch, who witnessed the negotiations in Davis's imperially baronial office, called a handshake deal.

With the men having concluded their business, Davis smiled and Bright extended his hand. All that remained was the mere formality of having financiers and attorneys draw up the papers.

Things were going so well that the men headed to Davis's home to celebrate over dinner. And it all went well, until the men strolled to the foyer to say their goodbyes. And that's when it happened: the remark that changed the fate of the Dallas Cowboys forever, an anti-Semitic slur that killed the deal with Marvin Davis, who at that point was clearly the frontrunner to succeed Bum Bright as the third owner of the Dallas Cowboys.

Veatch was not present at the dinner, but one of Bright's top lieutenants was. The aide reported the story to Veatch, who played no small role. Veatch was the investment banker hired by Bright to execute the deal.

"Well, at least, you're not like one of those Hollywood Jews I was expecting," Bright said to Davis.

It did not go over well—at all. The late Marvin Davis was a large man, who may have weighed 350 pounds, Veatch said. He had blond hair and blue eyes. He was 6 foot-4—and proudly Jewish. As *Vanity Fair* once reported in a profile of Davis: "Marvin's father, Jack Davis, came to America from London in 1917, as a teenager. A fireplug of a man, he joined the British Navy after having been denied a college scholarship because he was Jewish."[42]

So, how did the No. 1 contender for being the Cowboys' next owner react to Bum's stupidly racist insult?

"He walked away," Veatch said. "That was it."

And had he *not* walked away, offended by Bright's remark, well, Veatch said, it's highly possible that Jerry Jones would have never owned the Cowboys, or for that matter any NFL team.

After that, Veatch said, "Davis no longer returned our calls." Frustrated with Davis not returning his calls, Veatch asked the aide if he knew why, and that's when Veatch heard for the first time the story about Bright's anti-Semitic slur that deeply offended Marvin Davis.

"That became a non-starter for Marvin," Veatch said.

So, did that open the door for Jerry Jones?

"Oh, for sure, for sure," Veatch said.

Was Davis serious about buying the Cowboys? Absolutely, Veatch said. He had sent his son, Hollywood executive John Davis, to Valley Ranch in Irving to inspect the team's headquarters and practice facility and get a feel for the multimillion-dollar deal his dad was in the final stages of cutting with Bum Bright.

"Marvin had a huge ego," Veatch said. "He put in a strong indication close to the price Bum was asking. But his ego would not permit him to fly to Dallas to complete the deal. He wanted Bum to come to Los Angeles."

That posed a problem, Veatch said, because Bright was horribly afraid of flying. It's the reason he didn't attend Cowboys road games and the reason he drove from Dallas to College Station to attend Texas A&M games. What he most feared was engine failure.

In the end, he agreed to fly to LA in the private plane of his fellow billionaire and friend, Ray Hunt, whose Lockheed JetStar had four engines. And what do you know—one of the engines *did* fail on the way home from the ill-fated meeting with Marvin Davis. "At least we've got three left," Bum said. Headed back home to Texas, Bum was down one engine and one very big deal.

Starting once again from scratch, he turned his attention to the next potential buyer: an Arkansas oilman named Jerral Wayne "Jerry" Jones.

CHAPTER FOURTEEN

From Hooterville to the Hall of Fame

T HERE ARE THOSE who say that Bum Bright's dismal tenure in owning the Cowboys is noteworthy for only one thing: he sold the team to Jerry Jones. But not even that rings true. Absent Bright's crude, anti-Semitic remark to a Hollywood executive, Jones might never have owned the Cowboys.

Bright's crudeness surfaced once again in remarks made to Clint's Valley Ranch partner Ted Rea after selling the Cowboys for $140 million. He got the better of the Arkansas oilman, he told Rea, or to put it in language Bright was comfortable using, "I fucked him like a tied goat."[1]

Even that says more about Bright than it does about Jones.

In 2015, *Forbes* magazine estimated Jones's personal net worth as more than $5 billion. (By 2021, *Forbes* had elevated his net worth to $8.8 billion.) The driver of that, of course, was the Cowboys franchise that Bright sold to Jones. In 2018, the same magazine wrote this about Jones' purchase from Bright:

"The Dallas Cowboys are the world's most valuable sports team for the third straight year at $4.8 billion. America's Team has the highest revenue [$840 million] and earnings before interest, taxes, depreciation and amortization [$350 million] of any franchise"—in the world. Soccer is an international sport, but the Cowboys continue to dominate the likes of such stalwarts as Manchester United ($4.123 billion), Real Madrid ($4.088 billion), and Barcelona ($4.064 billion). And, of course, in 2021, the Cowboys finished, for the sixth consecutive year, as the world's most valuable sports entity, with a colossal value of $5.7 billion.

Tied goat, indeed. The net worth of the Cowboys has appreciated *more than thirty-five times* since the tied goat signed the papers.

The authors of this book went to Jones's office in Valley Ranch in 2016, days before he moved the franchise to the Star, the team's sprawling, futuristic $1.5 billion practice and entertainment complex in Frisco, Texas, near the northern end of Dallas North Tollway, which begins in downtown Dallas—the city that snubbed both Clint Murchison Jr. and Jerry Jones.

Jones insisted we call him Jerry, who keeps in a glass case near his office the team's five Super Bowl trophies, two of which were won during Clint's tenure.

Jones begins by telling a story. When he bought the team in 1989, he was so elated with the purchase that he went to Texas Stadium by himself. At night.

"I shook hands with Bum, and that very evening, I drove to the stadium. I had them turn the lights on. The stadium was dark. I walked out there and lay spread-eagle in the star, in the center of the field. I just laid there and looked up at the stadium. It was that kind of moment."[2]

Jones encountered a foreshadowing of his spread-eagled moment years earlier. When he was a senior at the University of Arkansas, he played in the national championship game in the Cotton Bowl on January 1, 1965. His teammate and roommate at Arkansas, Jimmy Johnson, is the guy he hired to coach the Cowboys after saying sayonara to Tom Landry, in what remains one of the most controversial moments in Dallas history. Landry had been with the team 29 years, starting with its inception in 1960 and ending in 1989. He coached the Cowboys through twenty consecutive winning seasons, beginning in 1966, when Clint began yearning, openly, to flee the Cotton Bowl for a new venue in downtown Dallas.

Days before the 1965 Cotton Bowl game, against the University of Nebraska, Jones and his Arkie teammates went to Houston to get away from the hubbub in Dallas. The Houston Astrodome was near completion. The Razorbacks got a VIP tour. When Jones walked in, he couldn't believe his eyes, much less his skin, which felt cool and comfortable in the 72 degrees on which the Astrodome thermostat was locked.

"It was like going to Mars," Jones said. "How did it get here? How did it come to this point? Well, I had very similar feelings about Texas Stadium the night that I bought the Cowboys. The day after I shook hands with Bum, Texas Stadium became my Astrodome."[3]

And it all began, Jones said, with the dream of a true Texan icon—Clint. He lauded the Cowboys owner for masterminding a turning point in the economics of American sports, by making the stadium far more than a tired old venue, owned by a city charging exorbitant rent.

"The No. 1 contribution that Clint initiated," Jones said, his eyes seeming to light up with dollar signs, were the seat options, "which were truly unique. The right to the seat and the ability to transfer that right to another person."[4]

Such a scheme, Jones said, his eyes popping in admiration, was "brilliant."

We asked Jones what it means to have a stadium that serves as its own revenue-producing entity, a cash cow, if you will, a luxury that drove the San Diego Chargers and the Oakland Raiders to abandon loyal fan bases built up over decades, as though they were shedding wives with whom more than half a century of marriage suddenly meant nothing.

In the NFL, loyalty truly is a one-way street. Or at least it's become that way in the modern era.

President Barack Obama once called President Bill Clinton—Jones's friend and personal guest when the NCAA Final Four took place at Jerry World—the "Secretary of Explaining Things." When it comes to sharing the details of sports economics, *Jones* is the secretary of explaining things.

He has a way of explaining things that tell you this guy knows money and how it works as well as anybody. So, it's no surprise that he was the No. 1 supporter of the Rams leaving behind a fan base in St. Louis for the allure of Los Angeles (which, incidentally, is where Jones was born) and the promise of a stadium that, when it opened in 2020 in suburban Inglewood, eclipsed Jerry World overnight as the No. 1 cut of prime stadium beef anywhere in the world. Notwithstanding the fact the Rams had exactly zero fans in the stands all season long.

"A new stadium today," Jones said, "would and should take a team's revenue from the fourth quartile of revenue and lift it to the second or first quartile."

Think about that. *The stadium's role is to take the team's revenue from the fourth quartile of revenue to the second or first quartile.*

And how does it do that? "More suite revenue," he said without hesitating. "More seat revenue and more energized economic sponsorship interest."[5]

Of course, the paradigm was radically interrupted in the otherworldly season of 2020, when the NFL, as with all other sports, was reduced to a TV-only experience.

The stadium-first paradigm requires someone laying a foundation—and that someone, Jones said, was Clint. It requires someone else to put the concept on steroids, and *that* someone was Jones.

What the Cowboys founder introduced in the form of seat options at Texas Stadium was a stroke of genius, Jones said. For the options carried with them the ancillary and "priceless" dividend of passing ownership of a single seat from one generation to the next. And the next and the next.

"It lets you *re-seed* the stadium," Jones said, emphasizing the phrase *re-seed*, "and, yes, Clint introduced that. And, yes, it was truly brilliant."[6]

Jones seizing on the genius of Clint's foundation would, however, take a while to pay off. Jones's early moments as the Cowboys' owner were, at best, shakier than an earthquake in his native Los Angeles.

The current Cowboys owner has boasted in the past about having "a high tolerance for ambiguity" and thus a high tolerance for the one emotion that drives Jones far more than any other—risk.

When Jones geared up to buy the franchise Clint founded, his advisers told him he was out of his mind, certifiably nuts.

His agreeing to buy the Cowboys required Jones to purchase the 10 percent interest of two of Bright's limited partners, whose investment had been foreclosed on by the Federal Deposit Insurance Corporation (FDIC). At the time Jones bought the team, the FDIC owned 10 percent of the Cowboys, literally making them America's Team. Bright's immersion in the savings and loan meltdown of the late 1980s was why he needed to sell and sell quickly. Incredibly, there was also a clause in the Bright–Jones agreement in which Jones indemnified—that is, shielded—Bright from any potential lawsuits brought against him by his limited partners.

Tom Smith is the son of the late Edgar A. "Ed" Smith, who initially owned 15 percent of the Cowboys' franchise during Bright's tenure as owner and slightly beyond, lasting from 1984 to 1990. (Smith later increased his share to 27 percent, the amount he owned during Jones's first year as owner.)

"Jerry really, really wanted Dad to stay in, to avoid having to buy out Dad and his 27%," said the younger Smith. "And Dad was really excited about Jerry, because he knew there needed to be a change."[7]

His father found it endlessly appealing, Tom said, to be among the owners of America's Team.

"My dad came from nothing. He grew up on a farm in Collin County near Dallas. Years later, he was floating barges up and down the Mississippi. It truly was the American Dream."[8]

But when it came to Bum, the devil, of course, was lurking in the details. Always.

So, once, on a ride to Houston's Hobby airport, with Jones and the Smiths in the car, the issue of "indemnifying Bum" first reared its head, with Tom saying *he* was startled by Jones's admission. To which he responded pointedly: "Jerry, why would you *do* that?"

In Smith's words, Jones responded thusly: "I had to. I had to. He would not sell me the team unless I indemnified him—from the limited partners," among whom Ed Smith owned the largest share. So, who knows, when Bright bragged to Ted Rea in the crude story that ends with the words "tied goat," what the punch line may have meant was exactly that—the clause protecting Bum from potential litigation that he succeeded in getting Jones to agree to.

"He had some other limited partners that were more litigious than we were, that he, Bum, was more scared of," Tom Smith said. "But I will tell you this: Dad was not at all happy with the way the purchase price was allocated,"[9] meaning—in Smith's view—that an inappropriate share of the purchase price went to Texas Stadium Corp., which Bright owned exclusively, and not the owners of the franchise itself. As Tom Smith says, Bright was the sole owner of Texas Stadium Corp. And who had educated the once-skeptical Bum on the stadium being far more valuable than the franchise? Clint.

In the end, Ed Smith ended up spending a year as a minority owner under Jones, with the Cowboys' owner eventually buying out his 27 percent. To this day, Tom Smith said he and his late father believed that Jones buying the Cowboys was one of the best things that ever happened to the franchise, that it provided much-needed change at a time when the team desperately needed it. Even so, Jones admitted in our interview, using the word *candidly*, that his inaugural year of owning the Cowboys was one hell of a wild ride—and much rougher than anything he'd ever imagined.

"When I bought the team," he said, "the Cowboys had a negative cash flow of $1 million a month. The NFL's TV contracts for three straight seasons were flat. I wouldn't want anybody to dig into what I did in buying the Cowboys, because they'd lose respect for me as a business guy. It did not look pretty at all."

And soon, it got worse.

Texas Monthly once reported that the price Bright and Jones agreed on "was a reported $140 million for the football club and the stadium lease—the most that had ever been paid for an NFL franchise." But in the process of dotting *i*'s and crossing *t*'s, there was, as Shakespeare might have said, a "rub." A rather large rub, in fact.

"A $300,000 difference in the price was settled by a coin toss," *Texas Monthly* reported. "Jones flipped the coin, which hit the ceiling and a wall before landing in an ashtray. Jones, who had called tails, rushed to see the coin, while Bright remained at his desk. Heads was up. Bright would later buy a two-headed quarter from a magic shop and send it to Jones with a note that read, 'You'll never know.'"[10]

As it turns out, Jones had more to be scared about than Bum's wily ways. A young banker named Joel Fontenot helped Jones secure badly needed *permanent* financing, which in the short term alleviated the financial pressure the new Cowboys owner was under. It did so by refinancing short-term loans from various banks and individuals that Jones had cobbled together to complete the Cowboys deal.

Once the financing was secured, an exhausted and stressed-out Jones felt so relieved, Fontenot said, that he punctuated the moment by going to the bathroom and throwing up.

"Those were heady days," said Fontenot, who traveled with the Jones-led Cowboys for two years after the sale was complete. The sale, he added, was the last official act of then-NFL commissioner Pete Rozelle, who retired in November 1989, Jones's first season as owner.

Rozelle, who, incidentally, had been a fierce ally of the Cowboys' original brain trust—Clint Murchison Jr. and Tex Schramm—was less than thrilled with the terms of the sale, which he perceived as "disastrous," Fontenot said, noting the commissioner's insistence that Jones find more credible "permanent" financing, as fast as possible.

"Rozelle thought it would allow too much debt," Fontenot said.

But in Fontenot's view, what Rozelle failed to consider was Jones's ability to use the cash produced by his new toy—Texas Stadium—to retire the debt. And retire it quickly. By doing so, the new Cowboys' owner validated Murchison's vision from Day One that stadiums could and *would* emerge as viable profit centers—if only allowed to do so. The franchise owner, of course, needed control. Otherwise, it wouldn't work. By following the old model of city-owned stadiums serving merely as rental facilities, à la the Cotton Bowl, the team had no way whatsoever of using stadium operations to generate financial leverage. The Clint-begat-Jerry way forever shifted the dynamics by which NFL owners perceived the role of stadiums, which became far more important than they'd ever been in the past. That alone, Fontenot said, "led to great stadiums being built all over the league."[11]

In that regard, we the authors see an irony that harkens back to the beginning of *Hole in the Roof*. What Clint Jr. discovered, and Jones exploited, was indeed a gusher—not unlike the ones Clint Sr. and his Texas oil cronies found in the process of making them rich.

For Jones, though, the immediate concern after buying the team was how to dispose of a Mount Vesuvius of debt, thus easing Rozelle's primary concern. Enter Fontenot, who helped Jones obtain much-needed credible financing, secured through a bank called First City Texas. What *that* did was provide Jones with badly needed capital while at the same time helping him carve out a clever new turning point for American stadia. As Fontenot said, stadiums could then be used "to generate *real* money."

To his credit, Jones used his anxiety well. It served as a monster motivator. Almost immediately, he began to undo the immense fiscal damage caused by the Bum years and steer the Cowboys to a plain of profitability.

He took it upon himself to sell or lease unsold Crown Suites, of which there were more than 100. The turnaround of the team on the field in 1992 helped ignite an economic renaissance for Jones and the Cowboys. Jones soon began contemplating an additional level of suites called Crown Suites II. By the time Jones left Texas Stadium, there were about 400 luxury suites. Clint Jr. had built the original 178, and Bright added another 114, with Jones topping it off with 110 of his own. Their combined effort created a game-changing revenue generator, the likes of which have never been duplicated by any other franchise but that soon became the model for professional sports as a whole.

Jones even managed to work his magic on Clint's concept of the seat option bond. Jones took it to the next level, amplifying the already invented personal seat license, or PSL, which is like the seat option bond, except for how it enhances the owner's profitability. How is a PSL different from Clint's baby, the seat option bond? The PSL insures not a shred of liability for the stadium issuing the PSL.

Let us explain: The PSL did indeed evolve, like a meandering tree, from the roots of Clint's seat option bond concept. Both involve the purchase of season tickets for specific seats, but in Clint's plan, the seat option bond carried the obligation of returning the investment—with interest—to the person buying it. Whereas the PSL bears no such responsibility. In that regard, the PSL is much more lucrative, and in the process of selling thousands of them, Jones and other owners are able to reap additional millions.

But, if an individual fan can master the PSL game, the fan can also reap a reward, by selling the PSL for a profit. If not, well, the fan can lose money, and indeed, many do. In that way, they resemble the stock market.

If anything, PSLs underscore Jones's knack for chasing down every conceivable penny. By the time Jones purchased the team and the Texas Stadium lease in 1989, PSLs were nothing new. They were already in wide use throughout professional sports. But Jones had a gift for figuring out how to exploit them better than anyone ever has.

Early in the Murchison era, Clint had set aside 3,000 seats—1,000 in the $1,000 bond area and 2,000 in the $250 bond area (outside the 30-yard lines)—for promotional purposes. Over the years, Tex Schramm managed the inventory, sharing the seats with retired and active players, coaches, and their families, and various guests and VIPs. Once Schramm was gone, Jones discovered what he perceived as a treasure trove of seating and soon used it to develop his own PSL inventory.

Sadly, it fostered yet another schism in the pre- and post-Landry eras. Landry's son, Tom Landry Jr., had sat in the same seats for years, as part of the VIP allotment. But once, at a game, no less, a Cowboys' sales rep showed a potential buyer the very seats Tom Jr. was sitting in—at the time. So, of course, you can guess what happened next.

Around the same time, this happened: fans sitting in the first row of the upper deck, a handsome vantage point if ever there was one, arrived one season to discover that *now* they were sitting in the *second* row of the upper deck. Ever the money master, Jones had installed a whole new row of seats, simply to inflate the bottom line.

So, how did Jerry Jones develop his Midas touch?

The Jones biography has its roots in North Little Rock, Arkansas. His parents owned the neighborhood grocery store, Pat's Super Market (which looked nothing like a supermarket). Jones admits having inherited his entrepreneurial spirit from Dad and Mom. Even as a wee lad, Jones wore "a little bow tie" and greeted customers at the door of his parents' store.

After high school, Jones became a football player at (where else?) Arkansas, where one of the assistant coaches was a future Cowboys coach named

Barry Switzer, who called Jones "a different cat" from the moment he met him. Unlike any other Razorback, Jones spent his downtime selling life insurance.

He married his college sweetheart, Gene, whose grace and beauty catapulted her to the Miss Arkansas title in the 1960 Miss America pageant. Jones and his roommate, future Cowboys coaching legend Jimmy Johnson, started alongside Jones on the Razorbacks' offensive line. Jones wore No. 61 on his red Razorbacks jersey. Johnson wore No. 60.

Not long after meeting Gene, Jones remembers reading a magazine that chronicled the efforts of businessman Art Modell to buy the Cleveland Browns. Modell saw a future in pro football, which had exploded in popularity because of television and the 1958 championship game in Yankee Stadium, where the Baltimore Colts and Johnny Unitas beat the New York Giants in sudden death overtime. Even in black and white, that memorable game opened the door to television riches for NFL owners.

Colts–Giants also caused a light to flip on in Jerry Jones's head.

"That's what I want to do, I want to be *you*," he said of Modell.

Jones worked his way up from the bottom of the depth chart to become a starting offensive lineman and join the other seniors as co-captain of the 1964 national champion Razorbacks, whose Cotton Bowl victory anointed them national champions on the first day of 1965, when Clint Murchison Jr. was beginning to feel the approaching thunder of owning a winning team—in the same stadium.

In 1966, Clint's first winning season, Jones discussed the possibility of buying a minority interest in the Miami Dolphins. That led to a phone call with Barron Hilton, who owned the San Diego Chargers. At Hilton's request, Jones put together a $1 million line of credit (with, of course, the help of generous lenders). Jones was 24 years old.

He shared his Chargers dream with his Arkansas daddy, who in the son's word was "appalled." Jones paid heed to his dad and passed on the Chargers' opportunity, only to watch the AFL and the NFL join hands in a merger months later. It wouldn't be the first time that Jones's instincts proved to be right on target.

The Chargers' value instantly doubled, costing Jones $6 million in profit, which, of course, would be a whole lot more today.

With his dream of owning an NFL team in tatters, Jones turned his attention to wildcatting, borrowing money to buy land. Soon, he was drowning in debt. He loves to tell the story about trying to rent a car at Love Field in Dallas, where the attendant told him his debt was so bad, he'd been instructed to cut up Jones's credit card right in front of him. And so, he did.

Jones estimated his early income as being $36,000 in commissions, coupled with an interest debt of more than $116,000. But eventually, he did strike oil—selling his company for $175 million in 1986, a testament to risk-taking if ever there was one.

Jones has never been averse to having a good time. So, recovering from a margarita hangover acquired on a fishing trip to Cabo San Lucas with son Stephen, he remembers reading a newspaper that carried a story about Bum Bright wanting to sell America's Team. Stuck in a remote corner of Mexico, Jones somehow got Bright on the phone—immediately.

And on February 25, 1989, a reluctant Tex Schramm introduced Jones at a press conference. The Arkansas oilman was 46 years old.

"It's on live TV across the state of Texas," sports columnist and talk-show host Randy Galloway told the NFL Network during the Jones bio on *A Football Life*. "And I'm thinking, 'What in the world has just hit our town?' I thought Hooterville had arrived. It didn't go over well—at all."[12]

Jones told the assembled multitude: "This is Christmas to me. The Cowboys are America."

"We're all thinking, this guy hasn't got a clue. He's lost," Galloway said.

Jones vowed to involve himself in every phase of the Cowboys' operation, extending all the way to "jocks and socks," a remark that went viral in the prickly world of the NFL.

When it comes to "optics," Jones's couldn't have been worse. Days earlier, he was seen having dinner with Miami coach Jimmy Johnson at Mia's, which happened to be Tom Landry's cherished destination for Tex-Mex. Little did he know that a sportswriter for the *Dallas Morning News* was having dinner at the same time in the same place and called a photographer, who showed up within minutes to snap a now-famous picture. The photo of the two dining in a Landry hangout also went viral, in an age when *viral* was years away from being a commonly used word to describe a media explosion.

And then, the ultimate horrible-optics blunder: Jones canned the great Landry—a decision that in some circles in Dallas still paints Jones as a blasphemous villain. It was wildly, almost comically unpopular, and Jones took all the blame, despite Bright wanting to fire Landry for years without ever having the balls to do it.

Bright, of course, should have been the one to tell Landry that the new guy wanted to bring in his own coach, letting Landry resign with the dignity and grace that defined his character. It was reminiscent of Bright paying for but not having his name appear on the grossly unpopular, hate-filled ad in the *Dallas Morning News* that attacked President Kennedy on the morning he arrived in Dallas. Remember, as he told Bob Miller of the *News*, he had no regrets at all about the ad, despite what happened to the president. Even so, it served as a shining first example of Bright's cowardice. He may have loved the ad, even after the president had his brains blown out, but he never had the guts to attach his name to it.

When it came to dignity and grace, Tom Landry was the one who offered a how-to on that. He accepted with a rueful smile the pink slip from Jones.

"It was the most inadequate that I've ever been in my life," Jones said at his *Meet the Press*–like press conference. "And if you could grade that conversation from Jerry Jones, I got an F."

Jones later called Landry's firing "the greatest PR disaster in the history of sport." But again, Bright set him up for it.

Months later, the Cowboys embarked on their first season under the Razorback tandem of Jones and Johnson. It was the Cowboys' thirtieth season, and in terms of bad, it rivaled only their first. In 1960, they didn't win a game. In 1989, they won one, stunning the Redskins on the road. It was their first season without Landry as coach and Jimmy Johnson's first. He'd won forty-four games and lost four during his final four years at "the U" (Miami).

Right away, Johnson proved he had more in common with Landry than anyone realized. As luck would have it, yes, the Cowboys made the obvious choice with their first pick in the 1989 draft—UCLA's Heisman Trophy–winning quarterback Troy Aikman. A no-brainer there, but Johnson appeared to mimic Landry by picking in a later, supplemental draft Steve Walsh—whom he'd coached at the U—and setting him up as an instant Aikman rival. Aikman said later that Johnson's decision surprised him and, for a while at least, made him feel insecure.

It didn't stick, of course, but it felt a lot like Landry not being sure who to pick in a quarterback battle between Roger Staubach and Craig Morton. Aikman and Walsh slogged through a miserable preseason, and finally, wisely, Johnson settled on Aikman.

He apparently got a nudge in that direction from Brad Sham, the Cowboys' preeminent play-by-play man on radio. In his 2008 book, *Boys Will Be Boys*, author Jeff Pearlman shares the story of Johnson telling Sham on the eve of the regular-season opener in 1989: "You know what I'm thinking of doing. I'm thinking of starting"—at which point Sham "cut the coach off. 'Jimmy,' he said, 'if you start Steve Walsh the fans will burn your house down. You have to give this Aikman kid a chance.'"[13]

So, Aikman it was, which in retrospect calls for Sham getting a Texas-sized assist. Even so, the Cowboys finished the inaugural season of the Jones–Johnson era with a win–loss record of 1–15, surprising only the Redskins—with Walsh starting in place of the injured Aikman.

In some ways, though, the 1989 season is among the most momentous in Cowboys history, with Johnson pulling off a blockbuster trade during the season that, in retrospect, feels to this day like highway robbery.

Jones may contend that he, too, played a major role in trading Herschel Walker, but history proves otherwise. Johnson alone orchestrated the mechanics of the deal. Even so, give Jones a huge assist: he wrote Walker a check for $1.25 million (plus a house in Minneapolis and a Mercedes-Benz, as Fox Sports reported in 2017) just to get him to report to the Vikings, so as others before us have written, Jones and Johnson worked together beautifully. And for the sake of the Cowboys, it's a shame it didn't last.

Indeed, it's hard to believe in the Jerry reality of 2021, but Johnson's contract gave him full power to sign and trade players. At the time, Jones was focused almost entirely on the business side—on the franchise surviving. And he deserves major kudos for that alone. Johnson was, in effect, the de facto general manager, with Jones playing the role of bystander until after he fired Johnson in 1994, when he was gone within days of leading the Cowboys to their second consecutive championship.

Four games into the 1989 season, Johnson got the idea to trade Walker while taking a morning jog with his coaching staff. Absent a blockbuster trade, he saw the Cowboys going nowhere, whereas the Vikings saw themselves as being a single great player away from a Super Bowl. They coveted Walker *desperately*.

Before that, Johnson flirted with the idea of trading second-year wide receiver Michael Irvin to the Raiders—Irvin had played for Johnson at the U—but Raiders' boss Al Davis showed a surprising streak of compassion by asking Johnson, "Who's going to catch passes for you?"

So, Johnson traded Walker—the only marketable chip the Cowboys had—in a deal that, in the end, involved (for the Vikings) a devil's bargain of eighteen players and draft picks.

Dallas got linebackers Jesse Solomon and David Howard; cornerback Issiac Holt; running back Darrin Nelson; defensive end Alex Stewart; and a slew of incredibly delicious draft picks—a first-round pick in 1990 (this one alone allowed them to draft Hall of Fame running back Emmitt Smith); a second-round pick in 1990 (which became All-Pro safety Darren Woodson); a sixth-round pick in 1990; and five more picks labeled "conditional." The condition involved cutting five players previously acquired—Solomon, Howard, Holt, Nelson, and Stewart.

It's incredible to think that, initially, some of the NFL press thought the Cowboys got fleeced, that giving up Walker was sheer lunacy. But had they gotten only one of those players in exchange—the one being Emmitt Smith, who became the NFL's all-time leading rusher—it would have been worth it. As it was, they became instant contenders.

Johnson's monster gamble ended up ensuring his own legacy while branding the Cowboys the team of the '90s. What the deal led to also played a gargantuan role in the history of Clint's Xanadu, Texas Stadium.

For Jones, it was by no means instant gratification. The Walker deal happened in week 6 of the 1989 season. By week 16, the Cowboys said goodbye to their inaugural flop of a season, on Christmas Eve, no less, by having, in Jones's words, "every damned commode" in Texas Stadium—except for one—freeze up as the grim casualties of an overnight ice storm. Fittingly, the Green Bay Packers (who else?) trounced them, 20–10, before an announced crowd of 41,265.

The next season was better. The Cowboys finished with a 7–9 record and missed the playoffs for the fifth consecutive year. Even so, the NFL knew they were on to something, naming Jimmy Johnson coach of the year.

They won four in a row before Aikman suffered a separated shoulder in game 15, playing Philly on the road. Babe Laufenberg, who later became a Cowboys broadcaster, took over at quarterback. The Cowboys lost their final two, to Philly and Atlanta, killing any hope of making the playoffs.

Yet another sea change defined the 1991 season, the third in the Jones–Johnson regime and one of the shrewdest. The Cowboys signed Norv Turner as offensive coordinator. Before the season started, at an NFL owners' meeting on the big island of Hawaii, Jones told coauthor Michael Granberry that he was super-optimistic about the season because Aikman and Turner were already "in love."

The romance blossomed. The Cowboys used a wicked combination of powerful offensive linemen; Aikman's stiletto-sharp passing game; Emmitt Smith's ball-control, clock-devouring running; and Turner's near-perfect play-calling to carve out an 11–5 record.

They made the playoffs for the first time since 1985, Bum Bright's second year as owner.

Texas Stadium was beginning to feel like the old days. The proof was in the pudding of attendance. The Cowboys drew a near-capacity crowd of 64,530 on December 8, 1991, in a game against New Orleans that marked the largest home crowd in many a season.

They began the playoffs in the wild card round, traveling to Chicago to beat the Bears, 17–13. But the air blew out of the balloon the next week, when the Lions annihilated them in Detroit in the divisional round, 38–6.

Aikman had suffered an injury on November 24, in a game against the Redskins. Backup Steve Beuerlein played well, winning every game he started. So, Johnson stuck with him in the wild card game and, perhaps unwisely, rewarded him with a start 1 week later in the divisional round. The Beuerlein magic quickly evaporated. Too little, too late, Johnson inserted Aikman, hoping for "a spark" that, sadly, never came.

Even so, the prospects for 1992 looked terrific. Suddenly, everybody wanted to be at Texas Stadium, which by then was easily the best stadium in the NFL.

The 1992 season was arguably one of the best in the Cowboys' history. It's hard to make a case for any Cowboys team being stronger than this one. They finished with a 13–3 record in the regular season and marched through the playoffs like a Napoleonic army. They beat Philadelphia in the divisional round and, wonder of wonders, ended up in the NFC Championship Game for the first time since the 1982 season, when Clint still owned the team.

And despite playing in a mud bowl in San Francisco's Candlestick Park, the Cowboys delivered, beating the 49ers 30–20. It wasn't close. The 49ers were no match at all for what Johnson and his minions had put together.

There they were, the Dallas Cowboys, headed for a Super Bowl for the first time since the Clint-Tex-Tom-Roger days of 1978.

The Super Bowl played on January 31, 1993, at the end of the 1992 season, was Jimmy Johnson's finest hour as a football coach—and Jones's finest moment as owner.

The Razorbacks tandem had helped ensure their success by taking yet another colossal risk, which finished a close second in derring-do to the Walker deal.

In August, before the season started, the scary temperament and bipolar rants of defensive end Charles Haley became more than 49ers coach George Seifert could handle. The Niners took the odd step of trading Haley to San Francisco's then-rival, the hated Cowboys. Dallas had to give up a 1993 second-round draft choice and a 1994 third-round draft choice.

Pennies for what Haley could bring. After the trade, Raiders owner Al Davis called Johnson and said, "Congratulations, you've just won the Super Bowl."

The Cowboys didn't just win Super Bowl XXVII—they destroyed the Buffalo Bills, 52–17. The score would have been 59–17 had defensive end Leon Lett not gone brain dead by celebrating prematurely before crossing the end zone, which resulted in a Bills player ripping the ball from his grasp on Buffalo's 1-yard line.

Talk about a game that feels frozen in time. Barely a year later, Jones and Johnson would get a divorce. And who performed the halftime show in the Super Bowl between the Cowboys and Bills? Michael Jackson. He did his "moonwalk" before a crowd of 98,374 in the Rose Bowl in Pasadena, California. A short time later, one of America's highest-selling recording stars was accused of pedophilia. Michael Jackson died in 2009 at age 50, with the coroner ruling his death a homicide.

Reality and a sense of foreboding set in during the first two weeks of the 1993 season. Locked in a contract dispute with Jerry Jones, Emmitt Smith sat out the first 2 weeks. The Cowboys responded by losing both games, with every line of Johnson's face showing his frustration. Charles Haley added yet another notch of infamy to his bad-boy reputation by slamming his helmet through a wall at Texas Stadium, after the Bills throttled the Emmitt-less Cowboys in week two, 13–10.

In the ensuing days, Jones elevated his reputation among players by awarding Smith a record contract, something Clint's lieutenant, Tex Schramm, was never known for. In fact, Schramm was known for the opposite, fueling anger and resentment not only among the militant Duane Thomas but also such silver-blue loyalists as Lee Roy Jordan and Bob Lilly.

There were hints during the early weeks of the season that 1993 might end up fulfilling the Dickensian mantra, "It was the best of times. It was the worst of times."

Smith suffered a separated shoulder in the regular-season finale in New Jersey against the Giants, giving the Cowboys an NFC-best 12–4 record and a division title. He was named the NFL MVP.

A crazy season it was in so many ways. Leon Lett's tendency for brain farts surfaced again in the Thanksgiving Day game, when Texas Stadium was hit with a polar vortex ice storm, turning the artificial turf into a skating rink of ice and snow. Dallas was leading Miami 14–13 with seconds remaining, when the Dolphins' kicker attempted a long field goal. The Cowboys' Jimmie Jones blocked it, appearing to put the outcome on ice. But with the blocked ball rolling around Dallas's 10-yard line, Lett tried to fall on it and slipped, kicking the ball and making it live again. Miami recovered and kicked the winning field goal. Cowboys lost, 16–14, thus creating yet another memorable game in Texas Stadium and national television history.

Despite Lett's blunder, the Cowboys thundered through the playoffs, beating Brett Favre and Green Bay 27–17 in Texas Stadium and hosting the 49ers a week later in the NFC Championship Game. When Aikman suffered a concussion, the backup Johnson had signed for precisely this moment—Bernie Kosar—filled in perfectly at quarterback, and Smith continued to dominate. Dallas won 38–21, setting up a rematch with the Bills in Atlanta in Super Bowl XXVIII.

The Cowboys fell behind at halftime, 13–6, but with Smith plowing through the Bills in the second half, Dallas scored 24 unanswered points in winning their fourth Super Bowl title and their second straight under Johnson and Jones.

All seemed perfect in the Cowboy universe, but in truth, a franchise-ripping earthquake had just begun to rumble.

Soon after the Cowboys' second-straight championship, NFL owners conducted their annual meeting in Florida. An ebullient Jones entered a ballroom, where he saw Johnson, Norv Turner, and others, with their wives, having dinner. He went over and in a friendly way tried to make a toast to the team's good fortune. He was spurned.

Infuriated, and no doubt deeply hurt, he ended up in the hotel bar, where having more than a few drinks, he told a gaggle of sportswriters that "500 coaches" could coach the Cowboys and win. It soon became apparent to *Dallas Morning News* writer Rick Gosselin and others that, as ludicrous as it sounded, Johnson's days were numbered.

"When they won," Gosselin said during the Jerry Jones tribute on *A Football Life*, "there was not going to be enough credit in the room for the two egos."[14]

And there wasn't. Johnson had openly belittled Jones throughout the 1993 season, an embarrassing pregame show before the Super Bowl victory being just one example.

Fast-forward to 2019, when Jones admitted having regret over the falling-out with Johnson.

"I lost my tolerance for a lot of things," Jones said. "I probably should have had a little more tolerance with Jimmy Johnson. Seriously."

At the goodbye press conference, Johnson said that he and Jones had "mutually decided" to part ways. Bullshit. He was fired. Sure, maybe he'd gotten tired of the grind of coaching an NFL team, not to mention dealing with Jones, but anyone who knows him will tell you he would have loved to have won three in a row. No team has since Vince Lombardi and the Packers pulled it off in the 1960s.

Even without Jimmy J., the Cowboys came close. Jones shocked the football world (and Johnson) by hiring former Oklahoma Sooners coach Barry Switzer, who had been an assistant coach with the Razorbacks when Jones and Johnson played at Arkansas.

Despite years of success coaching a college team, Switzer was at best a peculiar choice, and his hello press conference did nothing to dispel the notion that Jones might have made a tremendous mistake.

His most famous sound bite, the one that made Jones blush, came when Switzer yelled at the multitude of media, "We gonna get the job done, ba-bee!"

It was also odd that Switzer would retain most of the assistants who had worked for and been hired by Jimmy Johnson. For the most part, though, the calculus worked.

The Cowboys finished with another 12–4 record and an NFC East title. They beat Favre and the Packers 35–9 in the divisional round of the playoffs and returned to San Francisco for a third straight NFC Championship Game against their archrival of the '90s, the 49ers.

From the moment it started, disaster flourished. The Cowboys fell behind 21–0 to start the game but made a late comeback and almost pulled it off. With a little more than 5 minutes left, they had a chance to pull within 38–35, and when 49ers cornerback Deion Sanders blatantly interfered with Michael Irvin in the end zone, it felt as though, by golly, they just might make it.

Inexplicably, no flag was thrown, and Switzer went ballistic. He grabbed a referee, provoking a 15-yard penalty that Aikman said after the game killed the comeback. Aikman had gone to the University of Oklahoma to play for Switzer, but when the coach instituted the wishbone offense, even after promising Aikman a passing-quarterback role at OU, the future Heisman Trophy winner transferred to UCLA. So, no, he was hardly a fan of Switzer's to begin with. Switzer's grabbing the referee laid another coat of ice on the Aikman–Switzer relationship.

There would be no three-peat, with the Niners winning, coronating Steve Young as the city's new hero. Young circled the field at Candlestick Park, conducting his own smug little victory parade, which Cowboy fans believe to this day never would have happened had Jimmy Johnson still been the coach.

The Bay Area crowd will never admit it, but they know it's true. They were damned lucky. The totally surprising, totally bizarre Jones–Johnson falling-out did as much as anything to make them Super Bowl champs.

Yes, Barry Switzer was still the coach, but the Triplets—Aikman, Irvin, and Smith—were still there, so the Cowboys had a chance.

For the third straight year, they finished the '95 season with a 12–4 record and won the NFC East. They got a break, however, when the defending champion 49ers melted down near season's end, meaning Dallas would escape Steve Young and Jerry Rice in the playoffs.

The Cowboys beat Philly in the divisional round, 30–11, and gut-punched Brett Favre and the Packers in the NFC Championship Game, 38–27—in a sold-out, wildly raucous Texas Stadium.

They headed to a then-league-record eighth Super Bowl, and despite Bill Cowher coming close to outcoaching Switzer and the Cowboys—with a surprise fourth-quarter onside kick that seized momentum for the Steelers—Cowher's team could not overcome the multiple interceptions of quarterback Neil O'Donnell, who elevated Cowboys safety Larry Brown to the unlikely status of Super Bowl MVP. (That one game allowed Brown to sign a lucrative free-agent contract with the Oakland Raiders.)

Switzer returned to form in the postgame press conference, screaming at a blushing Jones on national television: "We did it our way, ba-bee!"

The Cowboys became the League's first team to win three Super Bowls in 4 years. To this day, all five of their Super Bowl championships were won during seasons played in Clint's creation, Texas Stadium, giving it a truly unique distinction—no Cowboys championships were won in the Cotton Bowl, nor have any been won in their new home, AT&T Stadium.

To this day, Texas Stadium owns the copyright to the Cowboys' championship magic.

That's what happened *on* the field. What happened *off* the field figured heavily in the '95 season.

At the end of the '94 season, Jones believed the Cowboys' missing piece happened to have worn the red and gold of the 49ers—shutdown corner Deion Sanders.

What began was a series of major skirmishes as Jones the field general engaged in open combat, even with his own son. Acting on his own, Jerry cut a deal with free-agent Sanders that, on the surface, felt like open warfare against the League's newly instituted salary cap, which Jones had championed. Without discussing the matter with anyone else—after all, he is the owner—the elder Jones signed Sanders to a whopping 7-year, $35 million contract with a $13 million signing bonus.

Having been tasked with managing the team's salary cap, Stephen Jones freaked out.

The younger Jones reacted by grabbing his dad by the collar and shoving him against the door.

"You're really not going to hit me, are you?" a startled Jerry asked his son.

The elder Jones was right. Deion Sanders *was* the missing piece. He proved invaluable in allowing the team to win its fifth Super Bowl, albeit 26 years ago. During his first season with the Cowboys, they won the Super Bowl, whereas his old team, the NFC West champ 49ers, lost to Green Bay in the divisional round of the playoffs.

But there was more. The '95 season proved to be a seminal moment in Cowboys history, all because of Jones. He went to war in '95 and won every battle.

Chief among the year's footnotes was Jones's rise as a power broker in NFL politics.

David Moore, the Cowboys beat writer for the *Dallas Morning News*, offered details in a bit of history published in 2017. Five months after Jones bought the Cowboys in 1989, the owners convened in Chicago to replace the iconic Pete Rozelle as commissioner. No easy task. Rozelle presided over the explosive growth of the NFL, taking the job in January 1960, months before the inaugural season of the Cowboys and the Dallas Texans and the rest of the upstart American Football League. Rozelle retired in November 1989, Jones's first season as owner.

Its Old Boys Club tendency flaring again, the search committee presented only one candidate to replace Rozelle, that being New Orleans president and general manager Jim Finks. The newer owners in the League, including Jones, balked at not having a voice in the process. Philadelphia's Norman Braman, who Jones told us in our interview had become one of his closest friends, spearheaded the group. He and Jones became part of the block known as the Chicago 11. They abstained, leaving Finks three votes shy of approval.

Three months later, a new candidate emerged, Paul Tagliabue, who would not have been named commissioner had Jones and the Chicago 11 not intervened. But Jones wasn't done. He cobbled together a minority faction large enough to deny a push from NBC and CBS to extend their contracts with the NFL at a reduced rate.

As Moore writes:[15]

> The networks argue they are losing $75 million a year and can't continue beyond the expiration of the deal in 1993. Tagliabue and Cleveland's Art Modell, the chair of the broadcast committee, want to accommodate their partners. Jones kills a $238 million rebate on a two-year extension, taking roughly $8.5 million out of every owner's pocket.
>
> "You're a risk-taker, a wildcatter. We're not," one owner tells Jones. "We've got a plan to run our team. We may not be satisfied with how much, but we've got to know we have this revenue."

Tagliabue invited Jones to join the broadcast committee. The Arkansas wildcatter was on the verge of a Hail Mary that would change the NFL by hurling it in a new direction altogether. He set up a meeting with Rupert Murdoch, the Aussie-born billionaire owner of the FOX network, which needed its own Hail Mary to survive.

"I assure you I will do everything I know to do to make sure you're not a stalking horse," Jones tells Murdoch. "If you do your best to give us the best deal, we will take it, or I will holler so that everybody hears."[16]

FOX outbid CBS and the League's next TV contract jumped from $900 million to $1.1 billion—because of Jones. Compelling thought: Had Jones been unable to prevail, and Murdoch's American media empire ceased to exist, what effect would the absence of Fox News have had on America's political landscape?

The owners basked in the glow of Jones's freshly cut deal, but it didn't last long. Jones was about to provoke a new battle, one much more divisive than the television deal.

He informed the League that he would opt out of the trust agreement with NFL Properties when the deal expired during the Cowboys' Super Bowl season of 1995.

Jones launched his General Patton–like offensive on two fronts. He hoped to attain total control over the Cowboys' merchandise sales, which the League had previously controlled through its long-standing policy of revenue sharing, which, in our interview with him, Jones equated to socialism. In addition, he wanted his own sponsors, not NFL sponsors, and hoped to use Texas Stadium as the cash cow for facilitating those. Seizing control of the sale of merchandise was big but controlling sponsorships—and using the stadium as the agent of change—was much bigger. That alone represented a seismic shift in the way the League did business, elevating the role of the stadium to the colossus it is today.

Way back when the war started, David Moore wrote the following:

Jones believes that "he can better market the Cowboys brand and logo than the league. He strikes deals with Nike and Pepsi that net more than $40 million. He invites Phil Knight, the co-founder and chairman of Nike, to join him on the sidelines for a [Monday night] game against the New York Giants just a few miles from the NFL offices."[17]

What Jones was doing was what they call in football an end-around. He was selling sponsorships—not for the Cowboys but rather Texas Stadium— which became an illicit but transparent way to raise additional revenue. And ironically, Clint godfathered the concept, because it was done through the stadium and outside the scope of the League's socialistic policy of revenue sharing.

Jones shocked the League by luring corporate bigwigs to his corner. He sold one sponsorship to American Express, which became the official credit card of Texas Stadium. It was a clever way of one-upping the League and demonstrated how closely Texas Stadium was intertwined with the Cowboys' aura.

On *Monday Night Football*, Al Michaels said Jones's power play would "send shock waves throughout the NFL." Michaels was right.

The League responded by filing a $300 million lawsuit against Jones. Trying hard not to look intimidated, Jones stood his ground. But in the Jones bio in *A Football Life*, the Cowboys owner said being the defendant in a $300 million lawsuit filed by his fellow owners did make him flinch.

"It did make my eyes water," Jones said. "I knew I could lose the team."[18]

Again, the ultimate risk-taker. And in that respect, he was not at all unlike Clint Jr. and Clint Sr.

At the height of acrimony, Tagliabue invited Jones to a meeting in his Manhattan office, where the commissioner was so angry, he refused to look the Cowboys' owner in the eye. Jones exploded:

> "I have come all the way from Dallas, Texas, to meet with you and all your ass had to do was walk across the street. You have sued me. I haven't sued you. I don't even know if you've really read or any of these owners have read what you have sued me over.
>
> "But let me tell you one damn thing. You're going to read it and you're going to hear more about it."

As Moore writes: "Jones slams his fist on the table so hard it sounds like a gunshot. Papers fly everywhere as he storms out of the room and heads for the elevator."[19]

We attempted to interview Tagliabue for this book. Initially, he agreed. But as soon as he heard we might want to ask about Jones and the sponsorship issue, he responded in a way that coauthor Burk Murchison captured perfectly:

"He went dark on us."

Jones retaliated by filing a $750 million countersuit against the League.

Six weeks after leaving the New York meeting in a rage, Jones dropped his countersuit in December 1996 with the agreement that the League allow him full rights over sponsorships in Texas Stadium.

Under the old agreement, the League handled those entirely, with none of its member teams having a say. For example, the League had a soft drink deal with Coca-Cola, so each NFL stadium carried signage for Coke. The League had a separate deal with Adidas. The Jones revolution called for individual teams and stadiums to cut their own deals, giving Jones the power to snub Coke and Adidas by partnering with Pepsi and Nike and keeping their money for himself.

Jones later called the rewriting of the League's sponsorship rules "a quantum leap," one in which Texas Stadium played a decisive role.

As he told us during our interview, "Sure, every single one of the NFL owners is a capitalist. But get them in a room, and they're more socialistic than the old Soviet Union."[20]

That may be, but that is precisely how the NFL overtook Major League Baseball as America's national pastime. It is also the reason that owners have the power in the NFL, whereas players have the power in Major League Baseball. And in the latter example, capitalism reigns, which is why such teams as the New York Yankees, Los Angeles Dodgers, and Boston Red Sox enjoy a monetary clout that the Tampa Bay Rays and Milwaukee Brewers will never have.

It is true that, in Major League Baseball, Green Bay, Wisconsin, and Jacksonville, Florida, could not have a team. The Darwinian milieu that is Major League Baseball would give such a franchise no oxygen, as it barely does San Diego, Milwaukee, and Tampa.

In many ways, the "socialist," revenue-sharing method practiced unflinchingly by such men as Clint Murchison Jr., Lamar Hunt, and Pete Rozelle made the NFL what it is today—except for one thing.

One could argue in one way that Jones's early partner was Clint himself. For it was Clint who created revenue-sharing loopholes by making the stadium an entirely separate profit center, one that allowed for luxury suites, private clubs, and so on.

As he did in so many ways, Jones took the ideas introduced by the Cowboys' founder, including the stadium-is-king concept, and in the parlance of the day, put it on steroids. *Ka-ching, ka-ching.*

But in literary terms, Jones was less the writer and much more the *re*writer. Former Cowboys executive Joseph A. Bailey III, who endured as a franchise mainstay from the time he was 13 until ownership transferred from Bright to Jones, remembers that, in 1988, during the Bum era, the Cowboys fired off a confidential letter to the League, threatening to bolt from NFL Properties *and* its revenue-sharing program.

In a word, the Cowboys were frustrated, having spent heavily on promotion with little reward. They alone accounted for an outsized percentage of the sale of logo-bearing merchandise. But because of the way NFL Properties was configured, the Cowboys' pro rata participation in collective profit was not one penny more than any other team. With the letter, the Cowboys hoped to set off alarm bells among so-called free rider teams, who spent next to nothing on promotion. In the end, the Cowboys remained committed to the NFL's revenue-sharing ethos and took no further action. Until, that is, Jerry Jones bought the team in 1989.

The attack on the League's revenue-sharing foundation didn't start with Jones, but he gave it teeth and commandeered it in a way that no one before him ever dared. Given that Jones prevailed, it would also mark a turning point in the way the League regarded what we will call *franchise movement*. When Raiders owner Al Davis attempted to move his insanely popular franchise from Oakland to Los Angeles in 1980, the League wasted no time in blocking him with a court injunction. He countered with an antitrust suit against the NFL. In 1982, a federal district court—in Los Angeles, no less—ruled in Davis's favor, and the Raiders relocated to LA for the '82 season. And there they remained until 1994, when they returned to Oakland. And *there* they remained, until they moved to Las Vegas to inhabit their own twenty-first-century dream home, $1.9 billion Allegiant Stadium.

It's instructive to go to YouTube and listen to Pete Rozelle talk about Davis violating a sacred trust by wanting to abandon a loyal fan base in Oakland to move to a new city for one reason only: greed. The 1987 movie *Wall Street* seized the moment by exposing the virus running rampant in America in the form of Gordon Gekko, played masterfully in an Oscar-winning performance by Michael Douglas, whose motto was, "Greed is good."

Rozelle's successor, Paul Tagliabue—Jones's archenemy when it came to the sponsorship issue—was also the archenemy of franchise movement. Indeed, Tagliabue is the only reason the Saints still make New Orleans their home. Shortly before the start of the 2005 season, New Orleans was ravaged by Hurricane Katrina, which destroyed the city's levee system and inflicted $81 billion in property damage. It's estimated that the total economic impact in Louisiana and Mississippi may exceed $150 billion, making it the costliest hurricane in American history.

So how did Saints owner at the time, Tom Benson, respond to Katrina? He wanted to abandon New Orleans and move to San Antonio, where he lived. Tagliabue wasted no time in persuading NFL owners to chip in the first $15 million of a $184 million capital campaign to restore the Superdome. The rest came from FEMA ($115 million) and the state of Louisiana ($13 million) and the selling of bonds ($41 million).

So, when the Saints won the Super Bowl in 2010, quarterback Drew Brees and head coach Sean Payton were enshrined as forever saints in the city of

New Orleans. But the real credit goes to Tagliabue, who we've thought about a lot lately. When it comes to franchise movement, the prevailing lust in the NFL is a whole lot closer to Gordon Gekko than it is to Paul Tagliabue or Pete Rozelle. Largely because of Jones, The Stadium is the new god, and if landing your dream home means franchise movement, well, so be it. As the Raiders proved once again by screwing a loyal fan base, just as the Chargers did in leaving San Diego—their home since 1961—for the endless temptation of Los Angeles.

The irony of this, of course, is that one day, Jones may encounter a reality that is best summed up in a phrase by William Shakespeare and be "hoisted by his own petard." Tom Benson came within inches of moving his team to San Antonio, where the Dallas Cowboys have long been sacrosanct. Had Tagliabue not successfully intervened, could Benson have moved the Saints to San Antonio? Of course. Davis and the Raiders proved that long ago. American businesses move from one city to another all the time.

Just before the start of the 2021 season, the Buffalo Bills emerged as the latest team to trot out the threat of leaving to get what they want—a new stadium. And like so many teams, in a sport dominated by billionaires, they too are demanding that the taxpayers of Buffalo be the ones to pay for it. And *where* did they threaten to move should they not get what they want? Austin, Texas, where money, *so* much money, fueled by high-tech billionaires, now flows as freely as water.

As it turns out, Austin appears to have been no more than a threat. In March 2022, the *New York Post* reported that the "billionaire owner of the Buffalo Bills appears poised to get a record amount of public funding for a new stadium in what critics are calling an unprecedented giveaway. Gov. Kathy Hochul—a Buffalo native—is expected to announce in the next several days a deal in which New York State and Erie County agree to pay nearly $1 billion toward a new $1.4 billion stadium that will be located next to the current one, sources close to the situation told *The Post*. That would be the most public money ever spent on building a US stadium, University of Michigan sports management professor Mark Rosentraub told *The Post*."[21]

So, there you have it. But play along for just a moment. Let's say the Bills were actually serious about moving to Austin or any other city willing to build them what we call a Frankenstadium.

How *would* Jones respond to that? He would, of course, be unmoored by the prospect, but if the Bills had been serious about moving to Austin, what, if anything, could he do about it?

Nothing, absolutely nothing, as Al Davis—whom Jones once described as his role model for how to run a franchise—proved in the Gordon Gekko era of the 1980s. Had the Bills done that and actually moved to Austin, only one phrase would some it up: *karma's a bitch*. And to understand how that is so, let us return to the war between Jones and Tagliabue, which, of course, Jones won with a knockout punch reminiscent of a heavyweight champ.

But was it a victory whose final chapter had yet to be written?

When it came to the stadium/sponsorship war, Jones emerged the winner, but at the time, Tagliabue sounded a cautionary note that rings frighteningly true today.

"This attack on NFL Properties"—and as a result, the very concept of NFL revenue sharing—"is part of the pressure of getting teams to move," the commissioner once said in a television interview. "If everyone is going to do their own marketing, then everyone is going to try to move to the best market."[22]

Wow. Tagliabue was so prophetic. He said this in 1995, more than 20 years before the Chargers left a super-loyal fan base in San Diego to play three seasons (2017 through 2019) in a 27,000-seat soccer stadium that rarely sold out. It's why the Raiders abandoned the world's most committed fan base in Oakland for the devilish charms of Las Vegas and the $1.9 billion Allegiant Stadium that lured them there.

Of course, what none of them counted on was a global pandemic that would neuter the stadium's role in the woebegone season of 2020. So much for the NFL's Gordon Gekko "greed is good" mentality when trapped in the coven of COVID-19. When it came to 2020, owners were staring hard at a fiscally grim season when all they would have was the $3 billion in television money. No small sum, but think about no tickets, no concessions, no parking, no suite revenue, and no on-site souvenir sales. Jones AT&T Stadium has a Victoria's Secret store, but in 2020, the secret was out—the owners were on the verge of losing their collective shirts. And it won't be good for the players. Even before the troubled launch of the 2020 season, there were mounting signs that the salary cap would have to be drastically cut back—not increased, as the players thought it would be.

Marc Ganis, cofounder of the Chicago-based consulting group Sportscorp and a confidante of many NFL owners, estimates that, during the 2020 season, revenues shrank by $100 million for each of the League's thirty-two teams, adding up to almost $4 billion in losses.

But never underestimate the power of the NFL—or its bus driver, Jerry Jones—to weave gold from straw. Before the 2021 season, the NFL announced a new 11-year television deal, which, according to the Associated Press, will give its owners a collective $113 billion in profit. The owners also added a seventeenth regular season game, adding even more profit. As *Forbes* reported in May 2021, Jones led the parade when it came to survivors:

"The pandemic has caused a world of chaos for the sports industry, but billionaire owners are thriving, with the average value of the world's top teams jumping 9.9%, to $3.4 billion."[23]

But let us go back to the pre-COVID world of Paul Tagliabue, who during his era had every reason to be concerned. What Tagliabue most feared was the escalating belief that the stadium was everything—a doctrine Jones accelerated, because he, for one, rightfully concluded that that's where the money is. Jones managed to accomplish the truly remarkable: he teleported himself from the doghouse (or maybe the outhouse) to the NFL's monetary throne. He became its treasurer, the printer of its currency. Why else would his fellow owners go from suing him for $300 million in 1995—essentially, wanting to get rid of him as fast as they could—to enshrining him in 2017 in the Pro Football Hall of Fame? Again, let us quote Watergate's Deep Throat ("Follow the money") and broadcasting great Don Ohlmeyer ("The answer to all your questions is money").

Which brings us back to the inspiration for *Hole in the Roof*, Clint Murchison Jr.

Clint owned the Cowboys in a radically different era, when advances in television technology were making it far too tempting for anyone to risk driving to a tired old stadium in a depressed urban era, à la the Cotton Bowl. As per his comment to Blackie Sherrod, he had the vision to see that televisions would one day be as big as movie screens, occupying entire walls and offering sound that made it feel as though you were *in* the stadium when, of course, you were not. Absent an upgrade in comfort and elegance to the stadium itself, Clint feared that he and his fellow owners would be forced to surrender to television—even while taking in outrageously high rights fees. What he feared most of all was that the NFL would become a studio game, which seers such as Gary Cartwright predicted would eventually happen anyway.

Which is why, until the early 1970s, the NFL blacked out *all* home games—including playoff games—without granting a single exception. Clint strongly believed that stadiums had to undergo a radical transformation to have even a prayer of competing with a color television in the comfort of a clean, safe, spacious living room, where fans could enjoy good food and even alcohol (which Clint was not allowed to sell in the Cotton Bowl or for that matter Texas Stadium, unless they drank it in a private club). No place like home—but in Clint's era, it became an even starker reality and the primary stumbling block to luring tens of thousands to the ballpark. What he never envisioned, in our opinion, was The Stadium becoming gasoline to the fire of an out-of-control greed machine. In other words, a Frankenstadium.

Tagliabue, we believe, was trying to put the brakes on a trend that worried him. He saw the rise of the Frankenstadium long before most.

Hurricane Katrina devastated the city of New Orleans in 2005, when the Saints were already making noise about wanting to flee. Tagliabue stopped them, and in the aftermath, the Saints became the balm for New Orleans's wounded soul. Absent Tagliabue's intervention, they might be the San Antonio Saints. (Curiously, Tagliabue's last season as commissioner was that year—2005—after which current NFL commissioner Roger Goodell took over.)

San Diego and Oakland had no such savior. They abandoned incredibly loyal fan bases for the promise of stadium riches elsewhere.

Cowboys executive Rich Dalrymple, who until 2022 served as Jones's top public-relations guy, was also interviewed for the Jones bio on *A Football Life*.

"When Jerry bought the Cowboys," Dalrymple said, "he had to buy the lease to operate Texas Stadium, and in doing so, a lot of other owners laughed at him. They said, 'This guy wants in the league so bad, he's dumb enough to buy the stadium too.'"[24]

In other words, Dalrymple said, Jones's NFL partners believed that stadiums and stadium management were "a financial ball and chain."

But not Jones, who was multiple steps ahead. Jones, in Dalrymple's words, "wanted to make Texas Stadium a viable place for people to come 365 days a year. In order to do that, he had to sell these sponsorships for the stadium that ultimately led the other owners to say, 'I need to get in the stadium business.'"[25]

In the end, what effect did Jones's sponsorship power play have on the business of the Cowboys and for that matter the League as a whole?

As he told us in our interview, "It increased the scope of our revenues tremendously."

Which is why Jones ended up in the Hall of Fame, a destination that once seemed impossible. Laughably so.

As Randy Galloway said, "Jerry was totally right. He turned millionaires into billionaires."[26]

Jerry Jones's reputation as a money maker is unrivaled. He may be an Arkie, but he's an Arkie with a Midas touch.

When it comes to football, however, Jones's success falls short, beginning with the '95 season. It's the bane of his existence as an NFL owner, despite his once admonishing a listener on a call-in segment on Dallas's all-sports radio station, the Ticket, snapping at him angrily: "I hope you enjoyed those three Super Bowls!"[27] Jones barking at the fan became what's known in the world of radio as a "drop," one the Ticket has played over and over and over. (By the way, as far as we know, that was the end of Jones appearing on call-in shows.)

Yes, we enjoyed those three, but Cowboys fans are spoiled, and 26 years is a long time to wait for an NFC Championship Game, much less a Super Bowl.

Indeed, the drought that continues unabated began in '96, barely 3 years into Bill Clinton's presidency.

With Switzer hanging on as coach, the team finished with a 10–6 record and won the NFC East. The Cowboys won their opening round playoff game, beating Minnesota, 40–15. Incredibly, it remained their *only* playoff victory until 2009, the year Cowboys Stadium opened in Arlington.

The next week, they traveled to Charlotte, North Carolina, to face humiliation from the Carolina Panthers, 26–17.

The absence of Jimmy Johnson's firm hand soon became painfully obvious, upsetting Aikman as much as anyone. Michael Irvin was suspended for the first five games of the '96 season, after being indicted on second-degree felony charges of cocaine possession and misdemeanor marijuana charges.

As Todd Archer wrote in 2007 in the *Dallas Morning News*, on the eve of Irvin being inducted into the Pro Football Hall of Fame: "With Irvin, Aikman, and Emmitt Smith making up the famed Triplets, the Cowboys won three Super Bowls from 1992 to '95, but then off-field problems littered Irvin's life. He pleaded no contest in 1996 to felony cocaine possession. He was fined and put on probation for four years and had to perform 800 hours of community service."[28]

Even so, the Irvin circus continued. Before the playoffs, he and offensive lineman Erik Williams were accused of sexual assault—an accusation that was later proven false. For the Cowboys, the damage was already done.

When the 1997 season opened, Switzer was still the coach. But the team finished 6–10 and did not make the playoffs.

When the 1998 season opened, Chan Gailey was head coach. He led the Cowboys to a 10–6 record and an NFC East title, but with Aikman saying he was "not comfortable" in Gailey's system, well, you won't last long. The Cowboys lost yet another opening round playoff game, 20–7, to the Cardinals.

But the 1998 season was memorable for another reason. Even with his team struggling on the field, courting mediocrity with each new snap, Jerry Jones somehow found the power to print more money.

In November of the '98 season, the Cowboys invited coauthor Michael Granberry to come and check out Jones's newest creation—the top-of-the-line Platinum Suite, whose 10-year leases, Jones told Granberry, would each contribute $2 million to the Cowboys' till. That's $200,000 paid out annually over a decade. In Jones's view, Texas Stadium's Platinum Suites were not just the best in the NFL; they were the best in any stadium anywhere, regardless of the sport being played.

By 1998, Jones had proven that skyboxes were gleaming necessities in the world of sports, especially with the skyrocketing cost of players' salaries. On the home front, the Dallas Mavericks of the National Basketball Association and the Dallas Stars of the National Hockey League were planning to abandon Reunion Arena, which opened in 1980, without a single luxury suite, and had thus become a modern-day liability in the world of professional sports.

When Texas Stadium opened in 1971, it had separate press boxes on each side of the field, one for print media, the other for electronic media. To get the space needed to build his Platinum Suites, Jones closed one of the press boxes, merging it with the one on the other side of the field. His reasoning? Why do we need two press boxes? He then used the space to build the Platinum Suites.

The annual $200,000 rental fee gave Platinum owners twenty tickets to each home game, with the option of buying an additional ten.

More than any of the 400 other suites circling the stadium, the Platinum Suites offered the whole enchilada—two rows of seats with reclining chairs; their own restrooms; their own heating and air-conditioning systems; a sofa; a full bar staffed with a bartender and a server; and six television monitors used to keep track of other games while the Cowboys provided the live action below. There was even a VCR for the kiddies to watch videos.

It was a lush, plush, one-of-a-kind experience, but the best thing about it, said Dr Pepper CEO Jim Turner, whose company leased a Platinum suite, was the rarefied atmosphere it created for entertaining clients and friends, even public officials.

"Some of our lease-holders tell me they do as much as $10 million a year in new business up in these suites," George Hays, then the Cowboys' vice president of marketing, told coauthor Michael Granberry in an interview with the *Dallas Morning News* in 1998. "Where else can you get the CEO of Haggar or GTE to sit down and visit for four hours and feel comfortable the entire time?" Hays, a longtime friend and confidante of Jerry Jones, retired from the Cowboys in 2004. He died in 2014.

Despite being a major source of income, the Platinums constituted less than one-forty-fourth of Texas Stadium's skybox inventory. The rest of the lineup included 178 of the original Circle suites; 114 on the Crown I level that circled the upper deck; and 90 more on the Crown II level just below the Crown I level.

The best deal going was still Circle Suites I and II—established by Clint. When Texas Stadium opened, all Circle Suite I and II owners were required to lay down a $50,000 payment, to purchase two hundred $250 bonds, which gave them control of the suites through 2008. When the terms of this 38-year lease expired in 2008, the Cowboys were required to return to each owner of Circle Suites I and II their original $50,000 investment, plus an additional $10,000 in interest.

Since Clint's days as Cowboys' owner, Texas Stadium's skybox population had doubled. In 1985, Bum Bright built the 114 Crown I suites that lapped the entire upper deck. Jones did him one better in 1993 by adding Crown II, which added 90 more—are your ears popping yet?—a full tier lower.

Fans hoping to sit in a skybox could lease individual suites, ranging from $3,500 to $15,000 a game. Or they could lease suites annually at Texas Stadium, paying anywhere from $35,000 to $200,000 a season.

Since moving to the new stadium in Arlington, the costs have become even more astronomical.

Chan Gailey continued as head coach for the 1999 season, but the Cowboys finished 8–8 and lost a wild card playoff game to Minnesota. The ugliest moment came in a game at Philadelphia, where Michael Irvin sustained a cervical spine injury that forced his retirement and for a few tense moments made it look as though paralysis might be inevitable. Predictably, Eagles fans booed Irvin as he lay on the field, unable to move.

As it was, Irvin became the first of the Triplets to retire, with more to come.

The drought dug in deeper with the 2000 season, when former defensive backs coach Dave Campo took over as coach. The Cowboys finished 5–11, in fourth place with no playoff berth. The team's biggest departure was Troy Aikman, who, fearing ongoing concussions, chose to retire.

Only Emmitt Smith remained from the Triplets.

Campo returned for 2001, finishing with an encore 5–11 record and a fifth-place finish in the NFC East.

"Five-11" Campo came back again in 2002, finishing with his third straight 5–11 and another fourth-place finish.

But here's the thing about Texas Stadium and its remarkable history. As bleak as the team's chances often looked, Clint's Xanadu had the power to create yet another historical milestone. It came in 2002, when Emmitt Smith broke Walter Payton's record for career rushing yards. Smith finished his career with 18,355 yards, a record he still holds. The 2002 season was his Cowboys finale. With the rebuilding Cowboys opting for youth, Smith signed with the Arizona Cardinals, with whom he spent the 2003 and 2004 seasons, with little left in the tank.

Time for Tuna!

Randy Galloway and other outspoken Cowboys' critics said the only reason Jones hired Bill Parcells in 2003—and gave him full authority—was in line with a mission to have taxpayers help fund a new stadium. It was all part of a massive lobbying campaign, and if it meant giving up control of the team, at least for a while, so be it. (It certainly hasn't happened since.)

Whatever, it provided much-needed oomph to a stagnant franchise, which had languished through three miserable seasons with Campo as coach, the only bright spot coming with Emmitt Smith breaking Walter Payton's record and ensuring the reputation of Texas Stadium as a place where big things happened.

In his inaugural season, Parcells guided the Cowboys to a 10–6 record *and* a playoff berth. Even so, they lost to Carolina in the wild card round, 29–10.

The next year, back to mediocrity. During Parcells's second season, the Cowboys finished 6–10, with no playoff berth.

It was more of the same in 2005, when Parcells took them to a 9–7 record but no playoff berth.

With the end of its Texas Stadium days inching ever closer, the Cowboys under Parcells finished with a 9–7 record in 2006 and a wild card berth.

A new development made week 7 fascinating. An undrafted free agent named Tony Romo replaced Drew Bledsoe at quarterback and remained on the Cowboys' roster until his retirement at the end of the 2016 season. The first major chasm showed up, however, in the Jones–Parcells relationship when Jones got his way by getting Parcells to agree, reluctantly, to the signing of flamingly controversial wide receiver Terrell Owens. The team's new narcissist-in-residence had once deeply angered Cowboys fans, during his days with the 49ers, by rushing to the star in the center of the field at Texas Stadium. Cowboys safety George Teague took a swing at him, which remains a staple on YouTube.

There was not a shred of evidence that Parcells really wanted "the player," as he called Owens, that it was all Jones, à la the acquisition of Deion Sanders that almost got Jones punched out by his own son. But Owens was there, and Romo was his quarterback. The two did help land the Cowboys into a playoff game, albeit one that became the first entry in the oh-no-Romo playbook.

During 2006, Romo held for extra points. So, there the Cowboys were, on the verge of a wild card playoff victory at Seattle, needing only a chip-shot field goal for a victory. As fate would have it, Romo fumbled the snap, and with his miscue, Parcells's dreams as a Cowboys miracle worker rapidly disintegrated.

Which wasn't the only sad chapter in the wake of Romo's fumbled snap. In March 2007, Cowboys fans mourned the death of Wilford Jones, better known as "Crazy Ray," the team's unofficial but beloved mascot whose appeal crossed generations. Crazy Ray had attended almost every home game since the team's Cotton Bowl days but became a fixture at Texas Stadium, endearing sold-out crowds with a showman's mix of blue-and-white western attire, eye-popping magic tricks, and a piercingly high-pitched whistle. And, of course, he somehow did it all by galloping through the stands on a hobby horse. He could also rally a crowd better than anyone we've ever seen.

And then, more bad news.

Whatever his reasons, Parcells hung it up after the 2006 season, its primary highlight or lowlight being Romo's fumbled snap. Defensive ace and homespun Texan Wade Phillips became the Cowboys' new coach.

The Cowboys finished with a 13–3 record, one of the best in their history, and an NFC East title. They snared a first-round bye and home field advantage throughout the playoffs.

For the first time since 1995, it looked like they might have a Super Bowl contender.

But not so fast. Playing at Texas Stadium, the Cowboys lost 21–17 to the New York Giants, whom they easily could have beaten.

As for the Giants, they went on to upset the New England Patriots in the Super Bowl.

During 2008, the Cowboys reverted to mediocrity. They finished with a 9–7 record but no playoff berth.

The 2008 season was made even sadder, since the team's mediocrity was no way to say goodbye to Texas Stadium.

The final game at Clint's Xanadu happened on December 20, 2008, with the Cowboys losing to the Baltimore Ravens, 33–24.

The team's on-the-field moments at Texas Stadium ended not with a bang but a whimper. A week later, the Cowboys blew their 2008 playoff chances by losing to the Eagles in Philadelphia, 44–6. The most noteworthy thing about this game came years later, when movie director David O. Russell focused on the game as a seminal plot point in his Oscar-winning movie *Silver Linings Playbook*. It was yet another example of the Cowboys playing the villains in a Hollywood story that featured another team—the Eagles—as the heroes.

So, the authors of this book don't want to pass up the opportunity of getting something off our chests. Literally every depiction of the Cowboys in Hollywood movies and television shows is negative, and in the words of the immortal Howard Beale in the Oscar-winning movie *Network*, "We're mad as hell, and we're not gonna take it anymore!"

Geez, it even happens in kids' movies. In *Little Giants*, released in 1994, the team wearing blue stars on their metallic blue helmets—yep, "the Cowboys"—are, of course, the villains. It happened again in 2021, during the season finale for the brilliant television series, *This Is Us*. The family at the center of the show hails from Pittsburgh, so, of course, the Steelers are depicted in terms bordering on the saintly. But in the final episode of season 5, Beth Pearson is consoling her daughter Tess before a big family wedding. Tess doesn't like the dress the bride and groom want her to wear. So, Mama Beth is attempting to assure her reluctant daughter that her feelings are, well, perfectly okay.

"You cannot disappoint me," says Tess's mom. "I need you to understand that. You could wear shorts to this wedding, okay? You could root for the Dallas Cowboys. You could *murder* somebody. I'd be surprised. I'd probably ask a couple questions, but I'd assume you had your reasons."[29]

So, there you have it—an Emmy- and Golden Globe–winning television show has equated rooting for the Dallas Cowboys with murder! Such hostility has its roots, of course, and we contend it all got started during the "city of hate" era in the wake of the Kennedy assassination.

And then it became amplified when, beginning in 1966, three years after JFK's death, the Cowboys rolled off twenty consecutive winning seasons, almost entirely under the stewardship of Clint Murchison Jr. By early 1996, the Cowboys had racked up five Lombardi trophies as the winners of *five* Super Bowl championships. Only the Steelers and New England Patriots have won more (six each).

So, if the Cowboys spent years making mincemeat of your team, well, of course you won't like them. But for a franchise that hasn't sniffed an NFC Championship Game, much less a Super Bowl, in 26 years, why on earth would the Cowboys be threatening to anybody? Granted, a lot of people around the country, even the world, *love* the Cowboys.

But when it comes to Hollywood, they remain slow-moving targets. Everybody's favorite Big D punching bag.

CHAPTER FIFTEEN

No Dice for Dallas

T HE COWBOYS CARRIED their own *Silver Linings Playbook* into 2009, which will forever be remembered as a landmark season in the team's more-than-60-year history. This *Silver Linings Playbook* consisted entirely of the Cowboys heading to the most colossal stadium ever built—at least until 2020, when the Rams christened an even-splashier $5 billion home.

We say "silver linings" because the Cowboys' on-the-field product was as pedestrian as ever.

In April 2009, the Cowboys entered the NFL draft without a first- or second-round choice. Not drafting until the third round, the Cowboys picked a dozen players, who turned out to be their own corollary to the 1975 Dirty Dozen. This was a Dirty Dozen of mediocrity, an utterly forgettable draft that did not bode well for future seasons. Not a single player in this Dirty Dozen cracked the starting lineup, and most were waived before the 2010 season.

And it soon got even worse. On May 2, 2009, during a rookie mini-camp, the Cowboys' air-supported roof practice field (a tentlike structure) collapsed during a fierce Texas thunderstorm. Around seventy people were stuck inside, and twelve were injured, one gravely. Scouting assistant Rich Behm was left paralyzed from the waist down after his spine was severed. The Cowboys' special teams coach fractured one of his cervical vertebrae, and the team's assistant athletic trainer sustained a fracture to the tibia and fibula in his right leg. The tented practice facility was destroyed and never rebuilt.

The Cowboys opened the 2009 season in the team's obscenely lavish new home, then called Cowboys Stadium, as the season opener for *Sunday Night Football*. With a stadium capacity of 100,000, a figure that Jerry Jones had long fantasized about, even hinting at one point that he wanted to expand Texas Stadium to that magical number, the Cowboys packed in every small and large body they could find. The announced total: 105,121, which remains the largest crowd ever to attend an NFL game. Even then, the Cowboys succumbed to the New York Giants, 33–31.

Once again, Wade Phillips was the Cowboys' coach, and once again, he steered them to the playoffs. They finished 11–5 and won the NFC East. They won a wild card game, beating the Philadelphia Eagles, 34–14. But once again, they lost in the divisional round, falling to the Minnesota Vikings, 34–14.

And then came the destruction of Texas Stadium.

At the end of the day, Clint's dream lay in ashes.

Just after 7:00 a.m. on Sunday, April 11, 2010, thirty-eight-year-old Texas Stadium fell to the ground, blown apart by 2,715 pounds of dynamite, whose smoky rubble left four million pounds of concrete and two million pounds of steel and a mushroom cloud of collective memory. Three concrete buttresses remained, seemingly oblivious to the destruction around them. They simply wouldn't fall.

Bruce Hardy, the stadium's general manager since 1984, joked with Cowboys owner Jerry Jones that the buttresses symbolized the three Super Bowls the team won between 1993 and 1996. Others saw the buttresses as having created a spooky triad symbolizing the "Triplets" of that era, quarterback Troy Aikman, running back Emmitt Smith, and wide receiver Michael Irvin, all future members of the Pro Football Hall of Fame.

But those who knew the real history of the House that Clint Built believed the buttresses could symbolize only one thing. They served as a lasting reminder of the men who built the Cowboys—Clint Murchison Jr., general manager Tex Schramm, and coach Tom Landry. Their collaboration had built America's Team, making both the team and the stadium national icons.

The estimated 100,000 who gathered for the "official" attack on Texas Stadium nearly 9 years after 9/11 were far more adoring than the Saudi terrorist who had asked a federal official eerily pointed questions about "the hole in the roof."

Bands played, fireworks crackled in the overcast sky, and coated dignitaries gathered under a VIP tent on a bluff overlooking the site on a wistful, 60-degree morning.

"This ain't a sleeping night!" roared Norma Bowers of Garland, telling reporters she had arrived at 8:00 p.m. Saturday to snag a front-row spot near State Highway 183.

Fans paid $25 to watch the demolition from the stadium's Red Lot, which didn't open until 1:30 a.m. Irving police had to shoo away folks who started showing up at 9:00 the night before.

"The southern access road along Highway 183 looked like a shanty camp," wrote Brandon Formby in the *Dallas Morning News*. "Parking lots were packed with people camped out in tents, in lawn chairs, or asleep on car hoods. Amateur photographers had set up tripods on the dusty roadside, while drunks and large families weaved between them and the crawling traffic."[1]

Charter buses by the dozen unloaded passengers, only a few being sober. The night before, a 22-year-old named Andy Swearingen squeezed six friends from his Carrollton high school into his Toyota 4Runner ("Six in the front and one in the trunk," he bragged) and staked out a parking space across from the stadium, the *Dallas Morning News* reported. They were still drinking by 5:00 a.m.

Dozens tried to enter the middle of the main lanes of Loop 12 and State Highway 183 but were chased off by officers, who drove by and screamed, "Get out of the road! This is not rocket science!"

Ironies were as omnipresent as Cowboys folklore. The Reverend Billy Graham had opened the stadium in 1971 with a 10-day crusade. Graham's faithful included his fellow fundamentalist, Coach Landry. Fans had long joked that the hole in the Texas Stadium roof was put there so that God could watch his favorite team. So, it seemed strangely fitting that the person charged with pulling the trigger that would set off the fatal blast was an 11-year-old sixth grader, a former orphan, no less, the son of a preacher man from nearby Terrell. For the privilege of pushing the button that would bring down a stadium and erase nearly 40 years of memories, the kid had won a national contest sponsored by Kraft Macaroni & Cheese. It goes without saying that it helped immensely that the kid was a Cowboys fan and not (gasp) a Redskins or Eagles fan.

Casey Rogers had won the push-the-button contest by writing movingly about having founded Casey's Heart, a charity that provides food and clothing to Dallas's homeless once a month. A former foster child, Casey professed having a soft spot in his heart for the people who tumble through society's cracks, since he himself came close to being one.

Three years before he blew up the stadium, Casey and his dad, Reverend Russell Rogers, were eating at Burger King in downtown Dallas. A homeless man approached the elder Rogers, who shooed him away. Casey asked why. His dad told him the man wanted money but most likely would not be spending it on what he really needed. Casey felt an immediate empathy. He had been a foster child who went to live with Rogers and his wife, Shelly, soon after his birth. The couple legally adopted Casey when he was a year old.

"I was just like, look how great y'all helped me," Casey told the *Morning News*. "Why don't I help them?"[2]

Casey took to feeding the homeless in downtown parking lots and, whenever he could, reading to them—from the Bible. That led to the birth of Casey's Heart, which has helped the homeless ever since. The charity is now a ministry of Trinity Life Baptist Church of Garland, where Russell Rogers remains senior pastor.

During one of his many collection runs, a Casey's Heart donor told the boy about the Kraft contest to blow up Texas Stadium. More than 1,000 kids entered.

One of Casey's fondest memories was being a 6-year-old member of the Rowlett Eagles flag football team. He, like thousands of Texas school kids, had played on the same field as the Cowboys' greatest players.

"I was like, 'I'm standing where Roger Staubach was,'" Casey said.[3]

Emceeing Casey's big moment was ESPN's Chris Berman, who said of the stadium, "There was magic right away." He wasn't kidding. When the Cowboys played their first game in Irving in 1971, Duane Thomas ran for a 56-yard touchdown, the stadium's first.

But now, there was Casey, wiping it all away, with the push of a button. He pushed it, and moments later, the blast began.

There was a pause, however, before the implosion started, allowing Irving mayor Herbert Gears to feel strangely hopeful.

"You thought maybe for a minute that it would survive the attack from the dynamite," said Gears, who had managed to pay for the $7 million demolition by negotiating a nineteen-point transition agreement with Cowboys' owner Jones that must have felt at times like reaching peace in Vietnam.

Gears had pulled off another coup by getting the Texas Department of Transportation to pay, in advance, the sum of $15.4 million. That gave Tx-DOT the right to convert the former stadium site into a staging ground for highway reconstruction. Gears even struck a deal to have 95 percent of the stadium debris recycled into surrounding highway projects—more money for Irving.

Gears lived up to his name. He had spent years working tirelessly to keep the Cowboys at Texas Stadium—in a renovated home. Recalcitrant council members and previous mayors made the task impossible. The problem, Gears said, was that "a whole bunch of 'em just flat-out didn't like" Jones, who, at one point, Gears believes wanted nothing more than to stay in Irving.[4]

Jones was so unpopular, Gears said, that his name frequently appeared in political surveys circulated in Irving.

"Jerry would usually finish just a couple of points higher than Osama bin Laden," Gears said with a laugh. "So, really, I was kind of in a no-win position."[5]

Gears was so intrigued by Jones as a personality after years of dealing with him that he listed *King of the Cowboys*, a critical biography of Jones written by Jim Dent, as one of his three favorite books. *Black Beauty* was another. On the day we interviewed Gears, he couldn't remember the third.

And then much later, when we were fact-checking *Hole in the Roof*, Gears listed his third favorite as *Illusions: The Adventures of a Reluctant Messiah*, by Richard Bach.

"They were not necessarily my three *favorite* books," he said. "I would have to say they were my only three—the only three I've ever read. Guess you can tell I'm not exactly an avid reader of books."[6]

Gears can play the hayseed all he wants, but the truth is, nobody understood the machinations of the Cowboys' search for a new stadium better than he did.

He knew by Demolition Day that Dallas County had truly blown it. Dallas *County* was to blame, he said, for the stadium ending up *outside* Dallas County, which omitted both Dallas and Irving from further consideration by Jones.

On Demolition Day, all Gears could do was watch, fantasizing about a Might Have Been but realizing, yet again, what a huge role politics plays in almost everything in contemporary American society.

Soon, the concrete-and-steel monolith of Texas Stadium began a slow, sad crumble, rattling its surroundings and creating aftershocks as far away as Farmers Branch and East Dallas. (There was no small irony in this either, since as late as 2015, the stadium site would serve as the epicenter of dozens of earthquakes, which scientists blamed on oil companies drilling for natural gas deposits, in the practice known as *fracking*. Cowboys fans preferred to think that the quakes represented a form of Clint's revenge for his beloved stadium being blown to bits.)

Moments after doing the deed, Casey turned to his dad and yelled, "I did it! It's not there anymore."

For Bruce Hardy, it felt like a funeral, as it did for thousands of people watching on television and nearby hills.

"The roof started to fall on where my office was," Hardy said, "and then my heart went to my feet."[7]

As his own keepsake, Hardy kept all the keys used to open doors at Texas Stadium.

Jerry Jones had already moved the Cowboys to their incredible new venue, Cowboys Stadium, but he, too, felt moved by the sight of Texas Stadium imploding. Hardy said he was surprised, even shocked, when a tear-stained Jones kissed him on the forehead as the stadium disappeared.

"It was emotional, more so than you thought it would be," a solemn Jones told the press as he walked to his car. "When that roof started coming down, it was sad. That's about all you can say."[8]

Well, actually, there is more to say about the demolition of Clint's baby and America's Team ending up even farther away from Dallas than Irving. As Gavin Stevens said in William Faulkner's 1948 novel, *Intruder in the Dust*, "The past is never dead. It's not even past."

What the demolition symbolized to us—what's worth inspecting in the detritus of the rubble—is what Jones left behind.

And like an archaeologist probing the detritus, Herbert Gears grasped the meaning of "the dig" as well as anyone. Gears offers telling insight into why Jones's super stadium failed to end up in Dallas, noting first that the wrong person had been cast as the villain for Dallas saying no to the Cowboys a *second* time. That would be former Dallas mayor Laura Miller, who sports talk-show host Randy Galloway used to call "Madam No" for her perceived role in forcing Jones and the Cowboys to look elsewhere. Galloway's "Madam No" description came about in large part for her vocal opposition to American Airlines Center and then-mayor Ron Kirk using public funds to pay for it. The Cowboys seeking a new home—in Dallas—served as a sequel, and many assumed Miller, as the city's new mayor, would never be in favor of laying down a welcome mat for Jerry Jones. But, Gears says, it's actually a lot more complicated.

We tried to interview Miller for *Hole in the Roof*, but she declined our requests. Whatever role she played or didn't play in the Cowboys' quest for a new stadium is obviously a sore point. In either event, she took a public relations bashing, which Gears says was undeserved.

As Irving mayor in the early 2000s, Gears was no stranger to dealing with Jones, and their primary point of contention was the nineteen-point transition agreement that needed to be completed before the Cowboys' lease at Texas Stadium expired in 2008. In the end, those nineteen negotiated points added up to a carefully wrought agreement that gave Gears the $7 million that he and the city of Irving needed to blow up Texas Stadium. It should be noted that, once he decided to leave Irving, Jones wanted the stadium demolished, fearing it might pose potential competition to his lavish behemoth in Arlington.

But before any of that could happen, Jones had to sign his name to a laundry list of other conditions.

"We discussed—argued—about each of those 19 points," Gears says.[9] He remembers Jones bringing to each meeting supporting documents that addressed in detail each of the nineteen bullet points he and the mayor needed to work out. Jones was prepared—but so was Gears.

"At every single meeting, Jerry said, 'I will *not* paint the roof,'" Gears remembers with a laugh.[10] But Gears knew all along that, for Jones to win the point about demolishing Texas Stadium, the city of Irving was going to get its way on what *it* wanted, just as an earlier generation of Irving officials had taken a pound of flesh from Clint.

It was going to cost an estimated $800,000 to paint the roof, which, at the time, looked ghastly to anyone passing by on neighboring roads—on the teardrop property Clint Jr. had bought with his own money and flipped to the city of Irving, which gave Murchison back his original investment of $3.2 million.

Even so, Jones hated the idea.

"He just flat-out didn't want to do it," Gears said, "because they were only going to be there for three more years. But three years is three years."

And the final three years were anything but pretty at Texas Stadium. Anyone could see that the stadium had surrendered to the depths of degradation. Even best-selling author Ben Fountain noticed it. Texas Stadium served as the setting for his kickass acclaimed novel *Billy Lynn's Long Halftime Walk*. The protagonist poetically captures its nadir as he approaches Texas Stadium in person for the first time: "Give bigness all its due, sure but the place looks like a half-assed backyard job. The roof is a homely quilting of mismatched tiles. There's a slumpiness, a middle-aged sag to the thing that suggests soft paunches and mushy prostates, gravity-slugged masses of beached whaleness. Billy tries to imagine how it looked brand new, its fresh gleam and promise back in the day—thirty years ago? Forty?"[11]

Ben Fountain's prose notwithstanding, if there's one thing Jones understands as well as anyone, it's money. So, the idea of painting a roof that would cost $800,000 bothered him to no end, since, in retrospect, it was nothing more than window dressing, or rather roof dressing, for a stadium—and a city—he had every intention of leaving.

Then again, maybe we're wrong about that. Gears contends that, at one point, Jones did want to stay in Irving. And indeed, at one time, he spoke openly and enthusiastically of wanting to renovate and expand Texas Stadium to more than 100,000 seats, which for Jones had long been a dream figure for stadium capacity.

"Actually, Jerry was good to the City of Irving," Gears contends. "For the most part, he worked well with us over the years. Although, yes, several contentious issues had to be worked out, starting with the alcohol issue."[12]

It took at least two elections for fans in general seating areas to be permitted to buy and consume alcohol at Texas Stadium, which for years—like the Cotton Bowl before it—was a bone-dry desert on the wet-your-whistle frontier. And why? Texas had a long tradition of many, even most, of its counties being bone-dry, because of the herculean influence of the Southern Baptist Convention and other fundamentalist sects that, at least outwardly, defined drinking as an inroad to sin. And let's not forget dancing. God forbid should you contemplate both! No issue underscores Jones's relentlessness more than the one involving alcohol and its profit potential.

But it was not until Jones's third season as Cowboys' owner that he finally managed to change the policy, and even then, only beer and wine were allowed and could not be sold in the stands, only on the concourse, and in plastic bottles, not glass. As the *Chicago Tribune* noted in a story dated August 12, 1991: "For the first time, beer and wine will be sold inside Texas Stadium when the Dallas Cowboys host the Los Angeles Raiders in an exhibition game Monday night. Voters in Irving overwhelmingly approved a referendum Saturday [in August of 1991] that exempts the stadium from a city ordinance banning the sale of alcoholic beverages anywhere except restaurants."[13]

Churchly opposition had long been a point of vexation for Clint, Bum, *and* Jones, who deeply envied what Gears calls "the huge revenue component" that alcohol sales represented, which almost every other team in the League—at the time—got to bathe in.

As for the roof that sorely needed an $800,000 coat of fresh paint, Gears told the Cowboys owner, "You cannot win this argument," and in the end, Gears forced Jones to punt. Or rather, he stopped complaining about having to do it. Perhaps the best way to put it is that the $800,000 was part of a divorce agreement. To free himself from Texas Stadium and Irving, Jones had to go along. He had no other choice, lest he risk Texas Stadium remaining in play and serving as competition for concerts and sporting events.

"Some of the items in the greater list were very important to the Cowboys organization and would be controversial if they were pulled out," Gears says. "In regard to the totality of the public accepting the agreement, I had to win that argument. I said to Jerry, 'In consideration of the greater good of this agreement, you cannot win this argument.' That ultimately convinced him to agree to do it. He saw the sum total of the other components and felt the public perception was important. So, allowing me to win that argument about the roof was the only way to go."[14]

The truth is, Jones had reached an emotional ceiling with Irving. Or maybe a political ceiling.

This came at a time when a renovated or new stadium was still in play in Irving as a possible *future* home for the Cowboys. What Jones hoped to do with the half-cent sales tax he could siphon from DART was to use it toward underwriting a new or renovated stadium in Irving. And at the time, Jones appeared to be committed, having spent upward of $250,000 of his own money to defeat the DART initiative.

As it was, Irving held an election, asking voters to vote on whether or not they wanted DART service to continue in Irving. Keep in mind that Irving was and is a bedroom community, with most of its residents working in Dallas. Many of them liked having a low-cost way to get to and from work, without having to pay parking fees.

So, no surprise, the voters voted yes, they wanted to keep DART, which may have been the first indication that the Cowboys would not remain in Irving. Suburban Arlington, where they ended up, never once voted to allow DART service, even if it meant handicapping its residents by removing a valuable mass-transit option for getting to and from work. As a result,

Arlington voters have approved bond referendums for *three* major stadiums since the early 1990s—two for Major League Baseball's Rangers and one for the Cowboys. And had Ron Kirk not succeeded in keeping the Mavericks and Stars in Dallas with the construction of American Airlines Center, chances are they would have approved a new building for those two as well.

Even so, Gears says, Jones continued to believe that Irving remained his best possible choice. For a while, he supported the idea of a new stadium in the Las Colinas area, near D/FW Airport. The owner of the Las Colinas property was even willing to *give* his 105 acres of land to the city of Irving, just for keeping the Cowboys in the city named for the author who created the character of the headless horseman.

Irving soon had competition with a foe that Gears perceived as truly formidable. With flexibility it had at the time under its transient occupancy tax (TOT), Dallas County could hold an election and sling a whole bunch of money at Jones to construct a new stadium in Dallas County—maybe even returning the Cowboys to their original home, in Dallas. Making them once again the *Dallas* Cowboys was, Gears says, a powerful emotional advantage that, in his opinion, the city never really used in luring the Cowboys back to Dallas.

For Dallas County to keep the Cowboys—by keeping them in Irving or returning them to Dallas (both cities being in Dallas County)—was going to require a countywide election in November of 2003, but as Shakespeare would have deemed it, "Ah, there's the rub." And it proved to be a rub that Cowboys fans in Dallas and Irving would never overcome.

At the time, Gears says, the Dallas County Commissioners Court was top-heavy with Republicans, who were led by county judge Margaret Keliher, a Republican. The last thing she and her GOP colleagues on the court wanted, Gears says, was an election, when she and her allies would be locked in a fierce bid for reelection against Democratic challengers. Gears said:

> They believed that a stadium vote would lure thousands of new voters to the polls, many of whom would be minorities—Blacks and Hispanics who loved the Dallas Cowboys. But those same people, they feared, would never vote for them. Rather, they would vote for their Democratic opponents. The last thing they wanted was to lose those down-ballot races for judges, sheriffs, etc. So, to have that election in November was one they regarded as political suicide. And yet, in the end, it didn't matter. They got their way by not having the Cowboys' vote on the ballot, but they all lost anyway. And now, the Commissioners Court doesn't have a single Republican sitting on it.

Again, it wasn't that the commissioners opposed a vote for the stadium. They would have agreed to one in May 2004, but for Jones, Gears says, that was way too late. He had a timetable and needed to stick to it. Remember, as Randy Galloway, among others, had said, the only reason he chose to cede control of the football operation by hiring Bill Parcells in 2003 was his needing the stadium vote more than anything—regardless of where it ended up. With the Republican-controlled Commissioners Court saying no, the November 2003 election with a Cowboys measure on the ballot was never going to happen, meaning that Dallas and Irving would miss out on being the home of the Cowboys, when the Texas Stadium lease expired in 2008.

Even so, Gears contends, Jones wanted the Cowboys—if he could make the numbers work—to remain in Irving. At one time, the ex-mayor says, Jones had sixteen sites on his list of potential new homes for the Cowboys. A growing public perception at the time was that the Cowboys longed to return to their original home in Fair Park, where they began in 1960, but, Gears says, "Jerry Jones once told me that the Dallas Cowboys would never play in Fair Park."

Even in our interview with Jones for *Hole in the Roof,* the Cowboys owner said Fair Park was at a distinct disadvantage from the start compared to AT&T Stadium, "because the old Cotton Bowl site allows little to no ingress or egress on surface streets surrounding the area."

Here, we have to take issue with Jones: that is hardly a problem for the annual Texas-Oklahoma game, which puts more than 90,000 people in the stands each year during the State Fair of Texas, where as many as 200,000 people a day have been known to show up (except, of course, in 2020, when for the first time since World War II, the fair was canceled because of COVID-19).

Gears pointed out that DART has not one but *two* Fair Park stations, which in his opinion may have been another deal-breaker for Jones.

Could it be that Jones wanted a site where (1) he would not be constrained by the potential revenue mass transit would take away, or (2) he could not produce the kind of revenue he does at AT&T Stadium by charging each vehicle a whopping $75 for parking?

Initially, Gears says the Cowboys' infatuation was not limited to Fair Park. They considered another site in the old Industrial Boulevard area near the Trinity River—the street is now named Riverfront Boulevard— but that, he says, would have required "an incredibly costly environmental clean-up,"[15] with virtually none of the needed additional millions making their way to the pocketbook of the Cowboys owner.

Despite the role of the Commissioners Court—Gears blames Margaret Keliher alone for blowing the deal for Irving and Dallas—Dallas Mayor Laura Miller ended up the scapegoat.

"I have a lot of respect for Laura Miller," Gears says. "She's a tough nut."

She was rightly opposed, he says, "to giving tax breaks to billionaires."[16]

She and Jones did have one meeting, which Gears says didn't go well but might have been the starting point for negotiations that lasted weeks or even months, not unlike a scoring drive that ends in a touchdown—which in this case would have been the Cowboys getting their dream stadium in the city they used to call home. Was Miller the wrong mayor at the wrong time for the Cowboys? Possibly. But Gears says she should have never ended up the scapegoat, which he blames on—who else?—the news media.

Crayton Webb, who served as chief of staff for Dallas Mayor Laura Miller, echoes for the most part what Gears has to say, albeit with a caveat. Writing in *D* magazine in August 2009, just before the Cowboys moved into their new home in Arlington, Webb calls it "myth No. 1" that Miller "refused to meet with Jones and lost the stadium. Miller met with Jones and his team on numerous occasions. I know this for a fact because, as a member of her staff at the time, I was with her for many of those meetings."

The mayor was, Webb wrote, "not a fan of taxpayer-subsidized stadiums" and was quite concerned "about the cost of the stadium to Dallas taxpayers. But few know that it was Miller who persuaded Jones to even look at Fair Park to begin with. Unfortunately, I don't believe Jones ever seriously considered Fair Park as a viable location for his project. Whether you believe in taxpayer-subsidized stadium projects or not, no one can deny that having the Cowboys Stadium at Fair Park could have been great for Dallas."[17]

Years later, Gears remains resolute in saying that, if anyone was the villain, fingers should forever be pointed at the Dallas County Commissioners.

"Look," he says. "It's this simple: If, back then, you had had today's Dallas County Commissioners in Dallas County, the Dallas Cowboys would be playing in Dallas. Period. No two ways about it."

And maybe it all worked out for the best anyway. As Jones told us in our interview with him in 2016, America now defines itself not in terms of cities but rather large metro areas. By 2022, Dallas remained in the top ten of America's most populated cities. But that's nothing compared to the Dallas–Fort Worth metro area, which by early 2022 was threatening to oust

Chicago from the number 3 spot, which would make New York, Los Angeles, and Dallas–Fort Worth the nation's largest metro areas.

In that regard, as Jones said, with a knowing wink, "Arlington," which is halfway between Dallas and Fort Worth, "was the perfect choice."

CHAPTER SIXTEEN

Frankenstadium

Wᴴᴇɴ ꜱᴀᴍᴜᴇʟ ᴍᴏʀꜱᴇ invented the telegraph in 1844, his fingertips tapped out a nervous first sentence:

"What hath God wrought?"

If Clint Murchison Jr. were alive today, he might be asking the same thing.

"Believe me," we can almost hear him say, "*this* was never my idea."

This is the all-consuming craze of the twenty-first century.

This is the national mania known as super-stadium seeking, which eats up football, baseball, and other sports, and doesn't care how much money it bleeds or how many fans whose loyalties it tears to shreds.

This is the trend we call Frankenstadium.

Did Clint play a role in creating the Frankenstadium?

Yes, but as you must know by now, it's a lot more complicated than anyone realized, so thanks for letting us take you on the journey.

As we told you before, even high schools are building Frankenstadiums. In 2017, Katy, Texas, unveiled a $72 million high school facility, which carries luxury boxes for corporate sponsors. And, yes, Katy taxpayers paid for most of it. And you're right—it's obscene.

Stadiums no longer cost millions—today, most easily surpass $1 billion (the new one in suburban Los Angeles now exceeds $5 billion)—and almost all happily extort revenue from taxpayers, who are programmed to surrender to owners who proclaim: "If you don't build me my stadium, I will move!" Out of a deep sense of fairness, we should note that SoFi Stadium in suburban Inglewood, California, the new home of the Rams and Chargers—who are merely renting from the Rams—is one of the few being built without a penny of taxpayer money.

Even so, it too is obscene, and both teams spared no expense in making threats to get them where they are. They gave the finger to two great American cities, St. Louis and San Diego, and just flat out didn't give a damn. And they were not alone. The Raiders did the same in once again shafting Oakland to move to Las Vegas, which pretty much says it all.

After the Chargers spent *years* making threats as the cornerstone of maybe the poorest public relations campaign in history, San Diego voters got their own form of payback in 2016, when they voted—overwhelmingly—to say no to a new stadium. So, they kicked the NFL out of "America's Finest City" with what may have been a forever goodbye:

"Don't let the door hit you in the ass on the way out."

And then there was Clint, whose motives, as we hope we've shown, were born of necessity, not greed.

Texas Stadium cost $31 million, financed through the new concept of seat option bonds, which meant that those who used the stadium ended up paying for it. The Cowboys incited controversy when they fled the Cotton Bowl, with some critics saying they had shut the door on an egalitarian era in which Blacks, Hispanics, and poor whites could share the same primitive seating with affluent neighbors from wealthy areas. But what could be more egalitarian than having the actual users of the stadium pay for the stadium, rather than fleece taxpayers as a whole?

As Clint Jr. told Blackie Sherrod, who quoted him in the *Dallas Times Herald*, "This fairness business is a strong point with us. We're not charging everybody for the stadium, just the ones with preferential seats and parking. The 'poor people' that all these protestors seem concerned about, they don't have to help finance the stadium. There will be plenty of seats for them, and they will be better seats than the Cotton Bowl and better parking."

In the final analysis, $11 million of the overall cost of Texas Stadium came from Clint's checkbook. Texas Stadium endured through 2008, after which the Dallas Cowboys moved to the ultimate Frankenstadium in Arlington, Texas. For the 37 years it existed, Texas Stadium *did not take a penny* from the city of Irving. Arlington taxpayers, to use just one example, paid $325 million, plus interest, of the $1.2 billion cost of AT&T Stadium.

Granted, 50 years ago, times were different. For one, every single home game in the National Football League was blacked out until 1973, when, under a threat from President Richard M. Nixon, the rule was amended: if the home team sold out the game 72 hours before kickoff, the game could be televised on local television. If not, the game was blacked out.

The NFL has suspended blackouts of home games on a year-to-year basis since 2015.

But ironically, that was the year when the Frankenstadium virus gave way to a full-scale epidemic.

In the first quarter of 2015, the Chargers and Raiders dropped a bomb-shell, on their home cities and the pro football world in general. These once-bitter rivals announced jointly that, unless stadium issues were resolved in San Diego and Oakland—unless those cities ponied up new stadiums, *and fast*—they would pack up and move, together, to a new $1.7 billion stadium in Carson, California, 18 miles south of Los Angeles.

It was the first of many threats that carried with it an Alice-through-the-looking-glass, acid-trip component.

The juice fueling the Chargers–Raiders threat was, of course, their own craven desire for a Frankenstadium, as in, "How much can we both rake in?" In today's sports universe, *where* a Frankenstadium is built doesn't matter, as long as it carries with it the lure of billions. If you don't believe us, take a visit to the neighborhood that surrounds AT&T Stadium in Arlington, where the gleaming cash cow known as "Jerry World" is flanked on all sides by bail-bond dispensaries, payday loan outlets, and massage parlors.

The Chargers–Raiders conspiracy failed to work, but did that mean the two would stay put? Of course not! Greed is a mighty river.

If fans in San Diego and Oakland scoffed at what they perceived as hol-low threats from the Chargers and Raiders, well, now they know better. The Chargers ended a 15-year stadium dance in early 2017 by finally leaving San Diego, where they had played since 1961, to become the second team—a ten-ant, nothing more—in the $5 billion stadium that Rams owner Stan Kroenke built in Inglewood.

And get this: for the privilege of making the move, the Chargers have agreed to pay the NFL a $650 million relocation fee over a 10-year period.

Their landlords in Tinseltown will, of course, be the Rams, who aban-doned St. Louis in 2016 to return to LA, which they'd fled 20 years earlier, amid a chorus of resounding apathy. Let's face it, most people in and near the nation's second-largest city would much rather watch the Bears, Cowboys, Packers, or Giants on NFL Sunday Ticket, because most of them come from those places.

Despite LA having never offered evidence that it's anywhere close to a viable NFL city, Kroenke and his top ally, Cowboys' owner Jerry Jones, power-blasted the Rams past the Chargers and Raiders.

In January 2016, the League voted 30–2 (you can guess who the two were) to allow the Rams to move to LA, while granting the Chargers the bridesmaid option of being a tenant in the Rams' Frankenstadium. Whose architect, by the way, is HKS, the Dallas-based firm that also designed Jerry World.

SoFi Stadium played host to the Super Bowl in February 2022, and its landlord, the Rams, even managed to win it, with newly acquired quarterback Matthew Stafford (who grew up in the posh Dallas neighborhood of Highland Park) being the difference maker.

Stafford and the Rams fared much better than the Cowboys, whose drought of failing to appear in either the NFC Championship Game or the Super Bowl reached an embarrassing 26 years. And counting. The only NFC teams courting a deeper dive are the woeful pair of Washington and Detroit.

This feels like a good time to remind you that the title of our book—*Hole in the Roof*—carries with it a double meaning. As the NFL buckles up for the 2022 season, it is by no means a pretty picture. In February 2022, League officials complained to the bipartisan House Committee on Oversight and Reform that, according to the *Washington Post*, owner Dan Snyder's Commanders were impeding the committee's access to thousands of documents "related to the investigation of the team's workplace, another sign of increasing tension between the team and League over the handling of the probe."[1]

The investigation began after the *Washington Post* reported in 2020 that female employees of the team had experienced shocking episodes of sexual harassment, in particular its cheerleading squad. And, well, as everyone should know by now, it's never a good thing when the US Congress launches hearings on how *you* do business.

But in early 2022, the Cowboys incurred their own cheerleading scandal, when, according to documents obtained by ESPN, the team paid a confidential settlement of $2.4 million to four members of their cheerleading squad after they accused a team executive of voyeurism.[2]

The news got worse a few days later when Nataly Keomoungkhoun broke a story in the *Dallas Morning News*, reporting that a 25-year-old congressional aide who grew up in North Texas — and who once worked for former president Donald Trump — is suing Cowboys owner Jerry Jones, alleging that he is her biological father.[3]

And, of course, it didn't stop there. All of a sudden, the NFL was drowning in litigation, making us wonder if the Gordon Gekko mantra, "Greed is good," ought to include the caveat, "Until, that is, someone sues your ass off."

Some of the messiest headlines focused on Frankenstadiums and greed and the bitter feelings they conjure up.

To wit: the shiny red apple of the Rams landing what may be the ultimate Frankenstadium was found to have in its center a large and expensive worm.

The NFL and Kroenke ended up having to pay $790 million to settle a lawsuit filed by St. Louis interests over the team's defection to Los Angeles, according to a joint statement issued by city and county officials in Missouri in November of 2021.

Nor did it stop *there*.

As the CBS affiliate in San Diego reported in late January of 2022, "A lawsuit has been filed against the National Football League alleging that the league and officials with the Chargers violated NFL relocation policies when team owners approved the Chargers' move from San Diego to Los Angeles."[4]

Sour grapes notwithstanding, unhappy fans in St. Louis and San Diego appear to be having an impact, as evidenced by a stormy NFL owners' meeting in late October of 2021.

As ESPN reported at the time, Kroenke and his chief ally, Jerry Jones, angered fellow owners when Kroenke appeared to be welching on a promise to cover tens of millions of dollars in legal expenses related to his team's 2016 exodus from St. Louis to SoFi.[5]

Among those raising questions was Raiders owner Mark Davis, who, ESPN reported, "reminded the room that, in 2016, the L.A. committee recommended a rival Raiders-Chargers stadium project in Carson, California, by a 5-1 vote over Kroenke's project in Inglewood."[6] But through an alliance forged with Jones, Kroenke ended up the winner, albeit one who had to fork over a $790 million settlement fee.

So, what happened to the Raiders?

In March 2017, they announced the move to Las Vegas, where a $1.9 billion stadium opened in 2020, COVID-19 notwithstanding. The more religious among us might suggest that it was God's punishment for the occupants of Frankenstadiums to be forced to play an entire season without a soul sitting in the stands. Which also became the case for baseball's Texas Rangers, who played all of 2020 without a single fan in the gleaming, new $1.2 billion Globe Life Field, just east of AT&T Stadium, which many in North Texas refer to as "Jerry World."

So much for the fans of the Oakland Raiders, who have demonstrated since the team's inception in 1960 that they *love* the Raiders, no matter how badly they're treated. Seriously, at this point, it's like spousal abuse. The Raiders moved to Los Angeles in 1982, only to return to Oakland in 1994, and then left again to play the 2020 campaign in front of nobody in the gambling capital of the world.

Jones, who many today perceive as the NFL's de facto commissioner (he has that much power) lobbied heavily for a team in Vegas, the mere thought of which would have terrified Clint's generation of owners, who feared the potential of what gambling could do to the game they loved.

Only the future will let us know how *that* turns out.

In March 2022, Atlanta Falcons wide receiver Calvin Ridley was suspended for a full season for betting on NFL games. This despite the fact that NFL owners, with Jones at the forefront, are now counting on fans betting on games as its biggest growth industry. This alone is arguably the most notable distinction between today's NFL and the era of Commissioner Pete Rozelle (1960–1989), who, aligned with League owners, harbored apocalyptic fears about the evil effects gambling might one day have on the game. In 1963, Rozelle suspended Green Bay running back Paul Hornung and Detroit defensive lineman Alex Karras a full season for betting on games. Now, critics say, the NFL is openly and brazenly courting a double standard.

When it comes to stadiums, the League also operates as one, as in greed is good. Even if, at times, it carries with it strange side effects.

So far, the Rams–Chargers experiment in LA hasn't exactly flourished, at least not for the Chargers. The Rams averaged 71,229 a game in 2019, during their last season at Los Angeles Coliseum. The Chargers averaged 31,750 a game at their Carson, California, home in 2019, compared to 57,024 a game in 2016, in their final, lame-duck season in San Diego.

To be fair, Jones's Frankenstadium had the League's best average attendance in 2019, drawing 90,929 per game. But here's the most telling point from the 2017 season: on one weekend in Los Angeles, the Texas–USC game at the Coliseum outdrew the Rams and Chargers *combined*.

For the Chargers, it has been laughably bad. From its 3-year stay at a soccer stadium from 2017 through 2019, Chargers' management had to call a halt to introducing the home team before kickoff, because its temporary home in Carson was almost always filled with the crowd as a whole rooting for the Chargers' opponent. Pregame introductions were canceled because the boos filling the stadium were drowning out the PA announcer. Such is the state of the NFL, which to us feels like one of the warning signals of cancer. It also happened to the Rams during their Super Bowl season of 2021, when it rapidly became apparent during a road game for the San Francisco 49ers, that most of the SoFi crowd was, well, rooting for the Niners, not the Rams.

In the end, it boils down to this:

Will Frankenstadium kill the goose that laid the golden egg? Time will tell. And even in 2022, you'd be a fool to suggest that COVID-19 will merely go away without having a lasting impact on the fate of Frankenstadiums. For the winds of an unwelcome change are already being felt.

"Your season-ticket holders are the single-most important group that you have," says Joseph A. Bailey III, who left his executive post with the Cowboys to spend his final years in the NFL as an executive with the Miami Dolphins. Bailey made his remarks just before the start of the 2020 season, for which the Cowboys said they would not be selling season tickets. "Whether you win or lose, they are going to come out. It's a community of people. As season-ticket holders, you sit next to people you have sat next to for three years or four years or five years. Nowadays, some of these tickets end up with the opposition fans sitting next to you, and it destroys this community. So, what you end up with is a stadium of disjointed people. And that is a problem."[7]

But 2020 added a whole new wrinkle. "The kiss of death," Bailey says, "for any team sport is to make it a studio sport. And now they have a studio sport. It cuts the authenticity out of the equation for having fun."[8]

Is there anything worse than an empty Frankenstadium? Did Clint play a role in creating Frankenstadium? In a word, yes. But as we hope we have shown you, there is so much more to the story.

Since 1971, when Clint opened Texas Stadium, stadiums have played an increasingly important role in the alchemy of the NFL and, for that matter, *all* sports.

Until Clint, stadiums were largely rental facilities, suitable for playing a game and buying a hot dog and a soda and nothing more.

- Until Clint, most revenues in the NFL were shared equally, with teams dividing the increasingly lucrative television pie and permitting the "road" team its share of ticket sales and concessions.
- Until Clint, luxury suites and their progeny, personal seat licenses—which created a loophole in the revenue sharing dynamic—did not exist in NFL stadiums.

- Until Clint, private clubs—providing yet another source of owner-keeps-it-all revenue—did not exist. In addition to that, Clint carved out a first by controlling his own concessions, rather than license it to an independent contractor.

- Until Clint, no NFL stadium had been financed privately, with nary a penny of taxpayer money, by using a clever calculus that enabled those who would use the stadium to build the stadium—by buying seat option bonds.

Clint was the first NFL owner who saw that the role of stadiums was destined to change, or, in his view, sports would be headed for economic extinction. Clint the visionary knew that players' salaries, barely a pittance when the Cowboys began playing in 1960, would grow exponentially, as the money from television grew exponentially. And because he *knew* that would happen, he knew that owners would need new and deeper sources of revenue. The trend has continued, with Cowboys' owner Jerry Jones spearheading the deal that made the FOX network a carrier of NFL games, greatly increasing the League's television pie.

By 2009, when the Cowboys moved to their third home, the palatial palace christened as Cowboys Stadium, Jones had taken the Clint concept and juiced it up dramatically. With a seating-standing capacity of more than 100,000, the Frankenstadium known today as AT&T Stadium has hosted one Super Bowl, the NCAA Final Four basketball championship (attended by former presidents Bill Clinton and George W. Bush), the first College Football Playoff, the Academy of Country Music Awards, and dozens of other high-profile mega-events (Paul McCartney, Beyoncé, the Eagles, etc.) that underscore the stadium's identity as a stand-alone, revenue-producing gargantuan.

If Clint begat Jerry, then Jerry begat all the other imitators.

But there is a world of difference between Clint and the modern legion of imitators. As his own family contends, Clint was all about the fans' experience. For he believed that, without the fan having an experience that he or she would remember and treasure, the NFL and other sports would cease to exist. Most important of all, perhaps, was what separated Clint from almost every other owner: he never took a penny from taxpayers.

Not only that, but as the late Blackie Sherrod once said: "I don't think Clint was ever as dedicated to making money as a lot of those guys are. Many people have told me that Clint never took a dime out of the Cowboys. When he and his wife flew on the team charter, he made the Cowboys bill his office for their share."[9]

He cared deeply about architecture and aesthetics and used chunks of his own money to elevate both. He reveled in *sight lines*—fans being able to see *all* the action unfolding in front of them. He cared about fans having a safe, comfortable walk to get to their seats *or* taking a $5, round-trip bus ride that dropped them off at the stadium entrance. He cared about human beings having a comfortable seat, with plenty of back support and room for their kneecaps. Sure, naysayers say he introduced stratification to American stadia by ennobling luxury suites, but during his era at Texas Stadium, the percentage of people occupying suites—compared to its overall capacity of 65,000—was miniscule. As a man who understood economics, he knew that players' salaries would soon soar to astronomical levels—*as they did*—and the money needed to pay such salaries had to come from somewhere. How was it unfair to have the wealthiest fans shoulder the lion's share of creating the financing necessary to make the Cowboys competitive?

So, while Clint may well have been Dr. Frankenstein unwittingly creating a monster that would one day ravage the sport he loved, we contend that he would be appalled by what happened in San Diego and Oakland—and will, of course, continue to happen in cities where an owner's greed outweighs the interests of passionate, loyal fans, who will cease to matter if other fans and other cities can produce the revenue that the owner's appetite demands. Believe us when we say that, in today's NFL, the trend of dollar-hopping from one city to another will continue. For in so many ways, it's been reduced to a billionaire's game, with "fans" being nothing more than pawns on a chessboard of profit and excess.

So, what exactly *is* Clint's legacy?

Texas Stadium will forever be iconic, as will the hole in its roof, which has fascinated television producers and global terrorists alike and which, in its own way, lives on—at least in our memory. It began with a dreamlike run by Duane Thomas on a gorgeous afternoon that led to *five* Cowboys championships.

The man behind it all, of course, was Clint, whose amazing journey we were happy to share, from the Cowboys' humble beginnings in the Cotton Bowl, to Texas Stadium, to the Frankenstadiums that dot the land in snaring their own ginormous slice of America's cultural pie.

He was short, and he was shy, but he was truly a pioneer in American sports history.

NOTES

Prologue

1. Bryan Woolley, "The Rise and Fall of the Murchison Empire," *Dallas Times Herald*, April 14. 1985. Quotes originally came from an article published in *Fortune* magazine in 1953.

2. Woolley, "Rise and Fall of Murchison Empire."

3. Woolley, "Rise and Fall of Murchison Empire."

4. Robert Murchison, from an essay given to the authors.

5. Murchison, essay.

6. Woolley, "Rise and Fall of Murchison Empire."

7. Jane Wolfe, *The Murchisons: The Rise and Fall of a Texas Dynasty* (New York: St. Martin's Press, 1989).

8. Wolfe, *The Murchisons*.

9. Woolley, "Rise and Fall of Murchison Empire."

10. Woolley, "Rise and Fall of Murchison Empire."

11. Woolley, "Rise and Fall of Murchison Empire."

12. Woolley, "Rise and Fall of Murchison Empire."

Chapter 1

1. Connell Miller, "Right Place, Wrong Time: How the 1952 Dallas Texans Flamed Out After One Lackluster Season of Football," *Texas Monthly*, March 22, 2019.

2. Pat Toomay, "A Rivalry for a Song . . . and Chicken Feed," in a Page 2 feature of ESPN.com, accessed March 15, 2022, https://www.espn.com/page2/wash/s/toomay/020314.html.

3. Michael Meredith, the son of the late "Dandy" Don Meredith, interview by the authors.

4. Toomay, "A Rivalry for a Song."

Chapter 2

1. Toomay, "A Rivalry for a Song . . . and Chicken Feed,"
2. Toomay, "A Rivalry for a Song."
3. Thomas G. Smith, *Showdown: JFK and the Integration of the Washington Redskins* (Boston: Beacon Press, 2012).

Chapter 3

1. T. S. Eliot, "The Hollow Men."
2. Matt Mosley, "No Escape: With Heavy Hearts, Cowboys, NFL Played on After Tragedy," *Dallas Morning News*, November 19, 2003.
3. Mosley, "No Escape."
4. Mosley, "No Escape."
5. Don Meredith, interview by Michael Granberry, Beverly Hills, CA, May 10, 1982.
6. Meredith, interview.

Chapter 4

1. Clint Murchison, Jr., *Clint's Corner* (1970).
2. Keith Dunlap, "Who Was Bob Hayes? He's Still the Only Athlete to Do This," last modified January 20, 2022, https://www.clickondetroit.com/sports/2021/02/16/who-was -bob-hayes-hes-still-the-only-athlete-to-do-this/.
3. Gary Cartwright, article in *Dallas Morning News*, November 22, 1965.
4. Michael Granberry, article in *Dallas Morning News*, April 22, 2017.

Chapter 5

1. Larry McMurtry, *In a Narrow Grave: Essays on Texas* (New York: Simon & Schuster, 1968).
2. Craig A. Doherty and Katherine M. Doherty, *The Houston Astrodome* (Blackbirch Press, Inc., 1996).
3. Doherty and Doherty, *The Houston Astrodome*.

Chapter 6

1. Blackie Sherrod, interview by Michael Granberry, 2011. Sherrod passed away in 2016.
2. Michael Granberry, "Star Soloist," *Dallas Morning News*, November 7, 2016.
3. Donald Chipman, Randolph Campbell, and Robert Calvert, *The Dallas Cowboys and the NFL* (Norman: University of Oklahoma Press, 1970).
4. Clint Murchison, Jr., *Clint's Corner*.
5. Vincent Carrozza, interview by Michael Granberry, 2011.
6. Carrozza, interview.
7. Michael Granberry, "Stadium Debate Not a New Game: Before Leaving Dallas, 'Boys' Owner Battled for Downtown Digs," *Dallas Morning News*, May 2, 2004.
8. Granberry, "Stadium Debate Not a New Game."
9. Carrozza, interview.
10. Rev. Don Bryant, interview by Burk Murchison, 2011.
11. Lee Cullum, interview by Michael Granberry, Dallas, January 21, 2014.

12. Carrozza, interview.

13. Murchison Jr., *Clint's Corner.*

14. Murchison Jr., *Clint's Corner.*

15. Murchison Jr., *Clint's Corner.*

16. Murchison Jr., *Clint's Corner.*

17. Blackie Sherrod, "Murchison—On Fairness," *Dallas Times Herald*, January 26, 1968.

18. Granberry, "Stadium Debate Not a New Game."

19. Dan Matkin, interview by Michael Granberry, Irving, TX, March 20, 2013.

20. Matkin, interview; Robert Power, interview by Burk Murchison and Michael Granberry, 2014.

21. Matkin, interview; Robert Power, interview.

22. Matkin, interview; Power, interview.

23. Matkin, interview; Power, interview.

24. Power, interview.

Chapter 7

1. Power, interview.

2. Power, interview.

3. Power, interview.

4. Melvin Shuler, from documents in the City of Irving Archives, Irving Public Library, Irving, TX. https://www.cityofirving.org/1865/Irving-Archives

5. Shuler, City of Irving Archives.

6. Shuler, City of Irving Archives.

7. Shuler, City of Irving Archives.

8. Shuler, City of Irving Archives.

9. Shuler, City of Irving Archives.

10. Robert Wilonsky, "How a star of TV's 'The Good Place' wrote an acclaimed play about the bad place—racist Dallas of the 1960s," *Dallas Morning News*, October 19, 2018. https://www.dallasnews.com/opinion/commentary/2018/10/19/how-a-star-of-tv-s-the -good-place-wrote-an-acclaimed-play-about-the-bad-place-racist-dallas-of-the-1960s/

11. Murchison Jr., *Clint's Corner.*

Chapter 8

1. Ray Hutchison, interview by Michael Granberry, December 19, 2011; John Boyle, interview by Michael Granberry, February 15, 2012.

2. Hutchison, interview; Boyle, interview.

3. Hutchison, interview; Boyle, interview.

4. Mark Curriden, "Ray Hutchison, the Power at the Conference Table," *Dallas Morning News*, October 14, 2012.

5. Curriden, "Ray Hutchison, the Power at the Conference Table."

6. Matkin, interview.

7. Power, interview.

8. Power, interview.

9. Power, interview.

10. Power, interview.

11. Power, interview.
12. Shuler, City of Irving Archives.
13. Matkin, interview.
14. Power, interview.
15. Power, interview.
16. Power, interview.
17. Power, interview.
18. Power, interview.
19. Power, interview.
20. Power, interview.
21. Matkin, interview.
22. Power, interview.

Chapter 9

1. Gil Brandt, interview by Burk Murchison.
2. Clint Murchison Jr., interview by Gary Cartwright, *Dallas Morning News,* 1965.
3. City of Irving comments about adding seats.
4. Bob St. John, "Texas Stadium: A Familiar Look," *Dallas Morning News*, January 26, 1969.
5. Michael Granberry, article in *Dallas Morning News*, December 14, 2008.
6. Warren Morey, personal communication to authors, 1991.
7. Michael Granberry, "Icon's History Goes Back to This Man's Drawing Board: Work on Landmark Remains Source of Immense Pride and Countless Stories for Architect," *Dallas Morning News*, December 14, 2008.
8. Granberry, "Icon's History Goes Back to This Man's Drawing Board."
9. Granberry, "Icon's History Goes Back to This Man's Drawing Board."
10. Granberry, "Icon's History Goes Back to This Man's Drawing Board."
11. Granberry, "Icon's History Goes Back to This Man's Drawing Board."
12. Michael Granberry, "His Courage Still Inspires," *The News*, November 22, 2013.

Chapter 10

1. Helen Parmley, "42,000 Pour In to Hear Graham," *Dallas Morning News*, September 18, 1971.
2. Parmley, "42,000 Pour In to Hear Graham."
3. Power, interview.
4. Power, interview.
5. Clint Murchison Jr., interview, *Dallas Morning News*, October 25, 1971.
6. Drew Pearson and Frank Luksa, *Remembering Texas Stadium: Cowboy Greats Recall the Blood, Sweat and Pride of Playing in the NFL's Most Unique Home* (Denton, TX: Zone Press, 2008).
7. Pearson and Luksa, *Remembering Texas Stadium.*
8. Sales literature released by Texas Stadium.
9. Bryan Burrough, *The Big Rich: The Rise and Fall of the Greatest Texas Oil Fortunes* (New York: Penguin Books, 2009).
10. Edwin "Bud" Shrake, "Some Home on the Range," *Sports Illustrated*, August 14, 1972.

Chapter 11

1. Pearson and Luksa, *Remembering Texas Stadium*.
2. Pearson and Luksa, *Remembering Texas Stadium*.
3. Pearson and Luksa, *Remembering Texas Stadium*.
4. Pearson and Luksa, *Remembering Texas Stadium*.
5. Pearson and Luksa, *Remembering Texas Stadium*.
6. Pearson and Luksa, *Remembering Texas Stadium*.
7. Pearson and Luksa, *Remembering Texas Stadium*.
8. Richard Peterson, CEO of Gordon McLendon's drive-in movie operation which extended to Texas Stadium, interview by Burk Murchison; Richard Peterson, personal communication.
9. Pearson and Luksa, *Remembering Texas Stadium*.
10. Julie Graham, interview by Michael Granberry, *Dallas Morning News*, August 8, 2018.
11. Graham, interview.

Chapter 12

1. Dick Hitt, *Classic Clint: The Laughs and Times of Clint Murchison, Jr.* (Plano, TX: Wordware, 1992).
2. Murchison, essay.

Chapter 13

1. Charean Williams, "Donald Trump in '84 Interview: I Feel Sorry for the Poor Guy Who Buys Cowboys," profootballtalk.nbcsports.com, posted July 13, 2017, https://profootballtalk.nbcsports.com/2017/07/13/donald-trump-in-84-interview-i-feel-sorry-for-the-poor-guy-who-buys-cowboys/
2. Jim Dent, Dallas sportswriter, interview by Michael Granberry.
3. Jack O'Connell, personal communication in journal shared to authors.
4. O'Connell, personal communication.
5. O'Connell, personal communication.
6. O'Connell, personal communication.
7. O'Connell, personal communication.
8. O'Connell, personal communication.
9. O'Connell, personal communication.
10. O'Connell, personal communication.
11. O'Connell, personal communication.
12. O'Connell, personal communication.
13. O'Connell, personal communication.
14. O'Connell, personal communication.
15. O'Connell, personal communication.
16. O'Connell, personal communication.
17. O'Connell, personal communication.
18. O'Connell, personal communication.
19. O'Connell, personal communication.
20. O'Connell, personal communication.

21. O'Connell, personal communication.

22. James Francis Jr., Bum Bright's top aide, interview by Burk Murchison and Michael Granberry, April 22, 2013.

23. Burk Murchison, interview by Michael Granberry.

24. Francis Jr., interview.

25. Francis Jr., interview.

26. Francis Jr., interview.

27. Francis Jr., interview.

28. Francis Jr., interview.

29. Francis Jr., interview.

30. Francis Jr., interview.

31. Francis Jr., interview.

32. Francis Jr., interview.

33. Francis Jr., interview.

34. Francis Jr., interview.

35. Francis Jr., interview.

36. David Casstevens, article in *Dallas Morning News*, January 29, 1985.

37. Casstevens, article in *Dallas Morning News*, January 29, 1985.

38. Casstevens, article in *Dallas Morning News*, January 29, 1985.

39. Blackie Sherrod, article in *Dallas Morning News*, May 3, 1987.

40. Blackie Sherrod, article in *Dallas Morning News*, May 3, 1987.

41. Blackie Sherrod, article in *Dallas Morning News*, May 3, 1987.

42. Mark Seal, article in *Vanity Fair*, November 2005.

Chapter 14

1. Ted Rea, interview by Burk Murchison.

2. Jerry Jones, interview by Burk Murchison and Michael Granberry, June 14, 2016.

3. Jones, interview.

4. Jones, interview.

5. Jones, interview.

6. Jones, interview.

7. Tom Smith, interview by Michael Granberry.

8. Smith, interview.

9. Tom Smith, interview by Michael Granberry, 2021.

10. Joe Nick Patoski, "Turnover!," *Texas Monthly*, October 1, 2012.

11. Joel Fontenot, interview by Michael Granberry, 2021.

12. *A Football Life: Jerry Jones*, which debuted December 1, 2017, on the NFL Network.

13. Jeff Pearlman, *Boys Will Be Boys: The Glory Days and Party Nights of the Dallas Cowboys Dynasty* (New York: HarperCollins, 2008).

14. *A Football Life: Jerry Jones.*

15. David Moore, article in *Dallas Morning News*, February 23, 2014.

16. David Moore, article in *Dallas Morning News*, February 23, 2014.

17. David Moore, article in *Dallas Morning News*, February 23, 2014.

18. *A Football Life: Jerry Jones.*

19. David Moore, article in *Dallas Morning News*, February 23, 2014.

20. Jones, interview.

21. Josh Kosman, "Buffalo Bills' Billionaire Owner Set to Get $1B in Public Funds for New Stadium," *New York Post*, March 11, 2022.

22. News Wire Services, "Tagliabue Says Suit Filed to Keep Up with Jones," *The Buffalo News*, September 20, 1995.

23. Mike Ozanian, "World's Most Valuable Sports Teams 2021," *Forbes* magazine, May 7, 2021.

24. Rich Dalrymple, interview in *A Football Life: Jerry Jones*.

25. Rich Dalrymple, interview in *A Football Life: Jerry Jones*.

26. Randy Galloway, interview in *A Football Life: Jerry Jones*.

27. Sound bite from "The Ticket," archives of KTCK-AM (1390), Dallas, Texas.

28. Todd Archer, "Irvin Finally Gets His Hands on Hall Invite," *Dallas Morning News*, February 4, 2007.

29. *This Is Us*, episode titled "The Adirondacks," aired May 25, 2021, NBC.

Chapter 15

1. Brandon Formby, article in *Dallas Morning News*, April 12, 2010.

2. Formby, article in *Dallas Morning News*, April 12, 2010.

3. Formby, article in *Dallas Morning News*, April 12, 2010.

4. Herbert Gears, interview by Burk Murchison and Michael Granberry, with an additional follow-up interview by Granberry.

5. Gears, interview.

6. Gears, interview; additional follow-up questions by Granberry in 2021.

7. Formby, article in *Dallas Morning News*, April 12, 2010.

8. Formby, article in *Dallas Morning News*, April 12, 2010.

9. Herbert Gears, interview by Michael Granberry, 2021.

10. Gears, interview.

11. Ben Fountain, *Billy Lynn's Long Halftime Walk* (New York: Ecco, 2012).

12. Gears, interview.

13. "Beer Man Joins Cowboy Crowd," *Chicago Tribune*, August 12, 1991.

14. Gears, interview.

15. Gears, interview.

16. Gears, interview.

17. Clayton Webb, "Who 'Lost' the New Cowboys Stadium for Dallas?," *D*, August 12, 2009.

Chapter 16

1. Mark Maske and Nicki Jhabvala, "NFL Tells Congress That Commanders Are Blocking Access to Documents from Workplace Probe," *Washington Post*, February 10, 2022.

2. Don Van Natta, Jr., "Cowboys paid $2.4 million to settle cheerleaders' voyeurism allegations against senior team executive," ESPN.com, February 16, 2022.

3. Nataly Keomoungkhoun, "Woman Sues Dallas Cowboys Owner Jerry Jones, Says He Is Her Father, Court Documents Say," *Dallas Morning News*, March 9, 2022.

4. City News Service, "NFL sued over Chargers' relocation from San Diego," CBS8.com, January 25, 2022.

5. Seth Wickersham, "Los Angeles Rams Owner Stan Kroenke Angers NFL Owners with Financial Pivot Related to Lawsuit on St. Louis Move, Sources Say," ESPN.com, October 27, 2021.

6. Wickersham, "Los Angeles Rams Owner Stan Kroenke Angers NFL Owners."

7. Joseph A. Bailey III, interview by Michael Granberry.

8. Bailey III, interview.

9. Granberry, "Stadium Debate Not a New Game."

INTERVIEWS

Greg Aiello, former Dallas Cowboys and NFL executive

Milton Babbitt, lead architect for Ford, Powell, and Carson on Dallas Cowboys Valley Ranch headquarters

Joe Bailey, Dallas Cowboys COO, 1970–1989

Sam Blair, former sports columnist and editor with the *Dallas Morning News*

John Boyle, Irving city attorney (1966–1970)

Gil Brandt, Dallas Cowboys vice president of Player Personnel, 1960–1989

Anne Marie Bratton, daughter of NFL Commissioner Pete Rozelle

Clay Bright, son of Bum Bright

Ben Brooks, attorney specializing in public finance with the Bracewell & Giuliani Law Firm

Don Bryant, pastor and former Fair Park resident

George Burrell, former associate of Clint Murchison Jr.

Vincent Carrozza, Dallas developer and downtown historian

Richard W. Cass, president, Baltimore Ravens

Joe Cavagnaro Jr., former Texas Stadium general manager during the Bright years

Roy Coffee, former attorney and friend of Clint Murchison Jr.

Gary Coffman, former executive vice president with Woodbine Development Corp

Bob Colombe, Clint Murchison Jr.'s longtime barber

Willie Cothrum, youngest Dallas city councilman in the history of Dallas and supporter Murchison's plan to build a downtown stadium

Tom Coughlin, Triland Development, Inc executive vice president of marketing on the Cowboys Center project

Richard Cronin, son of Gene Cronin, lead broker on the acquisition of the Texas Stadium site

Lee Cullum, Dallas journalist, niece of Bob Cullum

Jim Dent, former Dallas Cowboys beat writer, bestselling author

Nick DiGiuseppe, former partner in Triland International, Inc, JV partner with Dallas Cowboys in Cowboys Center at the Valley Ranch

Ken Dowe, former DJ and radio entrepreneur

Cathy Duncan, former Irving city finance director

Lee Folkins, played for the Cowboys in the 1960s

Joel Fontenot, former banker with First City Texas

Jim Francis, former Bum Bright business partner

Richard Freling, former attorney with Jenkens & Gilchrist Law Firm

Gerald Fronterhouse, former chairman and CEO of First Republic Corp

Wendell Gardner, assistant to Texas Stadium architect Warren Morey

Herbert Gears, Irving city councilman (1998–2004); mayor (2005–2011)

Henry Gilchrist, early partner and lead attorney with the Murchison family with the Jenkens & Gilchrist Law Firm

Rick Gosselin, sports columnist covering the NFL for almost 50 years

Craig Hall, real estate developer and Dallas Cowboys limited partner during the Bright years

Tom Hardin, early business manager of the Dallas Cowboys during the Murchison era

Bruce Hardy, general manager of Texas Stadium during the Jones years

Cliff Harris, Dallas Cowboys Hall of Fame safety

Carol Hermanovski, interior designer of the Dallas Cowboys headquarters at Expressway Tower and later at Valley Ranch

Tim House, Triland Development, Inc executive vice president of planning on the Cowboys Center project

Walter "Walt" J. Humann, prominent Dallas businessman and public servant

Ray Hutchison, attorney and municipal finance expert who developed the seat option bond plan

Michael Jenkins, CEO of LARC, Inc and head of design and sponsorship sales on the Cowboys Center project

Stephen Jones, COO, executive vice president, director of player personnel of the Dallas Cowboys

Jerry Jones, owner, president, general manager of the Dallas Cowboys

Margaret Keliher, former Dallas County judge

Kevin Kendro, assistant director of archives and collections—Irving Archives and Museum

Kent Kilmer, executive vice president of retail development at the Cowboys Center project

Dana Kilmer, former Dallas Cowboys cheerleader and head of development of cheerleader rehearsal hall at the Cowboys Center project

J. Peter Kleifgen, former executive in Clint Murchison Jr. organization

Bill Lamont, son-in-law of John D. Murchison Sr.

Mark Lamster, architecture critic of the *Dallas Morning News*

Alicia Landry, wife of Cowboys coach Tom Landry

Tom Landry Jr., son of Cowboys coach Tom Landry

Mitch Lewis Jr., son of public relations executive Mitch Lewis

William (Bill) Lively, former director of the Dallas Cowboys band at Texas Stadium

Lindi Loy, daughter of Cowboys trumpeter Tommy Loy

Tom Luce, former attorney with Jenkens & Gilchrist Law Firm

.

Frank Luksa, former sports columnist with the *Dallas Morning News* and the *Dallas Times Herald*

Al Lurie, former executive in the Gordon McLendon Organization

Patrick Magill, architect in charge of renovations at Texas Stadium after Warren Morey's retirement

Ken Marvel, former attorney with Jenkens & Gilchrist Law Firm

Dan Matkin, Irving city councilman (1965–70); mayor (1970–1977)

Robert McCulloch, former attorney for the estates of John D. and Lupe Murchison

Bart McLendon, son of Gordon McLendon

Don Meredith, first player signed by the Dallas Cowboys

Michael Meredith, son of Don Meredith, filmmaker

Robert A. "Bob" Miller, former *Dallas Morning News* columnist

Paul Moser, grandson of Gene Cronin, the real estate broker responsible for consolidating Texas Stadium site

Curt Mosher, former head of public relations for the Dallas Cowboys during Murchison era

Robert Murchison, youngest son of Clint Murchison Jr.

Clint Murchison III, eldest son of Clint Murchison Jr.

Pettis Norman, played for the Cowboys in the 1960s

Chris O'Neil, former executive vice president of Bright Realty

Darwin Payne, prominent Dallas historian and author

Drew Pearson, Dallas Cowboys Hall of Fame receiver

Alan Peppard, former journalist with the *Dallas Morning News*

Richard Peterson, former executive with McLendon Theatres Corp

Regina Pistor, wife of Charles H. Pistor, former chairman and CEO of First Republic Bank Dallas

Janet Shuler Powell, daughter of early Texas Stadium advocate Melvin Shuler

Robert Power, Irving city councilman (1963–1967); mayor (1967–1970)

Becky Power, wife of Irving mayor Robert Power

Joe Putnam, Irving city councilman (1973–1983); mayor (1999–2005)

Marvin Randle, Irving city councilman (1971–1977); mayor (1977–1981)

Ted Rea, former CEO and partner in Triland International, Inc, JV partner with Dallas Cowboys in Cowboys Center at the Valley Ranch

Boots Reader, former chairman and CEO of Bright Bank

Don Rorschach, Irving city attorney (1970–1999)

Russ Russell, former publisher of the *Dallas Cowboys Official Weekly*

Ralph Sanford, C&W singer and friend of Clint Murchison Jr.

Steve Schiff, son of Herbert Schiff, former business partner of Bum Bright

Martha Ann Schneider, wife of Steve "Cotton Tail" Schneider

Bill Schneider, son of Martha Ann and Steve Schneider

John Schneider, son of Martha Ann and Steve Schneider

George Schrader, Dallas city manager, 1972–1981

Charlie Scudder, staff writer with the *Dallas Morning News*

Paul R. Seegers, former chairman and CEO of Centex Corp

Brad Sham, sportscaster best known as "Voice of the Cowboys"

Blackie Sherrod, sports columnist with the *Dallas Morning News*

Marshall Simmons, former attorney with Jenkens & Gilchrist Law Firm

Bill Simms, former attorney with Jenkens & Gilchrist Law Firm

Jerry Smith, former advisor to the John D. Murchison estate

Thomas E. Smith, son of Ed Smith, former minority partner in the Dallas Cowboys during the Bright-Jones years

Roger Staubach, Dallas Cowboys Hall of Fame quarterback

Leonard David Stone, former executive director of the Dallas Symphony Orchestra

Ted Strauss, friend of Clint Murchison Jr.

Tom Swiley, former executive with First Republic Bank Dallas

Bill Thau, retired attorney with Jenkens & Gilchrist Law Firm

Duane Thomas, Cowboys running back in the 1970s

Bryan Trubey, lead architect of AT&T Stadium

BB Tuley, former financial executive with the Bum Bright Organization

George M. Underwood III, Dallas Cowboys limited partner during the Bright years

Jack Veatch, former Salomon Brothers investment banker

Joe Walker, former president and CEO of JW Bateson Construction Corp

Charlie Waters, Dallas Cowboys All-Pro safety

Mike, Lee, and Al Weir, principals in Weir Brothers, the contractor that demolished Texas Stadium

Dan Werner, manager of business operations of the Dallas Cowboys spanning the Murchison/Bright eras

Helen Widener, wife of James Widener, staunch supporter of development of Texas Stadium in Irving

Coke Anne Murchison Wilcox, daughter of Clint Murchison Jr.

Don Wilson, longtime CFO of the Dallas Cowboys during the Murchison era

Truman Wolf, Tex Schramm's and Tom Landry's longtime barber

Anne Wynne, daughter of Bedford Wynne

Jimmy Wynne, son of Toddie Lee Wynne Jr.

Joan Wynne, wife of Bedford Wynne

John Zouzelka, former partner in Triland International, Inc, JV partner with Dallas Cowboys in Cowboys Center at the Valley Ranch

INDEX

Note: Page numbers in italics indicate images or caption information from photo gallery